The Naked Society

The Naked Society

Vance Packard

Introduction by Rick Perlstein

PUBLISHING

Brooklyn, New York

Printed in the United States of America
10 9 8 7 6 5 4 3 2 1

Ig Publishing
392 Clinton Avenue
Brooklyn, NY 11238
www.igpub.com

Library of Congress Cataloging-in-Publication Data

Packard, Vance, 1914-1996.
  The naked society / Vance Packard ; [introduction by] Rick Perlstein.
    pages cm
  Originally published: New York : David McKay, 1964.
    ISBN 978-1-935439-83-7 (pbk.)
  1. Liberty. 2. Privacy, Right of--United States. 3. Freedom. 4. Privacy, Right of. I. Title.
  JC599.U5P36 2013
  323.4'90973--dc23
                                      2013020662

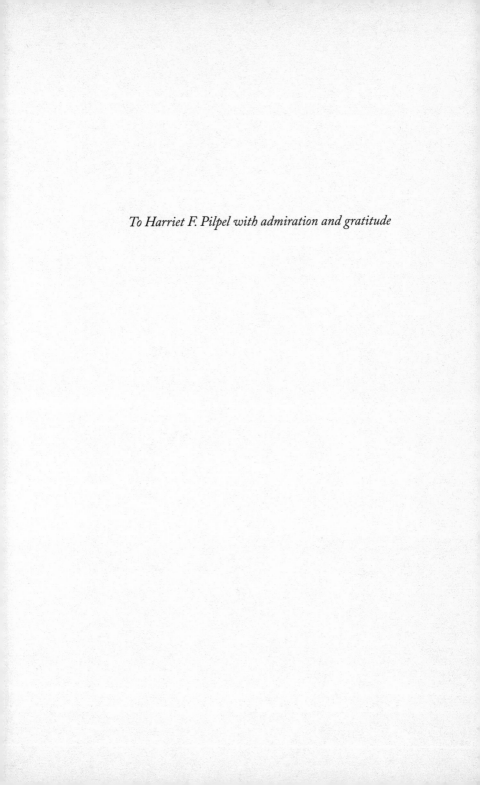

To Harriet F. Pilpel with admiration and gratitude

CONTENTS

INTRODUCTION

There is nothing worse than dated social criticism. So when the good folks at Ig Publishing invited me to write this introduction, my initial reaction was skepticism. What could a jeremiad about the epidemic of Americans spying on one another, published in 1964—thirty years before the invention of the Internet, thirty-seven years before 9/11, written in an age when the gravest insults to civil liberties consisted of congressional committees asking "Are you now, or have you ever been, a member of the Communist Party"—have to say to us now?

I picked up an ancient paperback copy of *The Naked Society* ("The explosive facts behind the hidden campaign to deprive Americans of their rights to privacy. Here's how snoop devices are being employed by Big Government, Big Business, and Big Educaiton in their sneak attack on YOU."). I began reading. I was in New York City—Penn Station, to be exact. I read Packard's framing questions: "Are there loose in our modern world forces that threaten to annihilate everybody's privacy? And if such forces are indeed loose, are they establishing the preconditions of totalitarianism that could endanger the personal freedom of modern man?" As I read this, I happened to notice a TV screen. Horrifying, apocalyptic images of buildings collapsing and shadowy terrorists alternated with messages like, "If you see anything suspicious report it to an Amtrak employee." And, "It's nothing, you think. *Can you be sure?*" After all: "It doesn't hurt to be alert."

I began reading with renewed, then steadily mounting, interest, my mind buzzing as the parallels between then and now presented themselves. Packard wrote, "the New York Police [have] about 200 plain-clothes men working virtually full time at wiretapping." That was then. This is now: the New York Police spend $1 billion on an intelligence unit, led by an active-duty Central Intelligence Agency Official, to infiltrate the Muslim community and spy on mosques. The NYPD admits the program has never produced a single terrorism lead).[1] Then: Packard quotes Sam Dash—who before becoming a household name as chief counsel of the Senate Watergate committee, was a leading civil liberties expert—that a "district attorney, in office, catches an occupational disease. He resents impediments in his way that prevent him from collecting evidence to convict criminals." Now: computer wizard Aaron Swartz earns an FBI investigation for the legal act of downloading federal court files; then, after harmlessly downloading too many scholarly articles from MIT's computer system, he is indicted by the office of United States Attorney Carmen Ortiz for charges that could have brought him thirty-five years in prison. Experts say he should have earned a slap on the wrist, if that, but prosecutors hound him so mercilessly he commits suicide.[2]

Then: welfare inspectors in Kern and Alameda Counties, California, stage late-night raids on 500 houses to investigate whether there is a man living in the household so they can cut off relief. Now: bills in states including Kansas, Texas, Arkansas, North Carolina, West Virginia, Florida, and Wyoming propose drug tests for welfare recipients (Republicans in Congress have introduced bills to submit recipients of both welfare and unemployment insurance to drug tests), and state legislators in Tennessee consider a law to kick families off welfare if their kids get bad grades.[3]

Then: "In cities where wiretapping was known to exist there was generally a sense of insecurity among professional people and people engaged in political life. Prominent persons were constantly afraid to use their telephones despite the fact that they were not engaged in any wrongdoing." Now: the Justice Department secretly obtains two months of telephone records of at least twenty *Associated Press* reporters and editors, including for home phones and cell phones; as of this writing, the government will not say why it sought the records, or how, nor whether a grand jury was involved. They only would say that U.S. attorneys follow "all applicable laws, federal laws, federal regulations, and Department of Justice policies when issuing subpoenas for phone records of media organizations," and that "we do not comment on ongoing criminal investigations."[4] Journalists have been both victims and perpetrators of such spying: just days before the AP story broke had come news that employees of Bloomberg News were availing themselves of a "Snoop" function that let them tap into the accounts of subscribers to the company's financial information network.[5]

Then: Packard writes of his horror that "cabled TV" will allow the "possibility of getting 'an instantaneous readout' home by home of what millions of people are [watching] in the entire country in about fifty seconds." Now: regarding the cables that connect our computers to networks of servers around the world, there have been too many horror stories to count, and more on that below. Then, "In some instances undercover men have been sent into plants to report on workers attitudes toward the union that is recognized or is seeking union recognition , and to report on union strategy"; in one case a detective insinuated himself so effectively into a textile plant the rank and file voted him onto the employee bargaining community. Now—well, too many horror stories to count on the labor front, too, but a great place to start is Human Rights Watch's 215-page report "Discounting Rights: Wal-Mart's Violation of U.S. Workers' Right to Freedom of Association" on how the world's largest corporation and its owners "violate their employees' basic rights with virtual impunity."[6]

By now you get the point. I have no doubt whatsoever that this is a book that should be read, and carefully. This runaway bestseller in its own time indicts us—not just because the privacy crisis that began taking shape in Packard's own time has grown so much worse, but because nobody any longer writes bestsellers about it. Re-reading *The Naked Society* can help us understand why.

II.

Vance Packard was born in 1914 in Granville Summit, Pennsylvania and raised in nearby State College, where his dad was a superintendent at the Penn State University farm. He majored in English there and worked for the literary magazine, earned a masters degree in journalism from Columbia University, and entered the newspaper business, eventually becoming a feature writer for the Associated Press, then a freelance magazine writer focusing on social science and human behavior.[7]

"He is of medium height, medium age, talks slowly, loses the thread of what he is saying, regains it, acts on the whole like a professor at a small college a little unsure of tenure and with an important lecture coming up with the president in attendance. At the typewriter he is something else again."[8] The *New York Times Magazine* said that in a profile when Packard was at the height of his influence, when that influence was very high indeed. His first book, *The Hidden Persuaders* (1957), on advertising, compared the hidden field of "motivational research" to "the chilling world of George Orwell and his Big Brother." The book also introduced the concept of "subliminal projection"—images flashed on screens too quickly for the conscious mind to register but long enough, Packard claimed, to instill longings in individuals they didn't know they actually had. The ad industry responded indignantly, and denies the practice to this day.[9] But the intensity of their backlash attested to the success of Packard's message: the book reached number one on the *New York Times* bestseller list. (As for whether subliminal project is still practiced, that remains an active debate decades later—for instance after Democrats alleged a George W. Bush ad emphasized the word "RATS" in a chyron reading "BUREAUCRATS" during the 2000 presidential campaign.[10])

Packard's successive books, *The Status Seekers* (1959); "under the gloss of prosperity," it argued, society was becoming more and more corroded by "new ways to draw lines that will separate the elect from the non-elect"), and *The Waste Makers* (1960). an exposé of "the systematic attempt of business to make us wasteful, debt-ridden, permanently discontented individuals" which presciently foregrounded environmental concerns) were also number one bestsellers, an extraordinary run. It was around that time that Betty Friedan heard Packard lecture and decided to turn the magazine article she was planning based on a questionnaire she circulated to her fellow members of Smith College's Class of 1942 on their experiences since graduation into the book which became *The Feminine Mystique*.[11]

Packard's work, in fact, heralded a golden age of American social criticism that played an outsized role in shuddering the country out of the somnolent fifties. The conventional wisdom, as the sixties began, was stated by the nation's young president in 1962: that most of the day's problems "are are problems, administrative problems"—that is to say, not really problems at all.[12] As I wrote in my book on the period, *Before the Storm*, those few writers who demurred were spending most of their energy begging people to acknowledge that serious social problems existed.

Three masterpieces of left-wing social criticism appeared around the same time in 1962 and 1963, the year before *The Naked Society* appeared. In *The Other America*, Michael Harrington argued forcefully that there appeared to be little poverty in the United States because in that poverty was hidden; Betty Friedan's *The Feminine Mystique* which said that women were miserable because they could not call out the name of their problem; and Rachel Carson's *Silent Spring*, on the subtle, progressive degradation of the environment. Such figuration of the implicit—hidden persuaders; problems with no name—were articulated most explicitly in the New Left manifesto penned by Tom Hayden in 1962. The Port Huron Statement said that America's alleged consensus of happiness might "better be called a glaze above deeply felt anxieties." James Baldwin entitled his 1963 collection of essays *The Fire Next Time*; the Establishment was aware there was kindling on the ground.[13]

With Packard, such books helped demonstrate how eager readers were for work that could articulate how civilization they were supposed to be celebrating was failing them. *The New York Times Book Review*, in a long and glowing front page essay they devoted to *The Status Seekers,* noted the paradox: that Packard's "books on various shortcomings of American society—hidden persuaders, status seekers, waste makers—have without exception been welcomed with almost fervent enthusiasm by many members of the society they partially condemn."[14] Not so partially, actually. Wrote biographer Daniel Horowitz, whose *Vance Packard and American Social Criticism* came out in 1994, Packard "went farther in asking his readers to question basic assumptions about the beneficence of the American society and economy" than just about anyone else—and was devoured by readers nevertheless.[15]

The Naked Society was published in March of 1964, one month after the Beatles arrived on the tarmac at Idelwood Field, two months before Lyndon Johnson's Great Society speech resounded with the Packardian aspiration that "the city of man serves not only the needs of the body and the demands of commerce but the desire for beauty and the hunger for community," and just as Barry Goldwater was campaigning in the New Hampshire primary on behalf of a conservatism (as 1960's *Conscience of a Conservative*, arguably another monument to the new critical wave, put it) that "knows that to regard man as part of an undifferentiated mass is to consign him to ultimate slavery."[16] It spent twenty-three weeks on the *New York Times* bestseller list.

Packard had been kicking around ideas with his publisher for his next project for a year. First, he began researching a book about private investigators.[17] But his clipping file soon became dominated by a parallel obsession: the extraordinarily detailed questionnaires applicants for employment as diverse as gas station attendant and corporate executives, probing everything from Cold War "security risk" (Lockheed: "Does he [she] have relatives abroad?" "Has he [she] traveled abroad?" "If [employee] is youth or woman, what is reputation of parents or husband?") to the most intimate matters of personal conduct and psychology. At that, he had his subject: a survey of "the numerous rights heretofore considered characteristically American that we seem to be in danger of scuttling," from "the right to be different" to the "right to a fresh start."

III.

There are two broad reasons why it can be valuable to revisit a long-ago text like *The Naked Society*. The first is for all the ways it remains relevant to us—how it helps us grasp the evolution of the world we live in now. The second is for such a work's irrelevance. An old book that suspends in amber mores that are alien to us now—the past as a foreign country—can be the best way to grasp the accomplishments of our own society. In that regard, *The Naked Society* is valuable, too. Specifically, it is a remarkable resource for students of gay and lesbian history, and historians of sexuality generally, a subject upon which Packard's findings are gloriously, triumphantly dated.

The mid-twentieth century was a moment of panic over any perceived deviance from sexual normalcy. One of the most fascinating patches of the book concerns the extraordinarily intrusive psychological testing children were subject to in schools. One consisted of eleven pictures of a dog named Blacky (the "Blacky Test") purported to evaluate kids on "Dimensions" including "Oral Eroticism" (a cartoon captioned, "Here is Blacky with Mama..."), "Anal Sadism" ("Here Blacky is relieving himself (Herself...)," "Here Blacky is watching Tippy..." ("Castration Anxiety [M] or Penis Envy [F])."

Employment applicants were even worse. In a stunning set piece, Packard takes the reader inside a polygraph examination of a poor soul named Bill who is applying for a job as a traveling salesman of consumer products:

"Ever fired for cause?"

"Never."

"Ever drink to excess?"

"I've been loaded a few times, but I guess that's not 'excess,' so I'll say no."

And so on. Until we arrive at this extraordinary passage:

"'Have you ever done something that you are really truly ashamed of?' Bill shook his head. My guide whispered, 'That question will sometimes smoke out the homosexual.'...

"Bill was unharnessed...The examination seemingly was over, and Bill was looking for his hat. Then Mr. Probe said pleasantly, 'Bill, one more question before you leave. There is nothing personal or offensive about this, but because of the kind of business you are going in and the fact you have been in the summer theater work, I think I should ask it. Are you inclined to be a homosexual?'

"Bill looked startled. He said, 'No.' But the question so unsettled him that he felt compelled to explain his situation. 'I have of course been surrounded by them in my work in the theater in the Midwest, and I've been exposed to this a lot in some of the bohemian areas where I've lived, and I have been approached. But the answer is no.' Mr. Probe didn't explain why sexual status had any significant relevance to the job for which Bill was applying."

The inquisition about "homosexuality," is mostly irrelevant. The polygraph stuff, however, throws us right back into the first category of reasons *The Naked Society* is worth reading. Lie detectors, then and now, are a scam and an affront to privacy rights. Packard writes of one psychiatrist's conclusion that they were more a "tool for mental intimidation" than a reliable apparatus for the detection of lies, and of a joint Harvard and MIT study that polygraphs may have no more than 70 percent accuracy. Even that was only in the hands of a competent investigator, unlikely in an entirely unregulated industry.

The spring the book came out, a Democratic California congressman, John Moss, began hearings on the subject. He was soon announcing, "I would never submit to a polygraph unless accompanied by my personal physician, my lawyer, and my psychiatrist." His subcommittee later concluded that "there is no such thing as a lie detector."[18] Unions, Packard noted, were lobbying for legislation to have them outlawed. They failed, of course—and their manufacturers still claim 90 percent validity, even though the National Research Council has found no evidence for their effectiveness. In *United States v. Scheffer* (1998), the Supreme Court left their use up to the states—and nineteen allow polygraph testimony to be admitted into evidence. Massachusetts, Maryland, New Jersey, Delaware, and Iowa eventually banned polygraph testing as a condition of employment, or in the investigation of wrongdoing by employers.[19] That, of course, means forty-five states have not.

IV.

We still stand naked in our society—more shiveringly than ever before. Consider the workplace. Packard profiles companies like Bishop's Service (motto: "A Man's Whole Life Precludes The Single Deed"), which maintained files of five million names for clients seeking executive talent; organizations like the American Society for Industrial Security, whose membership grew from 1800 to 2500 in two years; a staggeringly fast-growing company named Wackenhut that specialized in renting out former FBI agents (they are now the largest private prison company in the world). He also studies the prevalence of cameras in employee bathrooms, miniature transmitters installed inside toilet paper rollers, factory surveillance—"At thousands of plants no one is to be trusted in any sense in which we've traditionally known the word"—and what one expert called "psychological espionage": personality testing, sometimes in disguised form, was rampant, with a "special interest in trying to determine whether the applicant is adaptable enough to be a good team player...is money-minded (that is good)...is controversial or a 'screwball' (those are bad)." This despite the findings, according to the *Harvard Business Review*, of those tests' "dismal history" of scientific reliability."

So what is the state of the art now?

According to Ann Murphy Paul, author of *The Cult of Personality Testing: How Personality Tests Are Leading Us to Miseducate Our Children, Mismanage Our Companies, and Misunderstand Ourselves* (2005), 2500 such tests are on the market and being utilized by corporations now—an entirely unregulated industry (including the notorious and entirely unscientific Rorschach "inkblot" test)—not to mention their use in "the admissions process at private schools, the evaluation of learning and behavior problems, and the investigation of child custody and child abuse cases."[20]

Meanwhile, employment applicants these days do not have to establish their heterosexuality in order to get hired. Instead, they have to lay bare their credit ratings—quite possibly creating, in the not-too-distant future, a blacklisted underclass rendered permanently unemployable because of their bad financial luck some time in the distant past.[21] (So much for Packard's invocation of one of the rights heretofore considered characteristically

American that we seem to be in danger of scuttling: the right to a fresh start.)

And what about workplace spying? Google led me to an article in a newsletter called "Business Watch" that noted, "Employee monitoring is becoming a standard practice in just about every industry. . . . A 2001 American Management Association Association survey found that three-quarters of all major companies record and review employee communications and on-the-job activities." Most employers install software programs like "Investigator" which "allows an employer to monitor everything a user does on a computer, including opening windows and posting items in chat rooms. It then sends an activity report via email to the employer." Other programs flag taboo words selected by employers, or classify emails by the number of words sent, or measure the amount of time an employee spends composing, or even reading, email.

What is permitted, and what is not? In Wisconsin, I learned from "Business Watch," statutes specify that employees have a right to be free from intrusion in circumstances that "reasonable people would consider to be private, such as using the bathroom"—but that "much of what is considered private is ultimately based on what employers tell their employees to expect. 'If, say, they're committed to maintaining the security and integrity of the office by reserving the right to inspect lockers and offices, then it's clear lockers and desks aren't considered private space,'" the article quoted a lawyer named Tom Godar. Courts have generally upheld this and employers' rights to monitor just about anything else without disclosing to employees they are being monitored, I learned. And though the Electronic Communications Privacy Act prohibits unauthorized or warrantless electronic interception of oral communication, "there are several key exceptions: 1) Employers are allowed to monitor business-related activities if the monitoring is in the ordinary course of business, and 2) The employer is exempted from ECPA if its employees agree to be monitored." So it is that "employer-issued cell phones" have become "a monitoring technique that is gaining popularity, which allow employees to trace the whereabout of their traveling employees." Kind of like the ankle bracelets parolees where, only for traveling salesmen.

Scary stuff, and I braced myself to enjoy the jeremiad to follow. I was disappointed. The piece was called "Workplace Spying: How Far Can Companies Go," and I was halfway through it before I realized its answer was "not damned far enough, if you ask me." This was a business newsletter. "Don't Get Carried Away," the last section warned ("If the policy is too harsh, people will leave"), concluding with one last piece of advice: "Savvy employees are always looking for ways to beat the system . . . If you have electronic communications policies in place, make sure they are updated to include new technologies as they come out, such as instant messaging and camera phones."[22]

I also found an article on the blog of a store that sold security equipment asking if it was ethical to spy on employees. It concluded that, yes, mostly, it was, adding, "Let's be clear here. We intend for this question to be applied only to employers spying on employees. We feel it necessary to make this distinction, since there have been recent allegations of employees spying on one another, which is definitely viewed by most as being unethical."[23]

Packard (who died in 1996) would have loved that—having written of the tone corporate America was setting for the rest of society as one of "moral squalor." He raised alarms that "it was now possible for a technician to drive a special truck up a street and then report what channel each TV user on the street was dialing." I wonder what he would have made of Facebook? In the spring of 2013, a concerned public relations consultant named Peter Shankman posted there, "To the 43 of my friends who currently use the hookup app 'Bang With Friends,' including the 15 of you who are married, you should know that it's FAR from as private as you think."[24] Shankman set up a simple link for interested parties to work such magic themselves. I clicked it myself—and learned that among the five of my friends who had downloaded the app were an extremely prominent, extremely married political pundit.

Packard also all but lost his mind over cameras being used, for example, so apartment dwellers could inspect who was buzzing their residents, to police department store theft, to keep tabs on workplace productivity. What would he have said of the marketing email I received from the PMBC Group in the wake of the Boston Marathon terror bombing?

Hi Rick,

Ever since the travesty of 9/11, the video surveillance industry has spiked unconditionally, becoming a $3.2 billion market in the US by the end of 2007. Since then an estimated 1.1 million more security cameras have been distributed globally through retailers in 2010 alone. After video surveillance helped to identify the Boston Marathon culprits, we can all anticipate another drastic increase in sales and installations nationwide.

Video surveillance has actively developed, with the increasing demand, usage and advancements in technology. The Internet now allows police to review footage as ivideon archives all data in data centers located around the world. All the while, ivideon is streaming multiple cameras from different continents to one single easy to view interface.

As private video surveillance systems have become an integral aspect to criminal investigations, there has been an increased rate of installation. Personal cameras such as webcams, IP cameras, IP cameras with built-in ivideon, CCTVs, and DVRs can all stream live feeds both to the police as well as personal devices. Sharing these feeds can be done through ivideon's public TV, websites, blogs, social media platforms, as well as shared access.

Please let me know if you are interested in speaking with Vladimir Eremeev of ivideon to learn more about the growing video surveillance industry and how ivideon is paving the way for the everyday user.[25]

From the Cold War to the War on Terror. Back then, Packard reports, thirteen million Americans, one-fifth of all job holders, were scrutinized by a "loyalty" or "security" program (826,000 were conducted by the Department of Defense alone), and the House Committee on Un-American Activities maintained a card file of over a million names. "In all major cities the government maintains hotel rooms with eavesdropping equipment already installed through a nearby wall. When a person under surveillance goes to a hotel, 'the proper authorities arrange for him to be put in the proper room.'" (One such person was Martin Luther King, which was how J. Edgar Hoover amassed the transcripts sent anonymously to him in 1964 in an attempt to get him to commit suicide.[26]) How revealing, this sentence, in a section called "The Movement Toward a Garrison State Mentality": "Although not the least bit mitliaristic as a people, Americans are being swept toward being a martial—and thus watched-society."

Now just to take a single example, we have the abomination of the "No-Fly" list, more and more a vehicle of what the Canadian writer Murtaza Hussain has described as "de facto exile"; among the stories Hussain has recently catalogued in an article for al Jazeera is the Ph.D. student en route to a Stanford-sponsored engineering conference stuck in a "Kafkaesque legal limbo" in Malaysia for eight years; the multimillionaire businessman with close ties to Bill Clinton, Gilbert Chagoury, effectively banned from travel for no reason he has ever been able to determine ("I cannot accept being labelled a terrorist when I am known all over the world as a person who loves peace. It hurts."); one man told by FBI agents that he would be removed from the list if he agreed to spy on other Muslims; another placed on the list immediately after refusing to spy on fellow South Asians. "In the past year," Hussain says, "the number of individuals placed by the Obama administration on the federal No-Fly list has doubled to over 10,000, with at least 500 being holders of American citizenship. A further 400,000 individuals of indeterminate citizenship are on a separate 'watch list' which flags them as being 'reasonably suspicious and potentially subject to exclusion. The names of those on these lists are not being disclosed and neither is the reasoning as to why any particular individual may be flagged."[27]

Such outrages, of course, have become far to numerous to possibly catalogue in this space. Luckily we can turn to two recent books by David K. Shipler, the Pulitzer Prize-winning former *New York Times* reporter, *The Rights of the People* (2012) and *Rights at Risk* (2012), for a passionate, eloquent accounting.[28] Shipler's work is the closest we have now to what Packard was doing then. There is, however, a difference. Packard's book spent almost six months on the bestseller list. I wrote David Shipler to ask about his own sales. He replied, "My boookswere not on any bestseller list that didn't extend into the four digits—far from it." *Rights at Risk* sold so poorly that it was never released in paperback.[29] *Publishers Weekly* thought Shipler was overwrought concerning "less intrusive" electronic surveillance, which, after all, was nothing like "Hessians kicking down doors." And those contrasts, finally, brings us to the final reason *The Naked Society* is so usefully illuminating about our own time.

V.

The release of *The Naked Society* was a publishing event: full-page ads everywhere ("VANCE PACKARD ROCKS THE NA-TION WITH HIS MOST EXPLOSIVE BOOK YET!"); fawning, long reviews in papers like the *Wall Street Journal* ("We are farther down a dangerous road than it is pleasant to think about...") and the *Washington Post* ("The number or people who 'have a little list' on which you may find yourself is astonishing"); attention by top columnists booming its themes in magazines and on the editorial pages (Stewart Alsop launched a major exposé on polygraphs, for example, in the *Saturday Evening Post*).[31] Many reviewed it alongside another, similar book *The Privacy Invaders* by a former private investigator. The essays also frequently referred to the fact that 1964 was but twenty years before George Orwell's *1984*.

What comes across most forcefully from both the book and those reviews is how many revelations were judged outrageous by Americans that are almost entirely taken for granted today. Packard was horrified by a Manhattan district attorney who opined on network television "in favor of an astonishing bill being submitted to the New York State legislature. It gives a policeman who is armed with a search warrant the right to enter a premises, including a home, without saying who he is or what he is doing there." That is to say, he was horrified at just the thought of a prosecutor suggesting such a law. Imagine his shock if he could learn that, according to Profesor Peter Kraska of Eastern Kentucky University, the number of such real-world "no-knock" arrest warrants incrased from 3,000 in 1981 to 50,000 in 2005. I asked Professor Kraska if he could help me find more recent statistics. "No," he answered, "unfortunately no one keeps track of this."[32] According to the Cato Institute, forty people have been killed in no-knock raids.[33] No one gives a good goddamn.

Nor do we care much about what Packard calls "the Lively Trade in Facts About Us"—the intrusive collection and sale of mailing lists about what we consume, for instance—or that, "Each month more and more information about individuals is being stored away in some giant memory machine." The "progressive" candidate Barack Obama built his 2012 reelection campaign collecting just such "micro-targeting" information about voters, to no objection I can find—just celebration of its technological glories.[34] Packard was taken aback that, in a survey of 400 companies that check on the health of executives (an intrusion he found offensive in itself) "only one firm in ten permitted the executive to go to a doctor or clinic of his own choice." (No HMOs in 1964.) Other offenses then that don't register now: the 35 percent of former FBI agents working in investigation or security, spying on school bathrooms to avoid vandalism, the biographical X-rays people have to submit to for federal employment, "Washington's Version of 'This Is Your Life'"—still in effect: a friend of mine, for a minor job with the Parks Service had to submit a list of five people who had known him for at least ten years, complete with phone numbers. "I almost," he told me, "had to make people up."

When people learned about this kind of stuff in 1964, they began indignant. Though, in fact, not nearly enough for the *New York Times Book Review's* critic who found "a woefully common lack of indignation on the part of the bugged." He also quoted the American Civil Liberties Union: "A hallmark of totalitarian societies is that the people are apprehensive of being overheard or spied upon."

Well, hardly anyone is apprehensive now. I wonder: if a totalitarian society is one in which people are scared of their privacy being invaded, what do you call ours, in which no one seems much to care?

—*Rick Perlstein*

1. Matt Sledge, "NYPD Muslim Surveillance Report Details 'Collateral Damage of Progarm," *Huffington Post*, March 11, 2013, http://www.huffingtonpost.com/2013/03/11/nypd-muslim-surveillance_n_2855303.html; "With CIA Help, NYPD Moves Covertly in Muslim Areas," *Associated Press*, August 24, 2011, http://abclocal.go.com/wabc/story?section=news/local/new_york&id=8323847

2. "The Swartz Suicide and the Sick Culture of the DOJ," *Massachusetts*

Lawyers Weekly, January 23, 2013, http://masslawyersweekly.com/2013/01/23/the-swartz-suicide-and-the-sick-culture-of-the-doj/

3. John Celock and Arthur Delaney, "Drug Testing Bills Proliferate in State Legislatures," *Huffington Post*, April 11, 2013, http://www.huffingtonpost.com/2013/04/11/drug-testing-welfare_n_3063962.html

4. Charlie Savage and Leslie Kaufman, "Phone Records of Journalists of the Associated Press Seized by U.S.," *New York Times*, May 13, 2012

5. Amy Chozick, "Bloomberg Admits to Terminal Snooping," *New York Times*, May 13, 2013.

6. Discounting Rights: Wal-Mart's Violation of U.S. Workers' Right to Freedom of Association (Human Rights Watch, 2007)

7. "Vance Packard, 82, Challenger of Consumerism, Dies," *New York Times*, December 13, 1996.

8. Lewis Nichols, "Talk With Vance Packard," New York Times, March 15, 1964.

9. "Vance Packard, 82, Challenger of Consumerism, Dies," *New York Times*, December 13, 1996.

10. Julian Borger, "Dirty Rats Leave Gore a Subliminal Message," *The Guardian*, September 12, 2000, http://www.guardian.co.uk/world/2000/sep/13/uselections2000.usa

11. "Vance Packard, 82, Challenger of Consumerism, Dies," *New York Times*, December 13, 1996.

12. Rick Perlstein, *Before the Storm: Barry Goldwater and the Unmaking of the American Consensus* (New York: Hill & Wang, 2001), p. 209

13. Ibid.

14. John Brooks, "There's Somebody Watching You: T*he Naked Society*, by Vance Packard," *New York Times Book Review*, March 15, 1964, p. 1.

15. Daniel Horowitz, *Vance Packard and American Social Criticism* (Charlotte: University of North Carolina Press, 1994), p. 120

16. Barry Goldwater, *The Conscience of a Conservative* (Shepardsville, KY: Victor Publishing, 1960), p. 11.

17. Lewis Nichols, "Talk With Vance Packard," N*ew York Times*, March 15, 1964.

18. Lawrence Laurent, "Eavesdroppers Now Sophisticated Pests,"

Washington Post, May 23, 1964; Associated Press, "LBJ Sets Up Committee for Lie Detector Study," *Daytona Beach Morning Journal*, December 14, 1965.

19. Wikpiedia, "Polygraph," http://en.wikipedia.org/wiki/Polygraph

20. Ann Murphy Paul, *The Cult of Personality Testing: How Personality Tests Are Leading Us to Miseducate Our Children, Mismanage Our Companies, and Misunderstand Ourselves* (New York: Free Press, 2005), p. xiv, 157.

21. *Discredited: How Employment Credit Checks Keep Qualified Workers Out of a Job* (New York: Demos, 2013).

22. Mark Crawford, "Workplace Spying: How Far Can Companies Go," BusinessWatch, nd, accessed May 10, 2013.

23. Laura M. Sands, "Spying on Employees—Is It Ethical?," "Your Eye on Security Alerts, Blogs, News, and Videos," July 30, 2012, http://www.homesecuritystore.com/blog/2012/07/30/spying-on-employees-is-it-ethical/

24. Erik Serhman, "No Facebook Privacy for Cheaters (Or Anyone Else)," CBS Money Watch, May 10, 2013, http://www.cbsnews.com/8301-505124_162-57583881/no-facebook-privacy-for-cheaters-or-anyone-else/

25. Received April 26, 2013.

26. Taylor Branch, *Pillar of Fire: America in the King Years 1963-65* (New York: Simon & Schuster, 1998), 556-57.

27. Murtaza Hussain, "Exile the Obama Way," Aljazeera.com, February 5, 2013, http://www.aljazeera.com/indepth/opinion/2013/02/201324165957645514.html.

28. David K. Shipler, *The Rights of the People: How Our Search for Safety Invades Our Liberties* (New York: Knopf, 2011); *Rights At Risk: The Limits of Liberty in Modern America* (New York: Knopf, 2012).

29. Email, May 13, 2013.

30. *Publishers Weekly*, February 7, 2011.

31. March 18, 1964 *New York Times*, Doubleday bookstore; Edmund Fuller, "The Bookshelf: A Pair of Indictments of Privacy-Invaders," *Wall Street Journal*, March 26, 1964; Glendly Culligan, "Brothers of Assorted Sizes Are Kibitzing on Our Lives," *Washington Post*, March 18, 1964; for Stewart Alsop see June 15, 1964 *Edmonton Journal*.

32. Patrick Johnson, "After Atlanta Raid Tragedy, New Scrutiny of

Police Tactics," *Christian Science Monitor*, November 29, 2006; email May 11, 2013.

33. Radley Balko, "No SWAT," *Slate*, April 6, 2006, http://www.slate.com/articles/news_and_politics/jurisprudence/2006/04/no_swat.html

34. See, for instance, Alexis C. Madgrigal, "When the Nerds Go Marching In," *The Atlantic*, November 16, 2012, http://www.theatlantic.com/technology/archive/2012/11/when-the-nerds-go-marching-in/265325/

35. John Brooks, "There's Somebody Watching You: The Naked Society, by Vance Packard," *New York Times Books Review*, March 15, 1964, p. 1.

"Liberty lies in the hearts of men and women; when it dies there, no constitution, no law, no court can save it. . ."—Judge Learned Hand

PART I

THE MOUNTING SURVEILLANCE

1. The Individual at Bay
An Introduction

"Society is continually pushing in on the individual. He has only a few areas in which he can be himself, free from external restraint or observation."—U.S. Senator Edward V. Long of Missouri

By telescoping time a bit let us look in on a reasonably successful family in a typical city of the Land of Liberty, 1964.

Mom is at the department store trying on a new dress in the dressing room. A closed-circuit TV camera hidden behind a mesh screen is recording her moves to make certain she does not pocket any of the store's merchandise.

Dad is at a conference table in his office talking to a group of colleagues about the operations of his department. The colleague sitting next to him is an undercover agent hired from a nationwide detective agency by the president of Dad's company to keep tabs on the performance of key subordinates. Elsewhere an investigator is on the telephone chatting with Dad's banker about the size of Dad's account and any outstanding loans. It seems that Dad recently applied for an insurance policy on his personal property.

Son John, just out of college, is seated in a chair with a pneumatic tube strapped across his chest and an electrode taped to his palm. John has applied for a job as a sales representative for an electronics concern. He is now undergoing the usual lie-detector test to probe his honesty, his possibly dangerous habits, and his manliness. Meanwhile an investigator is talking to one of John's erstwhile professors concerning any political opinions the boy may have expressed during class discussions.

Daughter Mary, sweet girl, is still only a sophomore in high school. She is in the classroom struggling with a 250-item questionnaire. It asks her to reveal whether her parents seem to quarrel a lot, whether they have ever talked to her about sex, and whether she is worried about menstrual disorders. If Mary's parents happen to hear about this probing, they would be denied any information as to her various responses and how they were scored.

All these things obviously would not happen on the same day to one family but all of them happen every day to a great many individuals. All have become common enough occurrences to raise somber questions about what the future holds for late twentieth-century society.

Are there loose in our modern world forces that threaten to annihilate everybody's privacy? And if such forces are indeed loose, are they establishing the preconditions of totalitarianism that could endanger the personal freedom of modern man?

These are the questions we must ponder as we explore the recent enormous growth in methods for observing, examining, controlling, and exchanging information about people. Individually the new social controls we are seeing are cloaked in reasonableness. And some perhaps have comic overtones. But when we view them collectively we must consider the possibility that they represent a massive, insidious impingement upon our traditional rights as free citizens to live our own lives.

Many of these new forces are producing pressures that intrude upon most of us where we live, work, shop, go to school, or seek solitude. Millions of Americans are living in an atmosphere in which peering electronic eyes, undercover agents, lie detectors, hidden tape recorders, bureaucratic investigators, and outrageously intrusive questionnaires are becoming commonplace, if often only suspected, facts of life.

Privacy is becoming harder and harder to attain, surveillance more and more pervasive. Mr. Justice William O. Douglas of the

United States Supreme Court has commented: "The forces allied against the individual have never been greater."

The surveillance of citizens in the United States—and much of western Europe—has been growing year by year. One indication of its extent in the United States is seen in an analysis of our security system made a few years ago. It indicated that, even then, more than 13,500,000 Americans—or approximately one fifth of all jobholders—were being scrutinized under some sort of security or loyalty program.[1] In 1962 the Department of Defense alone conducted security investigations on 826,000 individuals.[2]

Surveillance of individuals for security, loyalty, or general behavior is most rampant in Southern California. In this area the majority of the families have one or more members under some form of watch, either as defense workers, public employees, studio employees, or as recipients of welfare benefits. For most of these people, at least one investigator is bound to call on next-door neighbors to inquire about their backgrounds or living habits.

The United States Government employs more than 25,000 professional investigators, not including counterintelligence and espionage operatives. Federal investigators, however, represent only a small fraction of the total number of people in the nation who earn their living investigating other people. There are hundreds of thousands of private, corporate, municipal, county, and state investigators.

Consider one private investigative firm that is little known to most Americans. Its world headquarters are in Atlanta. This firm bears the now outdated name of the Retail Credit Company. It offers a continent-spanning intelligence service with 6000 full-time salaried "inspectors" on "constant call," who operate out of 1500 offices in every state and Canadian province. It has sixty-four offices in Ohio alone and has representatives in Mexico and Europe. The company's inspectors conduct about 90,000 investigations every working day, reporting mostly on individuals. They investigate applicants for insurance and claimants of insurance, they also check people's credit, and they conduct investigations of job applicants for clients. Their firm has 38,000 client accounts that include many of the world's largest companies.

Much of the surveillance of individuals by trained investigators has been made easier by the proliferation of record-keeping in our increasingly bureaucratic society. I found it startling to learn how much information about one's private life is readily available to any skilled investigator who knows where to check accessible records and make a few routine inquiries. Detectives told me some of the presumably private information about myself—or just about any adult who is not a hermit—that an investigator could readily produce in most areas of the United States. They were referring just to an "easy" kind of checkout. An investigator in the New York State area could produce for a curious client most of the facts about you or me listed below, and it could be done within a few days. Here are the facts:

—Whether there are any significant blemishes on your record where you have worked.

—How much money you have in your checking account at the bank (roughly), whether you borrow money often and for what, whether you have been delinquent in paying back loans, and whether you have any outstanding loans.

—Whether you are a poor credit risk.

—Whether you have ever suffered from mental illness for which you were confined, been treated for a heart ailment, or been a victim of convulsive disorders. (This information can often be found in a public document—one's original application for a driver's license.)

—Whether you are a known sexual deviate.

—Whether you actually received that college degree, if you claim one.

—Whether you have ever been arrested, or had any lawsuits filed against you.

—A good surmise as to whether you were legitimately born, when and where, and the occupation of your parents at the time.

—Your net worth (provided you have a sizable unsecured bank loan), the value of your home, its layout and construction, its furnishings and upkeep, and what kinds of locks there are on your doors.

—Whether you have been involved in an automobile accident in recent years.

—Whether your loyalty has ever been questioned by any of the better-known investigative bodies, public or private.

—Whether you are a registered Democrat, Republican, or have failed to register a party preference.

When I expressed curiosity about my own credit rating one detective said, "Give me a couple of hours." Within that period he called and gave me data from a credit report on me. It contained a fairly thorough summary of my life, employers, agents, abodes, and offspring for the past two decades, and the precise assessed value of my home in Connecticut. He chuckled and added: "They say that, though you pay your bills, you occasionally take your time about it." He added that such reports often will provide a guess as to the person's annual income but that apparently my income was too erratic for a guess to be made.

Most American adults with jobs, cars, houses, charge accounts, insurance, and military or government records can assume that at least one specific dossier on them—more probably several—has been compiled. Most contain facts that are, by and large, relatively impersonal. But a great many hundreds of thousands of these dossiers contain thick reports with intimate details. Many also contain erroneous or adverse information.

The U.S. Civil Service Commission, which maintains a dossier on nearly everyone who has applied for federal employment since 1939, reportedly has nearly 250,000 dossiers that contain adverse information.

Its central index of approximately 7,500,000 dossiers is just one of the many central files on individuals that have grown to enormous proportions in recent years. The Defense Department maintains a central index of members of the armed forces, civilian employees, and a great many other people, including scientists working for defense contractors. The Federal Bureau of Investigation, of course, has its extensive central file. The House Un-American Activities Committee reportedly has accumulated a card file of more than a million names. The Association of Casualty and Surety Companies maintains a vast nationwide clearinghouse of information regarding claimants. Very recently its file contained 18,200,000 entries on claimants for bodily injury or workmen's compensation. The bureau investigates or scrutinizes about one fourth of all claims, which means it conducts about 500,000 investigations a year. And then, of course, there are the credit bureaus in every part of the United States as well as in Canada, England, and Australia that are affiliated with the Associated Credit Bureaus of America. Through rapid exchange arrangements any bureau can draw upon files kept on more than 100,000,000 individuals.

The private investigative firm Retail Credit Company has files on more than 42,000,000 individuals. These files consist of previous reports the firm has made on individuals, significant newspaper clippings, and available public records about individuals. The company points out to prospective clients that its massive files can strengthen and support any current investigations it makes.

A further indication of the increase in surveillance since the beginning of World War II is the tremendous amount of electronic eavesdropping that now occurs. An electronics expert familiar with the practices of U.S. intelligence agencies told me: "In all major cities" the government maintains hotel rooms with eavesdropping equipment already installed through a nearby wall. When a person under surveillance goes to such a hotel, "the proper authorities arrange for him to be put in the proper room," he said.

The United States of course is not the only country in which eavesdropping has been growing. The Russians have a very large head start. An American with Communist sympathies who had lived inside Russia a few years and then returned to America cited to acquaintances as one of his grievances about the Russian system that electronic listening devices were everywhere.

Of the many forms of electronic surveillance, wiretapping has had the most public attention in the U.S., not because it is the most pernicious and rampant, but simply because it has generated the most political heat. Unlike the hiding of microphones and cameras, which is more invasive of privacy, wiretapping is a federal crime, although the Justice Department for its own good reasons takes a tortured view of the law and an interestingly lax approach to enforcing even its own view.

The Justice Department and law-enforcement officials in a few states are pressing hard for clear-cut permission to wiretap in investigating certain suspected criminal activities. At one Senate hearing the Attorney General explained: "We are balancing off the right of privacy versus the need for better law enforcement. . . Many Americans, particularly those apprehensive about crime, would insist the "balance" tips far more heavily toward law enforcement.

During one session attended by the Attorney General, Senator John A. Carroll of Colorado raised a crucial point. He wondered if there was perhaps so much preoccupation with "racketeers, gamblers or prostitutes" that something far more fundamental to society was not being neglected: "the right of every citizen to his privacy."

As this book is being completed, late January, 1964, the Federal Communications Commission, after many years of virtually ignoring the mounting problem of electronic eavesdropping, has invited comment on proposed rules seeking to curb one kind of electronic surveillance. That would be the kind requiring the use of radio transmitters, whether for bugging or wiretapping. Even if we assume the rules are issued, their enforcement probably will be delayed pending court challenges brought by manufacturers. This action is long overdue. However, it seems doubtful that these proposed rules would significantly diminish eavesdropping because of the broad exceptions written into them. For example they make an exception for actions by law-enforcement agencies. They also except any situation where one party to the conversation knows of the eavesdropping.

Still another dimension of surveillance can be seen in the growing suspiciousness toward employees that has gripped much of U.S. industry. One of the nation's fastest-growing trade associations is the American Society for Industrial Security. Its membership grew from 1800 to 2500 in two recent years. And at a recent convention members were treated to a comprehensive display of bugging devices. A Washington newspaper called them "more frightening than any Black Widow spider." A spokesman for one of the displayers boasted that he didn't believe there was "any escape from this sort of equipment."

Along with the industrial espionage a new and more subtle surveillance is occurring throughout the land: psychological espionage of employees and school children.

The growing surveillance—and here I've just given a glimpse of its many manifestations—is inevitably exerting a significant impact upon the behavior patterns and value systems of the millions of citizens involved. The person who finds he is not trusted tends to strike back by becoming indeed untrustworthy. And the person who finds himself being watched, electronically or otherwise, tends unwittingly to become careful in what he does and says. This breeds not only sameness but a watchfulness completely untypical of the exuberant, free-wheeling American so commonly accepted as typical of this land in earlier decades. The American Civil Liberties Union has observed (correctly, I believe), "A hallmark of totalitarian societies is that the people are apprehensive of being overheard or spied upon."

The former district attorney of Philadelphia, Mr. Samuel Dash, who made an exhaustive survey of eavesdropping in several states during the fifties,[3] told a Senate committee: "In cities where wiretapping was known to exist there was generally a sense of insecurity among professional people and people engaged in political life. Prominent persons were constantly afraid to use their telephones despite the fact that they were not engaged in any wrongdoing. It was clear that freedom of communication and the atmosphere of living in a free society without fear were handicapped by the presence of spying ears."

The closing in upon the privacy of the individual comes not only from the outright scrutiny of individuals but also from multiplying rules and regulations and from ever mounting requirements for licenses. There is the new insistence that one be traceable from cradle to grave. Bess E. Dick, staff director of the House Committee on the Judiciary, complained to me: "There is a crowding in." You are required to "live just this way and no other way." She felt the typical citizen is robbed of eccentricity.

Among the numerous rights heretofore considered characteristically American that we seem to be in danger of scuttling are:

—The right to be different.

—The right to hope for tolerant forgiveness or overlooking of past foolishnesses, errors, humiliations, or minor sins—in short, the Christian notion of the possibility of redemption.

—The right to make a fresh start.

America was largely settled, and its frontiers expanded, by people seeking to get away from something unpleasant in their pasts, either oppression, painful episodes, poverty, or misdemeanors.

Today it is increasingly assumed that the past and present of all of us—virtually every aspect of our lives—must be an open book; and that all such information about us can be not only put in files but merchandised freely. Business empires are being built on this merchandising of information about people's private lives. The expectation that one has a right to be let alone—the whole idea that privacy is a right worth cherishing—seems to be evaporating among large segments of our population.

There appears to be little awareness today among the complacent that no one is secure unless everyone is secure from the over-eager constable, the over-zealous investigator, and the over-nosy bureaucrat. Totalitarianism typically begins when a would-be tyrant—whether a Hitler or a Castro—plays upon the anxieties of the majority to institute repressive measures against despised or troublesome minorities. Gradually the repressive measures are extended, perhaps inexorably, to larger and larger segments of the populace.

It was to protest the possibility of such an eventuality in the U.S.A. that Mr. Justice Brandeis issued his eloquent dissent in a case in 1928 involving surveillance. He said:

"The makers of our Constitution . . . sought to protect Americans in their beliefs, their thoughts, their emotions and their sensations. They conferred as against the Government, the right to be let alone—the most comprehensive of the rights of man and the right most valued by civilized men."

Today, as we shall see, the Bill of Rights is under assault from many directions. Thomas Jefferson's vow that he had sworn eternal hostility to every form of tyranny over the mind of man has a quaint ring to many people in 1964. Aldous Huxley commented that the classic cry of Patrick Henry that he wanted either liberty or death now sounds melodramatic. Instead today, Huxley contended, we are more apt to demand, "Give me television and hamburgers but don't bother me with the responsibilities of liberty."

It is worth noting that Mr. Huxley's prophetic book, *Brave New World*, written way back in the thirties about a technological society living in doped-up bliss under a watchful tyrant six centuries from now, has been banned from several U.S. schools. Also among the banned is George Orwell's *1984*, depicting life under the ever-present electronic eye and ear of a tyrannical Big Brother a bare two decades from now. When the U.S. Commissioner of Education was asked about the banning of these two classics from a Miami high school, he declined to comment because he said he had never heard of either of the books!

Many of the present invasions of our privacy originate in the kinds of life the citizens have chosen to pursue. Often such intrusions can be checked only by an aroused concern about individual rights. Other of the invasions, as we shall see, are susceptible to legal restraint. In general the legal checks are in a state of lamentable confusion, vagueness, or neglect. One judge has described the state of the law of privacy, for example, as "still that of a haystack in a hurricane."

In the chapters that follow, let us then try to understand what is happening to our privacy—and our freedom—as individuals in the face of the new kinds of pressure generated by our violently changing world. As we explore this subject we might bear in mind a haunting comment made to me by Representative Robert Kastenmeier of Wisconsin, who has led several battles for individual rights on the floor of Congress. He said:

"Basically I am not hopeful about the pressures that will in time make our country something of a police state. Unless we can bring a release from the prolonged Cold War and can check the inward drift of our country, I sense a losing game."

2.Five Forces Undermining Our Privacy

'The fantastic advances in the field of electronic communication constitute a great danger to the privacy of the
individual."—Chief Justice Earl Warren

In stable primitive societies the attitudes of the people in regard
to what is proper and decent in personal relations— including
respect for privacy—do not change much from century to
century. In the Western world today, however, swirling forces are
causing whole populations willy-nilly to change their attitudes,
ideals, and behavior patterns within decades. This is nowhere
more dramatically apparent than in the United States.

One effect of these forces is the undermining of respect for
privacy. And there is a straining after even better ways to sort,
inspect, control, and keep an eye on individuals.

I shall note here five of the forces produced by the changing nature of our society and technology with the hope that
the reader will bear them in mind as underlying factors when
we later examine their effects in detail. Throughout, our concern will be with these underlying forces, not with individual
villains.

1. The Great Increase in Organized Living

In the coming decade another 40,000,000 people will be added
to the population of the U.S., a figure approximately equal to all
the people now living in the western half of the nation. And by
the end of the present decade four-fifths of all Americans will be
living in metropolitan areas. Until quite recent times most of the
nation's citizens had little experience of urban living with its ten-

dency to reduce self-sufficiency and to require that the individual relate to large organizations.

Closeness of living does not necessarily destroy privacy. Holland is one of the most thickly populated nations in the world and yet, until very recently, individual privacy was greatly respected. But genuine considerateness toward others has not been a notable trait in the average American's make-up for several decades. And as America's empty spaces began filling up, the inhabitants developed an increasingly gregarious style of life. Perhaps they were over-reacting to what historian Walter Prescott Webb called "the nauseating loneliness of frontier life." And perhaps now the overreacting is changing. But a few years ago an Argentine visitor referred to modern Americans (U.S. breed) as "friendly as puppies—and just as nosy." A lag has developed between the habits of a people and the condition of their existence, so that personal privacy suffers.

Simultaneously there has been the continuous growth of giant organizations in U.S. society. Michigan State's Professor Eugene Jennings observed that "organizations consume our privacy." And Clark Kerr, now president of the University of California, has commented that the destruction of privacy seems to issue from the logic of organization itself.

As technology develops, it spawns large organizations—both business and governmental—to keep up with technology. U.S. society in a little more than a century has moved from being a nation of entrepreneurs to being a nation of employees. Most people today work for large organizations.

The larger an organization becomes, the more its managers seem to be obsessed with controls on the people involved, to keep the organization from flying apart. Since the top managers in bureaucracies cannot hope to know all the individuals in their organization they resort to appraisal forms, cumulative files, six-page application forms, and lie detectors as a means of "knowing" their people better. And being dedicated to rationality, the managers become obsessed with assigning numbers to people.

Congressman Kastenmeier relates that when his three-year-old son opened a $10 bank account the bank asked for the lad's Social Security number. It may well be that within a few years organizational logic will require that a Social Security number be put on each newborn person's birth certificate—and follow him to his grave.

Officially, one's Social Security number is a well-guarded secret and cannot be used to keep track of people's whereabouts. But I was told that some states have been using Social Security numbers to trace deserting fathers. And private detectives told me they had often got a man's number merely by calling the personnel director of a company where the man was known to have worked. The standard form that investigators of one national investigative agency are supposed to fill out when checking up on a man specifies that his Social Security number be established.

Urban living has played a part in making citizens more fearful of being beset by criminals. In many urban areas these anxieties have a sound basis. In the first three months of 1963 the FBI's Crime Index indicated that the volume of serious crimes had risen seven per cent during the preceding year. A growth in population and a growth in temptations in a nation increasingly swollen with material goods could help to account for much of the increase.

Law-enforcement officials cry out for more effective tools and techniques for catching the criminals. They argue that criminals have become so slick in developing organizations based on business models and in using the aids of modern technology that the law enforcers must be permitted to become slicker and rougher. *The Police Review* carried the headline: LEGALIZED WIRETAPPING ABSOLUTELY NECESSARY, in quoting Brooklyn's district attorney. The late New York tabloid newspaper, the *Daily Mirror*, editorially called for the fingerprinting of all Americans.

News accounts of the prevalence of criminals have persuaded

many millions of Americans, too, that the police must indeed become slicker and rougher. Much of the public anxiety about crime, incidentally, seems to be concentrated in urban redevelopment areas. Here the residents usually live in relatively expensive new apartments built in the midst of low-income areas where the people often are of different ethnic, racial, or religious backgrounds and may be envious, resentful, or disdainful of their seemingly rich, stuck-up new neighbors.

At any rate we have the paradox of a society trying to put men on the moon when millions of its urban residents do not dare to walk alone at night in streets or parks near their homes.

The same society that breeds criminals by the millions demands that its police catch the criminals, even if they must trample on constitutional rights and existing laws to do so. There is little awareness that lawlessness is a symptom of national character and that the character must change before the symptoms can be significantly affected. To cite an extreme, a Methodist minister in Dallas charged, after President Kennedy's assassination, that "the spirit of assassination" had flourished in Dallas for some time. There were reports of small children in several public schools clapping and cheering when their teachers told them of the terrible event. The children were reflecting not only the intolerance of their parents but the new genteel lawlessness that forgives assaults, in violation of law, against people who are disapproved of for one reason or another. In Northern cities genteel citizens have condoned the use by police of lawless or heavy-handed methods against suspects who happen to be members of minority groups that have produced a disproportionate share of disturbance of the peace of their particular urban society.

The United States cannot hope even to start becoming a law-abiding society until the great majority of its citizens know in their hearts that the constitutional rights of every citizen must be respected.

2. The Movement Toward a Garrison State Mentality

Although not the least bit militaristic as a people, Americans are being swept toward being a martial—and thus watched—society. The impetus comes from the facts of the cold war, the space race, and the growing appreciation of how defense and space spending spur the nation's economy.

Tens of thousands of employees of federal agencies spend all or much of their time handling secret data. And then of course there are about 2,700,000 citizens in the U.S. armed forces who require varying degrees of surveillance based on their assignments.

More disquieting has been the spread of security precautions in U.S. industrial plants that do some business with the Pentagon. *Business Week* estimates that 24,000 industrial facilities are now under Pentagon regulations on security and that more than 3,500,000 industrial employees in the past fourteen years have had to obtain clearances.

Many of the companies are so anxious not to lose their contacts with the Pentagon that, to be on the safe side, they allow their security officers to push defense-type precautions into other areas of the company. In such instances little distinction in hiring and surveillance policy is made between employees working on defense contracts and those in the commercial, non-military phases of their company's operations. The industrial security chief for Temco Electronics was quoted in 1962 as stating: "Regardless of where a man is going to work, his background should be looked at as carefully as if he were going to work on classified material."

The fact that the United States has been involved in four hot wars during this century and in a prolonged cold war for most of the last two decades is responsible for the continual introduction of new surveillance techniques and social controls. What is disturbing, however, is that the government rarely relinquishes such wartime techniques and controls when the shooting ends.

In the national emergency of 1941 President Roosevelt, as Commander-in-Chief, quietly authorized his Attorney General, Robert Jackson, to resort to wiretapping in urgent cases involving the nation's security. This action was taken in the face of what seemed to be a flat prohibition against wiretapping for any reason. In 1934 Congress had voted such a prohibition when it enacted the now notorious Section 605 of the Communications Act.

Mr. Jackson found that one phrase, by straining, could be rationalized into an authorization to tap. That phrase said it was a crime to "intercept" and "divulge" messages. Mr. Jackson decided that for the emergency this could be stretched to mean that it was all right to intercept as long as you did not divulge. He chose to ignore a nearby phrase banning the "use" of any intercepted message.

The war emergency ended; but all of the U.S. Attorneys General since Mr. Jackson, including the incumbent one, have embraced his interpretation to justify wiretapping, when it seemed to be warranted, for "leads" only. And many local law-enforcement officials have echoed the Attorneys General. The interpretation has been mouthed so many times that people assume it is the "law."

Another hangover of wartime measures is the use of recording devices attached to telephones to monitor calls you make or receive. Before World War II there was occasional use of such devices at the War Department, with the switchboard operators scrupulously notifying the party on the other end of the line that the call would be recorded. As the war emergency approached, the demand for recordings became so urgent that the Signal Corps installed a great many of the devices and notice to the calling party was discontinued! By 1945 more than 2000 of them were in operation. An FCC report in 1947 related that "The wartime experience gained with telephone recording devices has resulted in an unprecedented commercial demand since V-J day." By 1947 there were 19,000 recorders in use in the U.S., three quarters of them by business organizations, with no legal requirement that the other party be notified. Meanwhile in Washington the use of monitoring continued to grow.

Consider a final example. Few people realize it, but a sedition statute that goes back to World War I and is still in effect declares it a crime willfully to make false statements about the U.S. armed forces that could interfere with their success or to make any kind of statements intended to discourage enlistments. This statute was revived in 1953 while the nation was in a state of emergency, while winding up the Korean War, and today the government refuses to declare the emergency ended. Perhaps it never will. Technically the Southerners who criticized use of federal troops during crises involving civil rights for Negroes could have been prosecuted for sedition since such statements conceivably might discourage enlistments in some areas. Similarly those Republicans who suggested that the Russians had not pulled their missiles out of Cuba could be prosecuted since this was contrary to official statements. No Attorney General in recent decades has chosen to enforce this statute in peacetime. But a would-be dictator could have a fine time using it to hound critics.

An even greater legacy of suspicion and surveillance has followed in the wake of the prolonged Cold War with the Soviet Union. The devious tactics of Communists provided very real grounds for acting vigorously to counteract them. But it is also unfortunately true that a good many people have focused all their anxieties and hostilities into a generalized fear of Communism, and that this fear has been exploited in many cases by members of the radical right to harass anyone with whom they seriously disagreed. Freedom to communicate thoughts and express unorthodox ideas has thus often, even in private discussions, been inhibited in many areas in recent years.

3. The Pressures Generated by Abundance

It may seem odd that affluence should undermine privacy, but it clearly has. There is evidence that much of the great increase in surveillance, investigation, and intrusion into people's privacy can be traced to conditions arising from abundance.

Consider the problem of launching and moving goods in today's superabundant economy. Styles in products are changing swiftly. The lifetime of product types is becoming ever shorter. And, there is increasing strain to find significantly new products or variants. All these factors have produced a greater preoccupation with secrecy. A company concerned with secrecy in industry begins to wonder who can be trusted and brings in the undercover agents to check on employees.

This pressure to move goods affects individual privacy in another way. Companies have been turning to more relentless selling tactics to attract our attention. Privacy diminishes as the hawkers telephone us several times a week, or shove their feet in the door while posing as survey makers.

Affluence has produced a tremendous increase in the use of credit and in the sale of all sorts of insurance policies. The sellers of both credit and insurance feel that to survive they must investigate the lives of prospects. Every insurance policy, for example, is a risk, a bet. The companies try to hedge their bets on policies of substance by arranging for a quiet investigation of the insured's finances and living habits. And so we have millions of insurance investigations, often accompanied by a "neighborhood check"—and the findings often reach files from which information is swapped or sold.

The growth in the amount of spare time that most Americans can enjoy has in at least one way made privacy more difficult to achieve for many of them. Americans have more time now to read newspapers, magazines, and books and to watch TV and listen to radio. They want not only to be informed but to be entertained and, often, titillated. Many enjoy gossip and scandalous facts about fellow citizens. And many of the mass media have relentlessly sought to provide them with a steady diet of gossipy information. The result of both the desire for such information and the media's efforts to supply it has in effect produced a combined assault on privacy. The dual nature of this assault is pointed up by Morris Ernst and Alan Schwartz in their definitive legal analysis of privacy as it is affected by the media.[1] At one point they note that the desire "of the mass media to make a profit at the expense of our privacy is a growing pressure." And they ask: "How should the ever-increasing thirst of the public for news and information be balanced against the sometimes desperate desire for privacy on the part of the individual?"

Finally we might simply note sociologist Kingsley Davis' observation that the explosive growth of both possessions and people "is causing an ever larger portion of our high level of living to be used to escape from the consequences of congestion."

4. The Growth of Investigation as a Private Industry

There are now not only thousands of firms offering their services as investigators but also a large number of management-consultant firms that derive most of their income from screening, assessing, or observing employees. And there are quite a few hundred psychologists who are happy to reap the bounty paid for screening, probing, and assessing managerial aspirants. Finally, a great many firms are eager to keep a steady stream of subjects harnessed to their lie detector machines. An official of one of the nation's larger investigative agencies told me with a grin: "A lot of money can be made with lie detectors."

Many of these enterprises with a vested interest in anxiety among business managers work strenuously to keep reminding the nation's industrialists of the untrustworthiness or undependability of a good many employees. The president of the giant William J. Burns International Detective Agency wrote an article for *Business Management* that was entitled: "Does Your Plant Invite Theft?" He offered a 27-point check list of danger spots that needed to be watched, and called attention to the value of undercover operatives.

And a giant investigative firm based in Miami, the Wackenhut Corporation, has been bombarding managements with a brochure headed: "How Secure Is Your Business?" It asks: "Are your employees thoroughly screened before they are hired? . . . Have your offices been checked for the presence of electronic listening devices?" etc.

The growth of investigation as a full-fledged and potent industry has been greatly assisted by a new and unprecedented phenomenon. That is the fact that many thousands of men who have received thorough and intensive training in surveillance and investigative techniques by the U.S. Government have made themselves available in the possibly greener pastures of private enterprise.

Such highly trained investigators include not only former military and Central Intelligence Agency specialists in espionage, policing, intelligence, and counterintelligence but graduates of such other intelligence agencies as the Secret Service, former Treasury agents, former General Accounting Office watchdogs, civil service investigators, postal inspectors, and special agents of the FBI. These graduates number in the tens of thousands. Some have gone into jobs completely unrelated to their government specialties, but many thousands are making at least some use of their government training in watching or handling people in their new careers.

One of the nation's more fabulous private investigators, John Cye Cheasty of New York, is a graduate of the U.S. Secret Service, the Internal Revenue Intelligence Unit, and Navy Intelligence units. (He attained the rank of commander in the Navy.) In commenting on the techniques he uses as a private investigator when he is developing reports on business executives or candidates for executive jobs, he said he felt that investigators such as himself could do the job better than the usual representatives from a company's personnel department. He explained:

"We have ways of getting information, ways of interviewing, that are different than the ways used by personnel departments. We can get to people we want to see faster because we have learned our techniques in the service. We have learned techniques for commanding attention, commanding the truth, and commanding the information without seeming to be aggressive or imperative about it. We can move in and take over an interview and get what we want."

The role of the ex-FBI special agents in U.S. society offers an interesting case in point since they command, however justifiably, the most awe from the public. Industry courts them for all sorts of roles. In 1962 the *Wall Street Journal* carried the headline: MORE COMPANIES FIND MANAGEMENT TALENT AMOUNG EX-FBI AGENTS.

There are now apparently at least three quarters as many ex-FBI agents as active FBI agents in the U.S. Approximately 6000 men are active agents, and the membership of the Society of Former Special Agents of the Federal Bureau of Investigation (national headquarters: 274 Madison Avenue, New York) is near 4500. Presumably not all former agents have bothered to maintain membership. The society prints a newsletter that serves as a sort of grapevine for the organization.

Among the ex-FBI agents are clergymen, admen, writers, professors, ranchers, bankers, oil operators, dentists, and a number of corporate presidents. They include at least one neurological surgeon. And of course there are a great many accountants and lawyers. The 1961 directory of the society listed as members two governors (New Mexico and North Carolina) and the attorney general of Florida (who gave as his regular occupation "special investigator").

An interesting concentration of ex-FBI men, incidentally, has existed, at least until very recently, on the working staff of the American Security Council (Chicago), a militantly right-wing organization that is supported by several thousand companies and other organized groups. It disseminates information about what it considers to be statist and Communist conspiracies; publishes reports on national and international military and political developments as seen by its business or military-oriented analysts; and in the recent past it has provided information on names of employees or applicants submitted to it by corporate personnel officers of many of its member companies.

Our main interest in the Council, however, is in the following fact: As of 1962, its president, its administrative director, and its Washington bureau chief were all listed as ex-FBI men in the 1961 directory of the Society of Former Special Agents of the Federal Bureau of Investigation, Inc.

The Society of Former Agents is considerably more than a fraternal organization. It is also a clearinghouse for information about jobs available, and it offers a directory of trained investigators available for special projects in just about every corner of the U.S.A. In the geographic part of the directory there is an asterisk after the name of each member who has indicated he is "available for work."

In Indiana, for example, about half of all the society's members are "available." They are located in seventeen towns and cities. In New Jersey the "available" members can be reached in forty-six towns and cities. And in California there are ex-agents "available for work" in seventy-three towns and cities.

One of the more interesting entrants among the ex-agents who indicated in the 1961 directory that they were "available for work" was a police captain in Knoxville, Tennessee!

A random sampling of the 1961 directory suggests that several hundred of the former special agents are in charge of handling personnel at business corporations as either security officers, personnel directors, labor-relations directors, or industrial-relations directors. The Ford Motor Company, incidentally, had 39 ex-FBI special agents on its payroll in some capacity.

A check of all the society members who left the FBI in the years 1930, 1940, 1950, and 1960 reveals that 35 per cent of those who now have active careers are in jobs involving investigation, policing, or security enforcement.

Some of the former FBI men have banded together to form their own nationwide organizations for investigative assignments. One is Fidelifacts, a loose network of more than 200 former FBI agents. They operate on a franchise basis and either pay each other for investigations or have an exchange arrangement. (The name was recently changed from Fidelifax to Fidelifacts because people seemed to assume that Fidelifax should be a photocopying company.)

Fidelifacts has full-time offices in such places as Boston, Stamford, Albany, Baltimore, Richmond, Atlanta, New York City, Detroit, Las Vegas, Miami, Chicago, Charlotte, Garden City, Phoenix, San Francisco, Los Angeles, Billings, Akron, Houston, Syracuse, and Minneapolis. It has in addition many part-time "resident reporters" operating in areas not yet large enough to support an office.

An outfit that has benefited spectacularly from the romance of the FBI label is the Wakenhut Corporation, headquartered in Coral Gables, Florida. It is such a fast-burning business rocket that it is still something of a mystery to a number of people in the investigative field. In less than a decade it has grown from four private eyes into the fourth largest investigative and security organization in the nation, with a staff of 3500, complete with a lie-detector division.

All its announcements, and all public reports about it that I have seen, have stressed the fact that it was founded by ex-special agents of the FBI and is led by ex-FBI men. This is correct. George Wackenhut, a husky, jut-jawed, energetic man with a bone-crushing handshake, founded the organization in 1954 immediately after serving a three-year hitch with the FBI. Three of his colleagues also were former agents. And several of his top executives today are ex-FBI agents. But the client signing a large contract with Wackenhut Corporation in the expectation that he would be getting the exclusive services of ex-FBI men would be disappointed. In 1961 less than one per cent of its total staff were listed as ex-FBI men in the membership directory of the Society of Former Special Agents of the FBI.

The business editor of the *Miami Herald*, in commenting on the phenomenal national growth of this local firm, mentioned that its FBI leadership gives it an advantage in signing up new industrial clients. He said Wackenhut has this special advantage in negotiating with industrial security officers "because a high percentage of industrial security officers were once with the FBI"!

5. The Electronic Eyes, Ears, and Memories

In the novel George Orwell wrote about the year 1984 he envisioned that the advances of electronics had enabled his fictional totalitarian leader to install a telescreen in each living space of the realm. In this way the tyrant could maintain virtually total visual and audio surveillance when he chose. As Orwell put it: "You had to live—did live, from habit that became instinct—in the assumption that every sound you made was overheard and, except in darkness, every movement scrutinized."

If Mr. Orwell were writing his book today rather than in the 1940s his details would surely be more horrifying. Today there are cameras that can indeed see in the dark. There are banks of giant memory machines that conceivably could recall in a few seconds every pertinent action—including failures, embarrassments, or possibly incriminating acts— from the lifetime of each citizen. And brain research has progressed to the point where it is all too readily believable that a Big Brother could implant an electrode in the brain of each baby at birth and thereafter maintain by remote control a certain degree of restraint over the individual's moods and behavior, at least until his personality had suitably jelled.

Fortunately for the human race, a good many people are becoming apprehensive about the wonders bestowed by electronic research. Fortunately also the expense of most of the devices prohibits their use against whole populations (though the prices are coming down), so the present uses are mostly selective. Nevertheless in the course of a year literally millions of Americans are watched or overheard electronically without their awareness at some time during any single week.

Let us pause for a moment to brief ourselves on the state of the "art" of electronic surveillance as of 1964. In subsequent chapters we shall see how the devices that have been developed are applied in many situations in ways that tend to annihilate the privacy and dignity of the citizens under scrutiny.

Each year several thousand TV cameras are sold to industry, and such giants as General Precision, General Electric, and RCA are among the companies selling them. Seattle's classified phone directory lists fourteen local companies offering to sell or install closed-circuit TV. Many of the TV cameras used in industry are for such prosaic purposes as watching instrument panels or furnace operations; others are for watching people.

In some instances the people involved know about the people-watching, as at the gates of an IBM plant doing research work in Endicott, New York. In others it is done secretly.

Mr. Max Kanter—president of ITV in New York, which rents or sells closed-circuit installations—explained that if you wish to conceal the cameras even the lens need not show. He said: "If there is screening material or mesh to conceal the camera, and if it is focused at some point beyond, the lens can look right through the screening material." (His charge for renting basic equipment for one week: about $200.)

The makers of TV cameras for surveillance have not only learned to miniaturize them to a thickness of only about four inches, but they have learned that by shooting into a mirror they can install the cameras vertically in a wall that has a four-inch air space. The fact that the FBI uses closed-circuit TV in some of its surveillance work came out in the trial of a Navy yeoman suspected of spying.

Hidden still cameras are also in wide use for recording the activities of people. A company called Cameras for Industry has been aggressive in selling plants, stores, banks, etc., on "Automatic Photo Systems" that can now be rented for "pennies a day." The cameras operate silently, can take thousands of pictures in a single loading, and, it is explained, they can either be used openly or be concealed. The camera can be triggered by a photoelectric eye. Or if a clerk is handing you a document he can first insert it in a number-stamping machine, and the act of stamping will trigger a hidden camera beamed at you.

Then there are the tiny cameras used by investigators or others seeking evidence. Some are built into cigarette lighters. As the owner lights his cigarette, his thumb action simultaneously triggers the camera.

The impetus for the development of many of these remarkable surveillance devices came from defense and space research and from efforts to keep up with the Russians in this area. Advances in infrared photography (in the dark) resulted largely from research for aerial reconnaissance, as did automatic tripping devices for cameras. Many early developments in closed-circuit TV were for use in surveillance of machines and dials as well as people at missile launching complexes. Transistors made possible miniature transmitters for use in satellites where every ounce counts.

And then there was the evidence of remarkable Russian techniques that inspired the U.S. Government to plunge into research and development contracts in the fields of surveillance and counterintrusion. The discovery of that tiny microphone imbedded in the Great Seal of the United States that hung behind the U.S. ambassador's desk in the Moscow embassy was more of a shock to our technicians than has ever been admitted. A man intimately familiar with the search for this microphone confided: "It was an advancement of the art by the Russians that we were not then up to. We were not equipped to spot it because they had placed across the street an enormous transmitter beamed to bounce signals off the buried cavity device, and that giant transmitter was operating in an ultra-high-frequency spectrum we were not equipped to detect." The British embassy inspired the Americans to tear the ambassador's office apart, literally, because our British cousins confided that they had detected at their own embassy a signal they couldn't identify.

More than one hundred hidden listening devices have in recent years been found in U.S. embassies and residences in Soviet-bloc countries. A picturesque example of Soviet advances in miniaturization was discovered accidentally by a U.S. military attache at a Moscow bar when he picked up a martini not intended for him. The "olive" in it, according to a *Time* account, contained a transmitter, and the tiny toothpick stuck in it was an antenna.

One step the U.S. Government is now taking to protect secret discussions in its embassies in questionable countries is to ship portable rooms to the embassies. Such a room is sent as a knockdown package and assembled inside the embassy. It is shielded on all sides to prevent transmission of sound and is so built as to permit visual inspection under, over, and all around the "room" for any wires.

U.S. companies now can make microphones and transmitters just about as small as anyone could conceivably desire. Transmitters now available can fit inside a lipstick tube or ball-point pen or appear to be a lump of sugar. Microphones smaller than a twenty-five-cent piece are being made and widely used.

At least thirty U.S. companies are now involved in manufacturing electronic eavesdropping equipment. One of the larger companies, Solar Research, Inc., in Oakland Park, Florida, claims that in 1962, for example, its sales increased fourfold within a year. Some sell only to law-enforcement agencies; others sell only surveillance equipment to law-enforcement agencies but sell counterintrusion devices to private concerns; and some seem interested in selling anything they have to anyone who has the money to pay for the devices. There is no law against manufacturing or selling bugging devices, and pitifully few laws, FCC regulations, or court decisions against their use. I had no difficulty, for example, in obtaining catalogues from several companies. And I saw on display in the window of an electronics shop on Forty-third Street in New York City a device that automatically starts a tape recorder when a telephone conversation comes onto a line.

When one West Coast manufacturer of "bugs" was displaying his new models to the convention of the American Society for Industrial Security, he cautioned that sales were "subject to pertinent regulation." But he added: "I cannot be responsible for the integrity of the user. . . . I'm not going to ask the buyer what he does with it." (A leading electronics magazine, incidentally, has advertised for $22.50 a "Be a Spy" correspondence course that includes instruction in bugging.)

As for tiny tape recorders, their manufacturers have been conducting large-scale advertising campaigns in large-circulation newspapers and magazines. A full-page ad for the pocket-size Minifon cited not only its value in recording routine memos, conferences, etc., but pictured its "wrist-watch" microphone ... its "inconspicuous tie-clip microphone" . . . how the recorder could be "concealed" in one's briefcase . . . and its "unique telephone pickup" for attaching to one's telephone receiver to record phone conversations.

In the course of my research I was given a number of demonstrations on the arts of bugging and de-bugging by people who were clearly experts. Those offering their services to the public as anti-intrusion specialists were perhaps most willing to discuss openly the problems involved. Raymond Farrell, manager of Bondwitt Sound Engineering Co., in New York, explained: "If we're serving the public, we're anti-intrusion specialists; if we're serving the law, lawfully, we're intrusion specialists."

As he and I were chatting in an office, he took out of his briefcase a transmitter the size of a small matchbook. At his suggestion we went down the hall to a room where two girls were chatting and with their permission placed it and its tiny microphone on a table several feet from them. We returned to the office where we had been talking. He closed the door and turned on his receiving box. The conversation of the girls came through loud and clear. He said the girls could be heard at least a block away, and perhaps two, depending on conditions.

The most impressive demonstration was put on for me by Ralph V. Ward of Mosler Research Products, Inc., in Danbury, Connecticut. He is one of the leading authorities in the free world on surveillance devices. His company and its predecessors pioneered in making miniature surveillance devices for federal agencies, including some in the international field. As vice-president of sales he spends a good deal of time in Washington taking orders and soliciting research and development contracts. "We have not run out of wonders," he said. The Mosler company now also makes much of its equipment available to state and city agencies and to licensed investigative agencies. And it offers to industry for slightly more than $300 a "security" kit that contains a host of tools for detecting bugging devices—but none of the bugging devices themselves.

The amiable Mr. Ward generously spent most of a day giving me a chalk talk on the problems involved in both bugging and de-bugging and demonstrated, item by item, the tools that go into the pigskin satchels sold to federal and other official agencies. The filled satchels are produced in lots of a hundred and contain both bugging and de-bugging tools. One interesting item was a microphone mounted in rubber a quarter of an inch thick. It can be slipped under a hotel door. Another device was the spike mike: a microphone attached to a spike nearly a foot long. It can be driven into walls or doors, which serve as resonators.

I shall try to describe here my understanding of the latest achievements in microphoning techniques and tools as they were explained to me by expert informants, including Mr. Ward.

The challenge today is not to make the "bugs" small but to make them more undetectable, for use in spots where the occupants are security-oriented and likely to make checks. A transmitter, no matter how small, is fairly easy to spot by an anti-intrusion expert with room-"sweeping" equipment. He hears a squeal in his receiver when his electronic "mop" gets close to a hidden transmitter. A buried microphone with a tiny wire leading to a remote tape recorder is vastly more difficult to detect. Thus the transmitter is considered to be most appropriate for quick hit-and-run jobs, whereas the mike wired to a remote recorder is preferred for permanent installations.

Some of the preferred places to tape hidden microphones in a room are at the back of desk drawers (because people usually don't go all the way back even when searching), in the upholstery, or the underside of a bed. If a long-term bugging with a transmitter is planned, there is an advantage in putting the transmitter in an electric clock or TV set or in a light fixture so that it can draw its power from the building's electric power source.

Another favored spot for hiding bugging devices is within the frame of a picture on the wall. Mosler sells a nice pastoral scene that has a very thin transmitter pasted inside the paper covering the back of the picture. (Price: $215.) A visual search would not detect this transmitter even if the picture were taken off the wall. These pictures are particularly esteemed for installation in hotel or motel rooms where persons under surveillance are going to stay.

The base of a telephone is also a choice spot for making a quick installation of a bug: Mr. Farrell demonstrated to me that

it can be done within one minute. There are two ways of installing the bug. A two-wire tap using a small transmitter in the base
gives you only the telephone conversation. A three- wire tap includes a wire that jumps the hook switch and thus broadcasts all
calls and in addition all conversation going on in the room when
the phone is not in use.

As counterintrusion skills have advanced, the profession-
als have sought to place their microphones beyond the probing
range of the metal-detection sweepers now widely used. This
means placing the mike behind the wall—and as far away as possible. Mr. Ward explained:

"Normally the best way to bug is through a pinhole that is
too small to see in the imperfections of the woodwork or the
plaster. Visually, you wouldn't find the pinhole." (Researchers are
at work to develop pinhole finders.) But even with a pinhole the
presence of a microphone buried in the wall may produce a slight
signal on the metal detector if it is just inside the plaster behind
the pinhole opening. Now, Mr. Ward indicated, the tube mike has
been developed. This permits you to put the mike several inches
back from the pinhole. The tube, which can be a plastic resonator,
leads from the pinhole to the mike and reduces the chances that
the microphone will be detected by any metal-detecting device.
Dr. Leo L. Beranek of the Massachusetts Institute of Technology, an authority on acoustics, has described devices that can be
placed on the outside wall of a room under surveillance. Voices
inside the room set up mechanical vibrations that may be detected by such a device placed against the outer wall. Most experts hired for counterintrusion work feel insecure unless they
can inspect all rooms around, above, and below the room they are
guarding for any signs of bugging activities.

As for the highly directional microphones that reputedly
can pick up conversations from great distances, a sizable folklore
on the reach of such microphones has developed. Published reports that they can pull in voices from 1200 feet away or through

closed windows are apparently without basis. But apparently some do bring in conversations 100-150 feet away under moderately noisy conditions and up to 500 feet if conditions are ideal (quiet).

The first of these miracle mikes to receive much attention was the parabolic microphone, placed at the focal point of a reflector. Such giant saucers were first developed on a large scale during World War II, before radar, and proved to be much more sensitive than the human ear in detecting approaching aircraft. An effective parabolic mike requires a reflector with a diameter of at least three and preferably six feet. This makes it somewhat cumbersome for most sleuthing purposes, but it can be concealed behind bushes, or in an open truck, or in the darkened balcony of a conference room.

Another kind of long-range mike is the so-called machine-gun type, consisting of a bundle of tubes of varying lengths, each of which brings the sound to a microphone at the rear. Such an arrangement of tubes tends to eliminate most sounds not almost directly to the front. Cumbersomeness is again a problem. The picture of the one I saw in operation indicated that the longest of the pipes was about seven feet. The man using it was behind bushes. A Senate subcommittee was told that this type of mike proved to be practical in gaining evidence of blackmail involving a motion picture actor in California. The blackmailer, being suspicious that the man might wear a bug, specified that the actor meet him at a remote place on a beach and wear only bathing trunks. The actor complied but a machine-gun mike a few hundred feet away in the dark was able to pick up enough of their talk to provide incriminating evidence.

Still a third type of long-range mike is produced by Electro-Voice, which specializes in developing microphones for broadcasters. Recently it developed a single-barrel mike about seven feet long. All major TV networks have used it to pick up the voices of questioners at presidential press conferences . . . to pick up the sounds of distant bands in parades . . . and to pick up—from the side lines—the voices and sounds of body impact of players at football games. The National Football League now has banned it because it was picking up and broadcasting too many obscenities. Electro-Voice has had inquiries from—and made sales to— a number of customers who may well have been investigators, but it has no knowledge of how many are actually being used in investigative work, since these users keep pretty quiet about their methods of operation. Its big mike costs about $1000. A simpler non-electronic way to eavesdrop on distant conversations—if the eavesdropper does not need recorded evidence—is to employ a lip reader with binoculars.

One of the most prevalent forms of bugging is a concealed mike-transmitter on the body. Miniaturization has made this feasible; and unfortunately there is little reason to fear prosecution.

Many experts favor placing the mike behind the tie, fairly low down so as not to pick up interference from the heartbeat. Tape recorders are now small enough so that there is little chance they will be detected if taped to the body.

However the experts prefer concealed transmitters rather than recorders. The transmitter will broadcast to a tape recorder that can be several hundred feet away, and even a fairly powerful transmitter can be made much smaller than a good concealable recorder. Also it can operate without reloading longer than a tape recorder. And even if a person is caught with it during a frisk the information obtained up to that point cannot be destroyed, and if necessary help can be dispatched. The transmitter can be carried on a coat pocket with its antenna going up to the armpit and down the sleeve. One of the best places to put either a transmitter or small recorder, according to a man who has submitted to police frisks to test his theory, is just above the coccyx. Another favored way of concealing a transmitter and mike is to pack them inside a king-size cigarette package designed to feel, to the touch, soft as a package of cigarettes.

To complete our rundown on bugging devices, there are a variety of tailing aids that can be attached to an automobile. One simple transmitter broadcasting a pulsing tone signal is mounted on four magnets and can be attached to any clean metal surface under the car in a matter of seconds. It can be heard for a mile.

The "art" of wiretapping—which is at least technically a more illicit form of eavesdropping—has also seen some advancements in recent years. One is a miniature transmitter that can be attached to the tapped listening post. This is not only more convenient, but has the advantage of reducing the chance the tapper can be traced if a tap is discovered.

Tappers frequently pose as telephone repairmen, and some who engage in tapping on a large scale even buy or build imitations of the green telephone-company trucks.

Tools for the more elementary kinds of direct wiretapping cost less than $25. And for $4.25 one can purchase a little device that feeds a telephone conversation into a tape recorder. It can be installed in three seconds by pressing its suction attachments against the back of the telephone receiver.

However, when one gets into transmitters, automatic recorders, and many of the microphoning tools that we've discussed, the prices soar. A professional eavesdropper is likely to require an expensive bag—or truckload—of tools. An examination of four catalogues issued by producers of surveillance equipment (Mosler, Tracer Electronics, Inc., W. S. J. Electronics, and R. B. Clifton Electronics Surveillance Equipment) gives some idea of an eavesdropper's overhead. Here are some sample prices:

—Transmitters for wireless wiretapping. Prices range from $65 to $200 depending upon whether signal must be broadcast one block or three.

—Picture frame transmitter, $215.

—General-purpose transmitter to be planted inside room, $95 to $137, presumably depending on quality.

—Transmitters for concealment on body, $150 to $220.

—Device for automatically starting tape recorder when conversation begins on tapped telephone line, and stopping when conversation stops, $76 to $105.

Since a few states ban even the possession of wiretapping equipment by private parties, the Clifton catalogue states at the end of its price list: "Caution—in many parts of the world there are certain laws which prohibit using some of the items above. It is the sole responsibility of the buyer (and not the seller) to ascertain through legal counsel how these laws may apply to the use of each item purchased." Tracer Electronics simply notes after some of its items: "Sold for use subject to pertinent regulations." And the proposed FCC regulations restricting use of radio transmitters for electronic eavesdropping, if and when promulgated, will in no way affect the selling of such devices, but will only make the users warier of their legal position.

A quite different kind of electronic surveillance—and control—has become possible through the development of the giant memory machines. Each month more and more information about individual citizens is being stored away in some gigantic memory machine. Thus far, the information about individuals is usually fed into the super-computers to serve a socially useful or economically or politically attractive purpose. But will it always be? This might especially be asked concerning those memory machines that are building up cumulative files on individual lives.

All the storing and accumulating of information makes one wonder. Dr. Robert Morison, director of Medical and Natural Science for the Rockefeller Foundation, has commented: "We are coming to recognize that organized knowledge puts an immense amount of power in the hands of people who take the trouble to master it." It may be significant that increasingly it is those who hold the office of comptroller in U.S. corporations who rise so frequently to the presidencies. Their control of the computers gives them an edge on information over their competitors.

If information is power, Americans should be uneasy about the amount of information the federal government is starting to file on its citizens in its blinking memory banks. There are, for example, the gigantic memory machines that the Internal Revenue Service is starting to use to check data from our tax returns against data accumulated about us from other sources, such as employers and banks. The computers also watch for unlikely patterns. Obviously these memory banks are useful tools for fair and efficient tax collecting. But what are the implications for two decades from now, in 1984? If future bureaucrats choose, they can build up so-called "cum," or cumulative files, on each taxpayer over decades, and thus will have, instantly recallable, a vast amount of personal information about the living habits of every adult in the realm.

One computer maker, Bernard S. Benson, bluntly concedes that concentration of power in the form of accumulated information can be "catastrophically dangerous." He suggests that individual privacy ultimately may be at the mercy of the man in a position to push the button that makes the machine remember. At an international conference on information processing sponsored by UNESCO in Paris, he reminded his colleagues that it was "high time" they started devoting part of their conferences to discussing how to insure that any new accomplishments will be beneficial to mankind.

Whatever the benefits, the marvelous new electronic devices with memories or ears or eyes are serving to push back the boundaries of each individual's privacy. As we shall shortly see, the electronic eyes and ears are being put to a host of ingenious uses for the purpose of people-watching.

These five forces that are at work in the society of the United States—and to some degree in most highly industrial societies of the world—have accounted for an immense growth of surveillance over individual citizens and a massive invasion of their privacy.

PART II

Some Specific Areas of Assault

3. How to Strip a Job-Seeker Naked

"Bill, one more question before you leave. . . . Are you inclined to be homosexual?"—Question that the author heard a polygraph examiner address to a young man being considered for a salesman's job

A few years ago a management consultant in Chicago told me, "We have developed techniques that strip people psychologically naked."[1] At the time I thought he was merely showing an entrepreneur's exuberance in promoting some psychiatrically oriented assessment sheets he had developed for personnel directors to use in assessing managerial can-didates for private industry. Now I find a gigantic trend, involving thousands of companies, toward investigating all or most job applicants, not just would-be executives, to the point where the individuals are often deprived of virtually every shred of privacy.

All across the country, managements are evincing a growing wariness about taking on new "teammates." They used to size up a man by looking him over and by determining his "trade reputation." That is no longer enough. The increasing suspiciousness is illustrated in a booklet widely circulated by the American Management Association. It is titled "How to Keep Bad Apples Out of the Barrel." The cover illustration shows two men—one at a file and one at a desk—eyeing each other suspiciously.

The booklet, by a professor of management at the University of Wisconsin, describes how a prospective employee's private life can be investigated by "personal interviews with the neighbors both at his present address and at two or three of his former locations." And the blurb explains, "With the workforce more on the move than ever before, companies now run the risk of finding themselves loaded down with all kinds of undesirable employees."

Possibly another reason for the growing wariness is that a company takes on a larger commitment than in earlier decades when a man is hired, because of all the payments that must be made by the company for unemployment compensation, Social Security, insurance, pensions. Also, many companies find it necessary to make commitments in the form of job-security agreements with the unions.

But the suspiciousness of managements is also encouraged by the proliferating investigative firms, search firms, and psychological testing firms who keep worrying them as insistently as the deodorant makers asking in their commercials: "But can you be sure?" Managements are warned that the ordinary employment interview is ineffective as a safeguard because the applicant is on his good behavior then. They are warned that ordinary application forms can be filled with a pack of lies. They are warned that letters of reference are farcical and only a fool would trust them. They are warned that even a telephone call to a former superior may produce false assurances because the former superior may be pleased to be well rid of the man or may fear a slander suit.

What is the answer? It is a probe in *depth*. This may cost anywhere from $15 to $250 depending on the importance of the job and the probing techniques used. Each year several million Americans are subjected to these probes, often without their knowledge. We shall explore three of the major approaches:

—The use of a straight sleuthing to do a "background" check or compile a life history.

——The use of lie detectors.

—The use of psychiatrists, psychologists, or psychological apprentices armed with tests to make a personality analysis.

There is some overlapping in the kind of personal information each is designed to uncover; but each also is assumed to be superior in uncovering certain areas of one's life, soul, and psyche. Let us examine them in turn.

1. The Use of Investigative Sleuthing

A corporate personnel director may simply turn to a local private eye. One such private investigator in the Baltimore area confided to the pages of *Police Review* his practices in making an employment check. He digs up everything he can about a prospect by talking with neighbors, former employers, and co-workers. "At no time," he asserted, "is the identity of the inquiring client made known to the persons being questioned about the applicant." (My own practice is to shut the door on any investigator who will not disclose at the outset who wants the information and why.)

Our private eye in Baltimore, after checking out his facts, turns in a report to the personnel manager. If his report contains "derogatory data," he said, the applicant may be granted the privilege of furnishing an oral explanation in a "private interview" with the personnel manager. He said that one personnel manager, in granting such a "private interview," usually "requests a tape recording of the interview [made without the applicant's knowledge] for subsequent evaluation with our office." If after the interview the man is not hired, "the recording is erased forever. If he is placed on the payroll, the tape is retained in his personnel folder for later inconsistencies that may arise in which veracity may be the issue."

If the applicant has been working in another town or state the client probably will turn to an investigative network, such as Fidelifacts, with its 200 ex-FBI special agents scattered in many cities. These ex-FBI men conduct *personal* interviews with former employers, check the neighborhood, the bank, the local police, and so on. The New York City branch of Fidelifacts reports that in one large sampling of its works it had turned up "adverse information" in 29 per cent of its investigations of prospective employees. (It cited wife trouble, evidence of drunkenness, absenteeism, indebtedness, poor job performance, etc.) The head of the New York office, Vincent Gillen, who has also worked as a lawyer and a professor, finds the horizons for such "pre-employment investigations" broadening rapidly. He said that originally these "PEIs" were designed to screen applicants for sensitive government posts and jobs in industry requiring bonding. "However in the last several years," he said, "their uses have broadened. We've investigated job applicants ranging from charwomen in a bank to the top corporate executives."

Franchise holders of Fidelifacts are likely to charge $8.00 or $9.00 for each source checked on an ordinary worker, perhaps $80 for a more thorough report on a managerial candidate. Mr. Gillen told me the fact that each man holding a franchise is a former FBI agent is a great sales point because of the high esteem in which the public holds the FBI.

John Cye Cheasty, the former Secret Service, Internal Revenue, and Navy Intelligence man, serves as a counsel to top managment and confines himself largely to checking out managerial personnel. He relates: "We were asked the other day by a client where they should start checking their personnel. We laid down this rule. If the man makes more than $8000 a year he should be checked coming in [to the company]. If, on the other hand, he comes in at a lower salary but is considered a potential executive you should check him out anyhow." In the past, he contends, companies have been content to judge a man simply on his "trade reputation." Now, however, he states, more and more companies are making "extensive pre-employment checkups" before hiring such people. And he added: "I think that industrial intelligence is one of the fastest-growing businesses in the United States today. . . ."

Much of the investigating of executives, especially in the financial world, is done by Bishop's Service. The "Bishop's Report" on a man is held in considerable awe in some circles, and a good one is widely regarded as a prerequisite for getting ahead. Actually this is only partially true. The president of Bishop's, William M. Chiariello, explains that his firm has actually made full investigative reports on about 10,000 executives. "The men who make decisions," he said, "can't escape the cold, hard facts of an investigation. I find that more and more business leaders . . . no longer rely upon their own appraisal." In addition to its 10,000 full-fledged personnel reports made for specific clients, Bishop's has in its files on the second story of a skyscraper in the Wall Street area of New York information on 5,000,000 people—or just about everyone of consequence in the U.S. business world.

A full Bishop's Report on a man is not cheap. The Bishop motto is "A Man's Whole Life Preludes the Single Deed." A report is likely to cost from $150 up. Those that were shown to me ran from twelve to eighteen pages and covered with seeming thoroughness the subject's career, his finances, his mode of life. Each page bore a stamp in the middle sternly reminding the client that all information thereon was "privileged and confidential."

Mr. Chiariello, who was trained as a lawyer, considers amateurish and unnecessary the use of electronics, gumshoeing, keyhole peeping, or posing as a government agent to get information. "The heart of the investigating process is interviewing and gaining public documentary evidence." His investigators work on salary rather than at piecework rates, the method of payment more common at large investigative firms. And he scorns the rule common with some firms that investigators must come up with "derogatory information" in at least ten per cent of the reports in order to "maintain a balance." The great majority of the Bishop's Reports, he states, are not only wholly favorable to the subject but in most cases are constructive for him because potential abilities and skills are uncovered.

In general, those engaged in investigative sleuthing try to check a man or woman out on the factual kind of information that can be learned by interviewing the person, his business associates and neighbors, or by searching records. Here are the major facts they are paid to uncover:

1. How is his work record? Frequently investigators go all the way back to cover every job held since leaving school, and

make certain there are no unexplained gaps. Some investigators, such as those working for Bishop's, also explore the school background. Investigators usually want to know not only how well the person performed his job but whether he had a healthy attitude toward the company.

2. How well has he lived within his means? This involves checking the credit bureaus for a rating and litigation bureaus for any suits or judgments, among other things. There is a widespread theory in business that a person who has at some time been lax about meeting financial obligations might also be lax in fulfilling his job responsibilities.

3. How has his home life been? Is there any evidence of an unhappy marriage or neglect of children? Investigators tend to be less wary of a man if he has both wife and children. As Mr. Chiariello explained it: "A man who is a bachelor can pick up and go, and even the man with a wife can pick up and go, but if he's a man with five children it is hard for him to disappear." In the case of a man being considered for an important executive job, many search firms and management consultants feel it is imperative that someone—either with the company or retained by the company—actually get into the man's home for a look around. The management consulting firm, the McMurry Company, has developed a "Home Interview Report Form" for companies making such a check. The form includes such points to be noted as: "Who dominates the conversation? Whose opinions are decisive? . . . What is the attitude of others in the home? . . . Toward travel? Toward transfers? . . . Are the daily activities of the home arranged for the convenience of the applicant or for others?"

Dr. McMurry stated recently that in appraising potential chief executives "it is imperative that the candidate's off-the- job circumstances be investigated as thoroughly as he is himself." Such a check "is best done by a personal visit to the candidate's home. This has the advantage that the *entire* household can be observed and that family members tend to speak more freely on their home grounds. It is thus easier to ascertain who is dominant in the family; the emotional climate of the home, and the extent to which the wife will be friendly and supportive or critical, deprecatory or a 'problem' in some other fashion."

Sales Management carried an article by one of Dr. McMurry's associates entitled: "Don't Hire a Salesman—Hire a Man & Wife Team." Dr. McMurry believes any effort to eavesdrop on a home by electronic means would be entirely inexcusable. He states that it is bad enough to invade the privacy of the individual's home by interviewing him there. He does feel, however, that situations might well arise when it would be appropriate for a man's superior—after the man has been hired—to make follow-up visits should he have reservations about the man's home situation or the man's performance.

4. Are there any court convictions on the person's record? The professor who wrote the AMA brochure on keeping bad apples out of the barrel stressed the fact that few people have actual criminal records but that this check is nevertheless regarded as necessary because permitting even a few with such backgrounds to enter the company gates could be "highly important." And he added ominously: "Convictions as apparently innocuous as traffic violations have enabled some investigators to uncover everything from felonies to clearly psychopathic behavior." The head of a leading investigative firm scoffed at this assertion. He said: "We have prepared any number of reports on extremely competent executives, who were extremely sane but were always in a hurry." Frequently information about many a person's legal tangles can be got simply by checking the credit bureau in the area where he has lived.

5. Is there anything in the person's health history to create concern? Some investigators look into this quite thoroughly. As the Baltimore investigator explained: "He could be suffering from a latent illness which could recur and result in a subsequent compensation claim against the company. Or he could be under a psychiatrist's care."

6. Is the person controversial in any way? This assumes greatest importance in checking out potential managers, but even a workman can be too controversial for the company's comfort. Mr. Chiariello said quite a few of his clients want assurance that the man conforms. He added, "Big business hates controversy in any of its employees." A number of other investigators mentioned that they watch out for controversial types. The president of one large investigating organization, when invited to explain what kind of things can make an ambitious man too controversial for big business, explained what he felt was the prevailing viewpoint in these terms:

"It is not necessary that the man be an active member of a church; most aren't, but they can be. But does he conform, or is he an avowed, loud rebel? ... Whether he he is Republican or Democrat is secondary, but is he what is commonly heard of today as *being an extreme liberal*? Is he a Communist sympathizer? Is he a man who *openly espouses the end of the Cold War*? Is he sympathetic to Castro? *Is he a man who thinks that extreme patriotic organizations do more damage than good? Is he a man who might feel that a Communist has as much right to talk as anyone else*? If he is an active Democrat, *is he a member of the Americans for Democratic Action or is he just a Southern Democrat? Is he a man who might be active in the present militant fight for integration*?"

Just on the basis of the definitions I italicized, quite a few million thoughtful Americans would seem to come under the cloud ot being "too controversial."

The company-client may be anxious to know whether a man is controversial because he is too leftish or "stateish." If it is affiliated with the strongly conservative American Security Council, some insight may be gained by inquiring at the ASC, which maintains a vast library on suspect organizations and their present or onetime members. A few years ago it was reported to have information on 1,000,000 individuals, though its president (an ex-FBI man) now insists it does not maintain a filing system on "individuals as such." As recently as 1961 its brochure said its files were a source of information for "the personnel screening programs" of defense contractors. And its files probably contain the various ready-reference check lists of names compiled by congressional committees and other official and unofficial investigation bodies looking for "lefties" or people assumed for some reason to be security risks.

2. The Use of Lie Detectors

Promoters of the lie detector for screening potential employees argue that the detector (or polygraph) can take up where regular investigative methods leave off. One leading user of the lie detector for pre-employment screening is Dale System, Inc., an investigative company that has headquarters in New York but advertises that its services are "available in every city and state." The polygraph, it contends, can "inform you with *more accuracy than a background investigation* whether your prospective employee is what he claims."

Several hundred firms have leaped into the lushly profitable field of offering their services in polygraphic people-probing.

Until a few years ago the lie detector was used primarily in police work, inscrutinizing people assigned to highly classified defense installations, in testing guards for Brinks, Inc. Today more than three quarters of all testing is on employees or prospective employees for private companies. An official of John E. Reid and Associates of Chicago asserts: "We have done work for every major corporation in the United States." The significance to business of the lie detector is indicated by the fact that the *Wall Street Journal* featured at the top of its front page a report on the growing use of them.

The Reid official, not content with proselytizing U.S. firms, had just returned from introducing his company's methods to businesses and industries in Australia and South Africa. An official of Employment Services, which administers lie-detector tests, recently estimated that 5000 Texas firms now require their employees to take periodic tests.

And the Dale System states that among others it works for W. T. Grant Co., Westinghouse Electric Corp., Howard Johnson, Mangel Stores Corporation, Grand Union Co.

A substantial number of firms now offer polygraph service at a variety of locations within the United States. For example, the giant William J. Burns International Detective Agency, with 15,000 employees, has entered the polygraph field and now has machines at many of its forty-one offices. It screens the personnel of clients at all levels either before or after employment. One official reports: "We have quadrupled our polygraph business in the past eighteen months." Its big rival, the Pinkerton National Detective Agency, also has entered the polygraph field. Another large outfit headquartered in New York with polygraph examiners in many cities now is Lincoln M. Zonn, Inc. It boasts membership in the American Institute of Management.

What is clear from all this is that each year tens of thousands of American citizens seeking ordinary jobs—and this includes prospective filling-station attendants—find that a condition of employment is that they must permit themselves to be strapped into a chair. And while in that chair they often must answer highly personal questions. One firm, hiring out the services of the lie detectors, reported that less than one per cent of the people asked to take the test refuse to do so. There is a ready explanation. Usually applicants for jobs at client companies must state when filling out the application form whether or not they will be willing to submit to polygraph tests as a condition of employment

The general theory behind the polygraph test is that people can't lie without creating physiological reactions within the body. A standard lie-detection machine tries to catch this lie at three points: in sweating palms, in the way the subject breathes, and in the reactions of his pulse and blood pressure.

For screening job-seekers, the lie detector is widely promoted as being particularly effective in learning five things about the applicant:

1. Are there any latent tendencies toward dishonesty? The regular investigation plus the application form have presumably already established that the applicant has no known record of dishonesty. But the lie detector, it is hoped, will make the applicant confess any dishonesties that only he himself knows, or dishonesties that occurred before the events were permitted to become a part of any official record. One polygraph examiner explained to me that records of juvenile crimes are usually not available to an investigator because the courts try to protect the youngsters. He added: "But on the polygraph you get any undetected crime, and this will cover juvenile offenses."

2. What are his real intentions in regard to job "permanency"? Will he have a roving eye for more attractive jobs? Will he take advantage of what he has learned here to move to a better job elsewhere? *Printing Impressions* quoted a businessman who defended his use of the polygraph on job applicants in these words: "Now, when I hire a bright young man, I have the detection service inquire if he's planning to use me and my knowhow as a one-year training course, or if he's seriously considering a career with my organization." Some of the polygraph testing services claim they can help a company reduce turnover by preemployment screening. (People may hesitate to take a better job that comes along because they have vowed to the lie-detection examiner that they planned to stay.)

3. Does he have dangerous habits not uncovered in the screening process? Is he a secret lush, or does he gamble secretly, or if married does he have a girlfriend on the side, or does he have a lot of unrevealed debts?

4. In his application did he falsify anything? Recruiters of managers report that about one managerial aspirant in twelve will on an application give himself a college degree he actually

did not receive. This presumably happens because personnel directors are becoming rigidly insistent upon college degrees even for jobs where a degree has little relevance.

5. Is he a homosexual, or does he have any tendencies in that direction? Many personnel directors seem to want to know about this whether or not it has any conceivable bearing on job performance. Others are more tolerant of applicants for jobs at low levels in the company hierarchy provided they are not obviously homosexual.

During the course of my research I had several opportunites to watch through one-way mirrors while men were subjected to lie-detector tests. In one unforgettable case the young man under examination had applied for a job as an on-the-road salesman for a client company handling quite ordinary consumer products. This test took place at a polygraph testing center of an organization that does a good deal of such pre-employment testing in several American cities. The organization has a number of examiners at the center where I was visiting. (The reason I have chosen not to identify the center will soon be evident.)

Apparently the room under view was a typical polygraph setup. It had a one-way mirror on the rear wall (behind which I sat) and a bug in the room so that observers such as myself in the darkened next room could both watch and hear the interrogation. We'll call the lad who hoped to be a salesman for the client company Bill. He was slim, blond, handsome, and understandably nervous; perhaps this was why he was so talkative. We'll call the examiner, a man about forty-five, Mr. Probe. He told me earlier that he had examined more than 3000 people. (He also told me the name of a well-known college from which he had been graduated. A colleague of Mr. Probe's who stood with me in the darkened room behind the mirror and served as a sort of guide mentioned that there was one man on their polygraph staff who had a college degree. The man he named was not Mr. Probe. I was left to wonder whether Mr. Probe, the lie detector, had fibbed to me.)

At any rate Mr. Probe had a marvelously relaxing, first-name manner with Bill. He sat behind a desk with a polygraph machine worth about $1300 built into it. In front of the desk there was a comfortable chair—its back to Mr. Probe—where Bill would later be asked to sit and be tested. But now they were having a pre-examination chat. Mr. Probe said, "Okay, Bill, I'll go over several of the questions I'm going to ask beforehand." (This is apparently standard procedure and is not done entirely as a courtesy. It helps give the subject a chance to confess voluntarily or to start worrying about questions that may be troublesome.)

Mr. Probe helped Bill light his cigarette and then said, "I know we all have skeletons in the closet, and I'm not trying to dig them up. I'm just asking you to be completely honest with me." He gave as an example the fact that some people lie a little bit about their college backgrounds. Some say they attended college when they went only one semester, and others say they have never stolen before and maybe they have. Then he told his new friend Bill: "I want to be able to write that you have a good, clean, smooth indication of truth. I'll be back of you all the way if that is the way it appears." Then he said, "Okay, Bill?" And added: "If you can't completely and honestly say 'no' to a question, let me know and perhaps I can rephrase the question."

And so Mr. Probe began his *pre*-polygraph questioning. "Have you ever stolen from previous employers?" Bill shifted in his chair a little and said, "As far as stealing, the only kind I can remember is ten years ago I stole some stationery from a company where I was working." Mr. Probe magnanimously waved this aside. He said: "I'm not interested in stationery and paper clips; there's a little bit of pilferage in all of us." Then he said, more solemnly: "Have you ever taken anything beyond what we discussed?"

Bill: "No."

Mr. Probe: "Ever fired for cause?"

Bill: "Never."

Mr. Probe: "Ever drink to excess?"

Bill: "I've been loaded a few times, but I guess that's not 'excess,' so I'll say no."

Mr. Probe: "Any mental disorders?"

Bill: "What do you mean, mental disorders? I guess I'm nervous at times."

Mr. Probe: "I mean anything mental that would impair your work and prevent you from being a good salesman for this company."

Bill: "No."

Mr. Probe: "Are you in good physical condition?"

Bill: "Yes, as far as I know, except for sinus trouble."

Mr. Probe: "Are you seeking permanent employment?"

Bill: "Well, I guess. What do you mean?"

Mr. Probe: "Do you have any plans to leave in the near future if you get the job?"

Bill: "Not that I know of."

At this point Mr. Probe explained that his client was not interested in spending $8000 to $10,000 to break in a man who would go to some other company. Of course, Mr. Probe said, no one can blame a man for going to a much better opening. "But right now do you have any other plans?"

Bill explained that he did have another job offer, in Boston, and he couldn't positively state that he hoped to have a permanent career with the company to which he was applying, since he had not yet worked for it. But he said he hoped to get this job and at the moment had no other plans.

Mr. Probe: "Have you answered truthfully all the questions on the application?"

Bill paused and explained that there was that thing about having a college degree. He had attended two colleges in the Midwest for about four and a half years but had never, to be truthful, finally got the degree.

Now Mr. Probe began to explain the mechanics of the

machine. He asked Bill to take off his vest, roll up his left sleeve, and sit in the subject's chair. Mr. Probe strapped the accordion-like rubber tubing across Bill's chest (to check his respiration), attached a blood-pressure-pulse band to his arm, an electrode to his hand to check the sweating of his palm and muscular movement.

"This machine," Mr. Probe said jovially, "is a scientific instrument to record involuntary changes that occur when people lie." (He was persuading Bill that the machine was infallible.) He added: "In conversation, I can sit here and tell you one lie after another, but we cannot lie to ourselves, and we know that nothing we can do will prevent changes from being recorded. It is an accurate instrument in the hands of a competent examiner. I know you are a little nervous now. We're not measuring nerves: we are measuring changes. I will ask you some questions that are irrelevant I'll give you two tests. Just answer yes or no."

I could see that three needles on the recording machine in front of Mr. Probe were already starting to make their squiggling lines on paper: the first recorded breathing, the second sweating, the third circulatory responses.

And now the questioning began with the machine in operation. In addition to the ones given in pre-exam, Mr. Probe asked such irrelevant questions as "Do you ever watch TV?" These presumably are control questions. Twice Mr. Probe admonished Bill not to move about so much. At least two new questions, according to my notes, were:

"Have you ever been arrested for speeding or getting a ticket?" (Bill tried to explain something about an incident in Indiana.)

"Have you ever done something that you are really and truly ashamed of?" Bill shook his head. My guide whispered: "That question will sometimes smoke out the homosexual." When Mr. Probe repeated the question about ever stealing merchandise, Bill said, "No." One of the needles drew an emphatic peak line and my guide murmured, "That doesn't look so good."

Now the machine was turned off and Mr. Probe was explaining that a couple of Bill's responses did give him a little concern. There was a reference to stealing merchandise. Bill conceded he did feel sort of funny when that one came at him, and he said he had also become tense when asked about mental disorder. It sort of made him nervous. Also the drinking question. Mr. Probe talked reassuringly and said, "All right, let's run through the questions again." Now the needles were behaving more smoothly, and my guide commented on this. He called it "a smoother picture." And then came the final question for the machine. Mr. Probe paused dramatically and said:

"Now, Bill, I'm going to have to ask you a very embarrassing personal question. . . . Bill, have you ever . . ." Long pause, while the needles fluttered to high peaks, then ". . . I guess that question won't be necessary, Bill." My guide whispered that this was a deliberate jolter designed simply to test out Bill's "total reaction capability." Presumably a good or pathological liar would have taken this unfinished question in stride.

Now Bill was unharnessed from the chair and there was a discussion of the test. Mr. Probe noted with approval that all the responses that had caused him concern in the first testing had "washed out" in the second. The examination seemingly was over, and Bill was looking for his hat. Then Mr. Probe said pleasantly, "Bill, one more question before you leave. There is nothing personal or offensive about this, but because of the kind of business you are going in and the fact you have been in the summer theater work, I think I should ask it. Are you inclined to be homosexual?"

Bill looked startled. He said, "No." But the question so unsettled him that he felt compelled to explain his situation. "I have of course been surrounded by them in my work in the theater in the Midwest, and I've been exposed to this a lot in some of the bohemian areas where I've lived, and I have been approached. But the answer is no." Mr. Probe didn't explain why sexual status had any significant relevance to the job for which Bill was applying.

The question was outrageous not only on the ground of unreasonable intrusion but on the grounds of vagueness. As stated, it would cause a great many million U.S. males to ponder how to respond. Mr. Probe obviously had never read the Kinsey Report on males, which showed that while four per cent of U.S. males questioned had been homosexually inclined most of their lives, a full third of the U.S. male adults interviewed had at some time in their lives had a homosexual experience.

Now Bill was leaving. A second examiner had joined me meanwhile in the darkened room, and the two examiners, who said they had gone to a different polygraph school than Mr. Probe, explained that they used different techniques to try to check a man out on homosexuality without putting the question to him directly. While the machine is on they ask one or more of these questions:

"Have you had any past or present physical ailments we should know about?"

"Are you holding back something important that was not covered in the examination?"

"Are you holding back information, any incident or *condition*, which might open you up to blackmail?"

One of the men added, laughing, "If you really throw the homo question to them directly while the machine is on the needles really jump."

With Bill safely gone, Mr. Probe joined our discussion.

He said Bill looked "real good" on the second chart. As far as homosexuality was concerned, there was nothing suspicious in his responses to the question about physical or mental ailments, or source of shame, he said, and added: "If I had been really concerned about this homosexuality in a job where he was going to be working, for example with youngsters, I would have thrown the question at him during the test itself." But here, he said, there was nothing definite. "I may verbally mention to the client his theatrical background and may mention he needs watching."

The examiners wanted me to watch more tests; but I said I had had enough. I had had enough to the point of nausea.

Subsequently I dropped Mr. Probe a note requesting a summary of the report he turned in on Bill. He sent me an extract. It noted the discrepancy about a college degree and the fact that he had been unable to state flatly that he was seeking permanent employment. But he did give Bill credit for being honest and pointed out that while slightly nervous on the second test there had been *no specific* reaction to any of the pertinent questions. And then, in his letter to me, he concluded:

"In rendering a verbal report of results of the interview and examination to our client . . . I pointed out that I did not have any substantiating evidence on which to conclude that this man had possible homosexual [sic] tendencies, but that it was a great possibility. I then advised our client of the discussion I had with the applicant regarding homosexual activities. It was recommended that should the client organization be desirous of ascertaining whether or not this Subject had homosexual tendencies that we could conduct a background investigation or re-examine him on the polygraph at a later date."

In short, on no basis other than hunch based on facts already presumably stated in Bill's application about his environmental background, Mr. Probe had raised in the prospective employer's mind a terrible question (in our society) about Bill's manliness.

It should be further noted that most if not all of the derogatory points he reported came not from anything on the polygraph charts but were based on facts discussed while the machine was not turned on!

This fact alone would lead the author to concur with the statement of psychiatrist Joost A. M. Meerloo that the lie detector is primarily a "tool for mental intimidation." Two Harvard psychologists and a graduate student in industrial management at the Massachusetts Institute of Technology who made a study of the polygraph as an examining tool reported much the same conclusion. The squiggles intimidate. As for the machine itself, these investigators pointed out that, though lying *will* produce physiological changes, "other factors often produce physiological changes which are very similar. For example there is the real danger that the changes which occur are not the result of a 'feeling of guilt' itself, but rather of recalling some information, or of a shift in attention, or perhaps a sudden fear of the consequences of being pronounced guilty."[2] Their report was entitled "Don't Trust the Lie Detector."

The three investigators concluded that the lie detectors might at best be 70 per cent accurate in drawing out truth. Major practitioners such as Dale and Reid claim 95 to 98 per cent accuracy. But such claims usually carry the qualifying phrase, "in the hands of a competent examiner."

If there is such a thing as a competent examiner, he is not much in evidence. Except in a few states (notably New Mexico and Kentucky) just about anyone can set himself up in business as a polygraph examiner by reading a book. Reid reportedly hires only college graduates and certifies them for polygraph work only after a six-month apprenticeship. But most of the polygraph schools run about six weeks and may require no college training whatever. (Enthusiasts of the polygraph talk of improving its accuracy by adding devices that will measure brain waves, heart action, and eye twitching.)

As to the ethics of forcing job-seekers to submit to such a degrading experience, one comment seems appropriate. Any company that treats its future employees to such an indignity deserves the worst from those employees in terms of loyalty, commitment, and honesty—and probably will get it. One hopeful development is that unions are finally starting to fight the polygraph and seeking legislation to get it outlawed. Perhaps they became alarmed because the examiners in some instances were grilling employees or applicants about union activities. Such questions have now been ruled unlawful by the National Labor

Relations Board. Unions in general have been so preoccupied with meat-and-potatoes issues in the past that they have paid too little attention to trends in the modern work world that are operating to undermine individual privacy and human dignity.

3. The Use of Personality Tests

Each year considerably more than a million job-seekers must bare themselves to a battery of personality and other psychological tests before they are hired. Since the wide-scale use of such devices for screening job applicants has already been quite thoroughly explored,[3] I shall confine myself here to noting some of the privacy-intrusion aspects. For example, upon reexamining one of several batteries of tests and forms I completed or examined a couple of years ago while posing as an aspiring manager or making believe I was one, I find I was requested to supply the following quite personal facts about myself (along with many more):

—What I think of my mother and father.

—Whether I find my children upsetting.

—How often I am bothered by either constipation or loose bowel movements.

—The degree to which I am disturbed by marital troubles at home.

—How much I am disturbed by loneliness, feelings of guilt, frightening dreams.

—How close I think I am to a nervous breakdown.

—Whether I consider myself ugly.

—How much I am troubled by itching.

—How far my wife, father, and mother got in school.

—Whether I am at all worried about my health.

And here are some of the sentences I was instructed to complete:

"One of the things wrong with me . . ."

"My greatest fear is . . ."

"I failed . . ."

"Most girls . . ."

"I suffer . . ."

"My greatest worry . . ."

Business critic Alan Harrington sees these test forms so widely used as a new type of confessional. "Instead of confessing to God through a priest or confessing to one's self through a psychologist, the Corporate Man confesses to the Form," he stated. "He acknowledges his strengths and weaknesses as they have been defined by others."

A great deal of confessing is taking place. Most of the nation's major corporations as well as hundreds of smaller ones will employ only applicants who have been psychoscreened. Virtually every aspiring manager under the age of thirty already has gone through at least one testing of his personality at some stage during the past decade.

Many dozens of testing firms have sprung up to conduct for client companies "depth" interviews of applicants, to test applicants on check lists about their anxieties and on inventories of their interests and opinions, and perhaps on "projective" tests in which the testees unwittingly reveal themselves by the way they complete sentences or draw pictures of a girl or a house. At least one of these projective tests, widely used, is disguised as an application form. The way you place the initial in your name, make check marks, allude to relatives, and follow directions are all presumed to be revealing.

Here are some of the factors the personality testers, on behalf of their client companies, are most anxious to discover about people—especially salesmen or managers being considered for hiring:

Is he or she emotionally sound? This concern may seem odd in view of the fact that a number of respected psychologists have observed that many of the most successful entrepreneurs are hypochondriacs haunted by anxieties and verging on the neurotic.

But in any case most of the testers—perhaps to be safe—give their highest scores to the well-rounded, stable, solid-citizen type. The tester measures toward the average.

Testing firms have rushed into print, and hawked to personnel officials, hundreds of testing tools. Currently the favorite tool for corporate screening is a tongue-twisting form straight out of the psychiatric clinic at the University of Minnesota Hospital called the Minnesota Multiphasic Personality Inventory. It contains more than 500 items that probe how close your responses come to those of psychiatric patients. They delve into your marital problems, religious feelings, sexual anxieties, ailments, political views, and so on.

Is he or she sexually sound? The *he* applicants in business should ideally be all-he; but even the testers recognize that the gal going into business as a career need not necessarily be all-she. A number of widely peddled test forms promise to ferret out the overly unmasculine male or overly unfeminine female. One favorite is the Guilford-Zimmerman Temperament Survey. The tester draws up a chart of your "personality" on ten different polar scales, which presumably determine how you range on ascendance-submissiveness, sociable-shy, and cooperative-critical scales.

The tenth scale is masculinity-femininity. The male whose masculinity chart line falls substantially below the norm may be considered suspect. It is used by testers for many dozens of companies, including one of the world's largest oil companies. Efforts to smoke out the overly feminine male or secret homosexual are also made by the use of the MMPI test mentioned above and the Strong Vocational Interest test. On the latter the true male is assumed to be interested in hunting and fishing and working with tools and to engage in other presumed he-man endeavors; the inadequate male is more cultural and sensitive in his interests. A number of outstanding psychiatrists and psychologists have dismissed the whole approach as fatuous, since the homosexual is frequently completely "masculine" not only in his body build but in his recreational preferences.

Testers working for corporate clients also show a special interest in trying to determine whether the applicant is adaptable enough to be a good team player . . . is money-minded (that is good) . . . is controversial or a "screwball" (those are bad) . . . and has a lot of steam in his boiler (this is considered not only good but crucial). This last can be caught, it is contended, on the "general activity, energy" scale of the Guilford-Zimmerman.

And the testers insist on trying to find out how bright an applicant is, though this should be quite apparent from the man's record and his behavior in a routine interview.

A rather morbid interest is being shown in efforts to determine how many years of active, efficient life the applicant has ahead. One psychologist at the U.S. National Institute of Mental Health has been perfecting a "psychomet," a machine that records how fast we can respond in twenty-two different mental and physical tests. His thesis is that one's rate of slowing down can be discerned in a man even in his thirties. Presumably personnel officials and testers will show a considerable interest in this machine if it is marketed. Another psychologist, Ward Halstead, has developed a Halstead battery that has for several years been used in selecting and promoting personnel in industry. It purportedly assesses the "biological" age of a man's brain. The Halstead thesis is that some brains deteriorate faster than others and that an applicant's brain may be old beyond his years. His test has been given to several hundred executives.

As to the validity of much that passes for the "personality" aspects of testing in screening personnel, I simply offer the comment of one of the nation's leading psychologists, Dr. John Dollard of Yale University. He recently stated: "There may be exceptions unknown to me, but generally speaking, projective tests, trait scales, interest inventories, or depth interviews are not proved to be useful in selecting executives or salesmen, or potential delinquents or superior college students." The *Harvard Business Review* carried a report (September-October 1963) of an analysis made by Professor Richard S. Barrett of New York University. He stated: "A dismal history has been recorded by personality tests."

And as for the ethics of it all, we might ponder the words of Dr. Douglas McGregor, distinguished behavioral scientist at the Massachusetts Institute of Technology, who states: "I can only confess to a degree of disquiet over the possibilities for manipulation and exploitation of my fellow human beings inherent in the administrative use of personality tests and clinical diagnoses of adjustment for purposes of placement. . . . The critical point is whether management has any moral right to invade the personality." Even assuming that personality can affect performance, he questions whether management "has a right to go behind the performance to the diagnosis of its causes *when those causes are personal and private.*"

Our disquiet at the possibilities of manipulation and exploitation, I would add, should also extend to the widespread use of lie detectors and detectives in the selection of personnel for business and industry. The lie detector is vastly more of an intrusion on one's privacy and an affront to one's dignity than the personality test. And the use of detectives to pry into the private affairs of a candidate would seem to me to be a sad comment on the lack of respect for the individual that such firms are demonstrating.

4. The Hidden Eyes of Business

"Your private 'television eye' puts you everywhere . . . in
your building—on the grounds, instantly . . . any time."—
Illustrated brochure circulated to business managements
by Bell Television, Inc.

Surveillance of the teammates on the job in private industry has
shot up at such a rate in recent years that the phenomenon might
seem to have pathological overtones. At thousands of plants no
one is to be trusted in any sense in which we've traditionally
known the word. No one's motives and integrity are to be taken
for granted.

One justification offered for stepping up the surveillance
is pilferage; but there has always been pilferage, and in today's
economy there is much more to pilfer. Then there is the alleged
constant hazard of theft of secret processes being developed.
During and after World War II such guarding of secret military processes became commonplace, but now the same rules of
guarding are being applied to new zipper designs, to a formula
for new shades of lipstick, and to mock-ups of a built-in light for
milady's leg shaver.

And finally there is, for tens of thousands of companies with
some part of their output in the defense or space program, the
anxiety that they may somehow lose the confidence of federal
inspectors. They worry that they may not seem sufficiently thorough in their surveillance of employees.

Their worry is compounded by a socially ominous role that the
Defense Department has thrust upon them. One security official
of the Defense Department explained the prevailing practice
to me in these words; "The defense contractors are authorized

to grant clearance for access to Confidential information in the absence of derogatory information. . . .Clearance for access to Secret and Top Secret information is granted only by the Department of Defense." (The Defense Department's Central Index File indicates there are approximately 1,700,000 active current clearances in defense industry for access to Secret or Top Secret information.) Perhaps this method of leaving confidential checks to the contractors saves the Defense Department a lot of bother in not having to investigate all manner of plumbers, janitors, and stenographers who happen to be employed by defense contractors—as well as technicians and engineers who happen to have jobs only mildly related to defense. But it has thrust tens of thousands of private contractors into the business of making judgments about employees as loyalty and security risks. In the author's view this is a dangerous and unhealthy role that has been assigned to the contractor. Businessmen should not be in the loyalty-assessing business. Lockheed Aircraft, as an example, must run loyalty and security checks on many of its employees. Acquaintances and former superiors are requested to fill out forms that ask such questions regarding the employee as:

1. "Did actions or statements at any time give reason to question loyalty to the United States?——Does he (she) have relatives abroad?"

2. "Has he (she) traveled abroad? When and where?

3. "If (employee) is a youth or woman, what is reputation of parents or husband?"

If the United States Government feels the need for loyalty security checks of people who conceivably could have access to the lower forms of classified information, it should do the checking itself.

For all these and other reasons, it is becoming more and more fashionable among corporations to have a tight surveillance program over employees. Some of the most oppressive surveillance systems exist in the drug companies that are engaged in bruising battles to get to the drugstores first with a new variant of a pill that they hope will generate public excitement. The entire 600-acre tract maintained by Lederle Laboratories at Pearl River, New York, is ringed by a 7-foot fence. The fence and buildings are watched by a 50-man police force and passes are required to enter most of the buildings. I am not suggesting that the company doesn't have grounds for precautions, but only that such a phenomenon offers a sad comment on our industrial way of life.

Other industrial plants are patrolled by police dogs. Auto makers set up air-defense systems with rooftop lookout towers whenever they start to bring new models out of doors.

One symptom of the surging preoccupation with security is the fact that at least three schools of higher learning (Michigan State, Long Beach State, and Northeastern) offer majors in industrial security. Another symptom is the growth of the American Society for Industrial Security. Its membership, as previously indicated, is soaring toward 3000. The society stages three-day seminars around the country that not only cover the latest surveillance and counterintrusion techniques but include lectures on such subjects as: "The Detection and Prevention of Employee Dishonesty" and "What Can Industry Do to Prevent Espionage and Sabotage?" At least several hundred of its members are in such seemingly non-security product lines as tobacco, retail sales, food, automobiles, rubber, medical supplies, transportation, steel, and aluminum.

Many employers assume that the new electronic eyes and ears are just substitutes for the old human eyes and ears used by business supervisors for many, many decades to check on performance. And they feel that a management has a clear right to know what all employees are doing at any particular moment while at their work stations or in their offices.

Even if the new electronic eyes and ears are visible and known to the employees they offer less freedom than the old human system, because in the old system the employee at least knew when he could relax for a moment when weary. Now he must assume someone out there is always watching even if his work is only spot-checked.

The new electronic system is considerably more unreasonable when the electronic eyes and ears (and one-way mirrors and peepholes) are hidden, as they frequently are. If an employee learns to suspect the existence of hidden electronic devices—and word gets around—he loses any trust he had in his employer. And this profoundly alters his attitude toward his job.

Let us consider in particular some of the evidences of the use of hidden cameras, hidden microphones, one-way mirrors, and electronics to watch the already well-screened employees. An official of the giant William J. Burns International Detective Agency explained: "We're getting into electronics more and more [in industrial use] because electronics never sleep. We're also getting into closed-circuit TV for monitoring."

A West Coast specialist in installing microphones reportedly planted thirty-nine in a single building owned by a company.

One favored use of closed-circuit TV may have value not only for surveillance but as an appeal to the vanity of the president of the firm. He has been persuaded that he should have a panel of monitors (or a panel of earphones) in some secluded spot in or near his office, for his use only. He thus becomes the all-seeing eye, the commander who knows he is running a tight ship.

The head of a fixtures-producing factory in New York is one of many such presidents who holds a steady hand on the pushbutton panel. A president of another firm has placed a hidden camera in a fake dehumidifier box that is labeled "dehumidifier" in the company board room, where many conferences (which he may not always attend) are held. As for bugging, the head of a large cosmetics firm has, at least until recently, reportedly been bugging the offices of his colleagues. And the head of a Pennsylvania department store has had a tap on the phones of all his managers. A man who served in a very high position in a multibillion-dollar corporation and ordinarily speaks with deliberateness and understatement flatly asserted: "I suspect I was bugged."

One head of an investigative "consulting" organization specializing in managers explained: "Let's suppose, for instance, you think a guy is having a bad time on his job. It might pay to leave a bug in there for a week just to see how he is treating people and how he is getting along. You don't try to hurt the guy or fire the guy. You want to know what areas you have to fortify in his performance."

More commonly, however, surveillance is done by fulltime operatives. They can cause cameras—either hidden or unobtrusive—to pan and tilt, by remote control, over the work areas and can see who is doing what in the recreation or coffee area.

Then there are the hidden microphones and other surveillance devices to detect how people perform. Testimony before a New York Joint Legislative Committee revealed that a large telephone office in New York had installed hidden microphones in the base of the pen sets of employees involved in dealing with customers, to check on the adroitness of their performance in handling the customers.

Housing consultant James Mills reveals that certain builders of large development tracts have been bugging some of their model houses to check on how well the salesmen follow the selling strategies mapped out for them. A salesman in the Midwest showed a substantial deviation from prescribed strategy while with a lady prospect. The recording indicated that he demonstrated with her how cozy the bed could be with two people on it.

Two other electronic devices for surveillance or analyses of employee performance are worth notine. According to Robert Cubbedge, in his recent book, *Who Needs People?* the Hancock Telecontrol Corporation has developed a panel on which a red light blinks if any man-operated punch press in the building is not in operation. Another device that has seen some use is a time-measuring computer that can be operated by a hidden operator. It has had some acceptance. An observer (often in a box) can secretly watch a man or woman performing a job that involves a good deal of talking, and indicate by punching keys how the conversation is going time-wise. Who dominates, who interrupts and so purportedly indicates personality traits and temperamental reactions? The instrument has been described admiringly in a publication of the American Management Association. Alan Harrington has suggested that any offstage listening to an employee as if he were a laboratory mouse seems to represent "a stunning moral misunderstanding of what life is all about." It seems to be a retrogression for a society that professes to be striving to enhance the dignity of man.

One of the spots in a plant often put under TV surveillance nowadays is the loading platform. A TV camera runs back and forth along a monorail. The camera is hidden by wood paneling. It photographs through a one-inch slit and can see right into each truck and observe its loaders. Some will contend that this is just a better way to guard against theft, but it also seems to bring us closer to the all-seeing, ever-present eye.

In many instances managements concerned about whether employees are loafing or stealing or talking behind their backs have installed microphones in the employees' toilets. One of the more interesting installations to come to my attention is in the office of a very large corporation in Manhattan. The company has gone to great pains to build a public image of itself as a thoughtful, benevolent employer, and it has affiliated offices in many parts of the U.S.A. Most of its employees are women, and by necessity quite bright, so that they might spot ordinary mikes.

Guess where the "security" executives have planted their microphones?

My wife couldn't guess in twelve tries.

They have placed miniature transmitters inside the toilet- paper rollers in a number of the washrooms. The cylinder in the center of the plastic roller, which holds the tension spring for the roller, has a hollow space slightly more than three quarters of an inch wide and more than four inches long. The "security" officer ordered a number of one-ounce, self-contained microphone-transmitters to fit the spaces. They can readily pick up conversation within thirty feet. Since the frequency of each transmitter can be adjusted within a sixteen-megacycle range it is possible for a single "security" aide at a remote post to listen in at random to any of ten transmitters.

As this is written, a bitter dispute has arisen in a building in the same area, housing 2000 male and female employees of the American Telephone and Telegraph Company. A hidden camera was discovered in the ninth-floor men's room (in an air-conditioning duct) by men who became curious about a soft clicking sound that they heard every few seconds. When the management was confronted with the discovered camera, it contended that it had been installed to find out who had been defacing the men's room wall. But the company—in early negotiations with protesting officials of the Communications Workers of America—refused to offer assurances that it would not use cameras in the future as it deemed appropriate. Furthermore, a mimeographed statement distributed by the union to AT&T employees was quoted in the *New York Post* as indicating that the company would, if judged advisable, use a camera in a women's rest room "under proper circumstances."

A leading management consultant told me of finding that the executives of one large Midwestern firm were holding all important discussions outside their executive suite because they were convinced that a union had arranged for members of the company's maintenance crew to bug all executive offices.

When contract negotiations are on between a management and a union, one side may bug a conference room in an attempt to surmise how much "give" there is in the other side's position.

And during the delicate, informal, feeling-out talks when no notes are to be taken, one side may try to get word to its superiors master-minding the terms. Raymond Farrell, the anti-intrusion expert, relates that in the course of one such delicate situation he was regularly doing a "probe" of the conference room for hidden mikes before each session. He found none, yet information somehow was getting out. The next day he stood at the door with an eight-inch-long probe strapped to his body and an inconspicuous hearing aid. When one of the delegates came through the door, Farrell's probe squealed in his ear. The man was invited to step outside a moment, and when asked to remove his transmitter, he sheepishly did so. It was strapped to his arm.

In California I was told that some of the so-called personnel security surveillance at motion picture studios is really designed to permit high-level voyeurism of the starlets.

To people who express resentment when they learn they are being watched all the time, a spokesman for a leading maker of closed-circuit TV systems for industry has a ready answer. He said: "The person most likely to scream he's a victim of TV 'people-watching' is most often the person who needs the watching most."

Thus far we've barely started to examine the forms that watching takes at the offices and plants of hundreds of companies.

Managements are admonished by consulting firms specializing in surveillance to tighten up their "controls" on people. The warning cry of the William J. Burns International Detective Agency is "It Takes More Than Fences to Protect a Plant Today!" Its dollar volume has been shooting up three times as fast as the national economic growth and in 1963 reached $40,000,000. The company was founded by the same man who once headed the U.S. Secret Service. Fingerprinting of employees is urged as "a commonsense and routine procedure in many plants which have learned the value of keeping complete dossiers on all persons working for them."

Another organization exhorting top managements to look to their "controls" is Norman Jaspan Associates. The amiable Mr. Jaspan, whose spacious office high above Manhattan is lined with Chinese grass paper, is called the J. Edgar Hoover of Private Industry. He asserts that he has more than a hundred clients who are listed on the New York Stock Exchange. Mr. Jaspan has thirteen full offices. He hammers away at several strategies to maintain control. Among them:

1. "Establish dual responsibility." This prevents any one person from having much responsibility over his records or transactions.

2. "Keep the nature of controls secret." This keeps the sly ones off balance.

3. "Utilize spot checks."

4. "Develop a created-error program." If the employee doesn't catch the error he may be either sloppy or a crook.

5. "Utilize important psychological safeguards." Bonding the employee, he points out, has psychological benefits as well as the obvious protection.

He summed up his ostensibly nice-guy approach on handling employees in these words: "The trick is not to catch people any more than you want to catch your children. You want to remove temptation, so you have to set up safeguards as you would watch children, so that they do not run wild." Every day in the week, he says, his organization gets "confessions" from corporate children who have gone wild. If their transgressions are not too serious, they may be put on a sort of probation.

Some of the safeguards he urges upon corporations, however, would not set well even with children. He sends undercover men into his client companies in the guise of office boys, porters, executive trainees, accountants, or engineers. He said:

"We take our industrial engineers out of the universities and they go to work as typical employees, where they evaluate systems, methods, procedures, controls, supervision. We keep them under contract for the first three years out of school as undercover people. . . . We now have 350 undercover men in the first three-year phase. After the three years the men are ready to become a part of our industrial engineering staff. We draw from MIT, also Cornell for the hotel field, and from Northwestern, among others. If the men are on their toes and not married, you can't get a better opportunity for a man."

One of his undercover men, he recalls, was sitting in a toilet at an electrical plant in northern New York State, when he heard keys fall on the floor in the booth next to him, and no one picked up the keys. A Jaspan man is trained to be curious, so this man stood up on his seat and looked over and saw a man tracing a blueprint of a new electronic tube. That was why he hadn't been able to pick up the keys. Mr. Jaspan states:

"Last year we uncovered $60,000,000 in frauds; 62 per cent of it was at the supervisory and executive level."

At least in total numbers, Burns appears to have more undercover operatives in U.S. industry than Jaspan. *Traders Graphic* in a long, friendly report on the Burns Company stated that it is supplying undercover service to about five hundred companies. And it found that some companies would no more think of dropping this kind of help than of canceling their insurance.

Burns, with offices in forty-one U.S. cities as well as correspondents in virtually every country of the free world, happily points out that one of the fastest-growing wings of its far-flung business is in supplying undercover men—and women—to industry. It has a covey of operatives who go into companies as fluttery-eyed stenographers. In its brochure —across the top of which are two searing eyes peering out —it promises: "No one is aware of their identity, including those with whom they may be working closely as a fellow employee—or even as an executive— on your company's regular payroll." Beside that statement is a photograph of a group of obviously high-level executives around a boardroom table; one man, presumably a Burns operative, has the floor and is commanding the fascinated attention of the other corporate leaders. "Only the topmost management," the brochure adds, needs to know. And it makes the further promise that when it has two or more undercover operatives within a company, neither is permitted—just as in military intelligence—to know of the presence or identity of the other.

One of the more impressive claims by a company offering undercover agents is that of the Wackenhut Corporation, which, as we noted, is headed mainly by ex-FBI men. It proudly distributes reprints of an article in the journal *Research Development* entitled "I Was an Undercover Scientist." It is written by a "Dr. John A. Z. Wyler," whose name, it is explained, is a nom de plume for a Wackenhut staff member. His lead is a corker:

"Ph.D.s can be crooks. They can also be careless, ignorant in some cases, vain and dangerous, particularly when they are employed in R & D [research and development], I know. I am a Ph.D. and have been employed in R & D. I have also been employed as an undercover scientist."

Dun's Review and Modern Industry reported on a survey that had been made of the views of a large number of company managements on the subject of "crime prevention" on their premises. It listed as one of the solutions that had been urged: "Planting private detectives among the employees: 'costs $25,000 a year but is well worth it,' reports one survey respondent."

In some instances undercover men have been sent into plants to report on workers' attitudes toward the union that is recognized or is seeking recognition, and to report on union strategy. A couple of years ago the Textile Workers Union became angry over the discovery that four detectives were on the payroll of a rug company. One of these detectives had proved to be so devoted to the employees' cause that he had been chosen by the rank and file to serve on the employees' bargaining committee.

Business organizations in the retailing field, it should be

added, have shown an obsessive interest in developing new ways to keep an eye on their customers. While merchandisers profess to court the customer as if he or she were a king or queen, the merchandisers also believe that both kings and queens have to be watched very sharply indeed. Otherwise they'll steal you blind, to use the language of the mart. It all adds to the soaring surveillance of people.

The trade journals justify stepped-up surveillance of customers by groaning about their mounting losses due to shoplifting. They cite increasing dollar losses without taking into account mounting population, mounting consumer spending, mounting self-service, and so on. If you start with the total volume of sale of goods to consumers, the losses due to both shoplifting by customers and pilferage by employees would appear to be a fraction of one per cent. But it is true that, in some of the vast stores, losses on occasion have risen above one per cent. The cry is out for help in stopping such losses. One result is a great growth in reliance upon electronic eyes and unseen human eyes for customer-watching.

Several department stores in a New Jersey chain have what they call "Trojan horses," which are concealed observation posts built into pillars or into simulated air-conditioning units. In eight stores they have about seventy-five such "horses," according to a report in the *Wall Street Journal*, based on an interview with the chain's security manager.[1]

A good many supermarkets in Southern California have closed-circuit TV eyes with monitors in the manager's office. Several department stores in Boston have been using television eyes.

Mr. Kanter of ITV informs me that his company has installed closed-circuit TV surveillance systems in more than twenty department stores. (His company's printed brochure lists twenty-two well-known department stores in the New York, New Jersey, Long Island area where closed-circuit TV installations have been made, as well as hundreds of other sites of installations.)

He states: "Three quarters of the name department stores in New York use television." Mr. Kanter pointed out an interesting social distinction concerning the delicate issue of whether the TV cameras in a store are openly displayed or concealed. The tendency among the mass merchandisers is to display the cameras openly and to place signs around announcing that the store is "protected by closed-circuit television." The managements apparently believe the psychological effect of visible cameras will have more of a deterrent effect in reducing shoplifting than could be gained by catching shoplifters in the act with hidden cameras. (Some of the openly displayed TV "cameras" in certain stores are dummies and cost less than a tenth the price of real ones.)

As you move into the ultra-chic stores on upper Fifth Avenue, however, the cameras, when used, are hidden, even though pilferage losses in some of these stores are relatively high. Apparently there is a feeling that the customers like to think of themselves as so affluent and socially secure that the mere thought that they need watching is offensive.

In all stores where cameras are installed, concealed or open, detectives can usually operate them by remote control. The cameras can scan selling areas by pan and tilt. When the detectives see something on the monitor that looks interesting, they can press a button and close in visually with a zoom lens to a close-up of the pair of hands. The hands they zoom in on may be a customer's or they may be the hands of a cashier at a cash register.

Dressing rooms, both male and female, are the areas of the department and clothing stores that seem to arouse the most intense suspicion on the part of detectives. Their assumption is that shoplifters will ask to try on several items and use the protection of the supposedly private dressing room to slip items under their clothing or into handbags.

Apparently two women employees (presumably detectives) of a famous department store in the Los Angeles area tried recently to satisfy their suspicion the hard, old-fashioned way by lying on their backs and peering under the partition of a dressing room. That at least was the charge made in court by attorneys affiliated with the American Civil Liberties Union of Southern California who presented a plea that the defendants, charged with shoplifting, had been victims of unreasonable search and seizure. They felt a civil liberties issue was involved, and as usual handled the case without fee. The ACLU brief stated that the women employees were peering up from under the partition to watch the prospective women customers try on garments "without any reason whatsoever to suspect the defendants were about to commit any crime." In one appeal the court supported the ACLU's position; but a higher court ruled against it Now it appears that an effort will be made to place the issue before the United States Supreme Court.

The simpler, more common way to maintain surveillance of dressing rooms (which is widely practiced) is by one-way mirrors or by looking through a peephole into a mirror so placed on an opposite wall that it gives the peeper a good view of just about every part of the dressing room.

The modern, if more expensive, way to peek is to install a hidden TV camera. Officials of two closed-circuit TV companies indicated warily that they may have made such installations. The president of one company said: "We do use cameras in the try-on rooms, but we don't talk about it. We try to see that the security officer [watching the monitor] is of the same sex as the people in the try-on rooms."

Alexander's five department stores in New York City have pioneered what is apparently a new concept in maintaining surveillance over customers. Since about fifty per cent of all the nation's shoplifters are teenagers and since at Alexander's the percentage runs even higher, the chain has hired and trained several dozen teenage boys and girls as detectives. These youthful gumshoes dress casually, often in shorts and open sports shirts, and mingle among their peer-group shoppers.

At least two of New York's most celebrated personalities who operate restaurants have installed concealed TV cameras about their premises.

Mechanical eyes of various sorts have been found to be most useful in observing customers who wish to cash checks at stores or to deposit or cash checks at banks. Americans now write about 18,000,000,000 checks a year. And some of them bounce. The number that bounce beyond recovery is not nearly as high as one might imagine from reading all the colorful news accounts about fraudulent checks becoming a "national pestilence." On the average, less than one check in 2000 presents a loss to the party accepting it.

But as stores have sought to increase the number of their customers from among people they don't know, by accepting checks, some have tried to protect themselves by using hidden cameras. In this practice they can cite the endorsement of a spokesman for the FBI. Experience may indicate, however, that the most effective way to deter the bum-check artist is to place the camera matter-of-factly right out on the counter. Regiscope pioneered this field with a dual-lens camera that simultaneously photographs on a single frame of film the person submitting the check and the check itself. There is little question of privacy invasion because a readily legible sign on the two-foot-high camera stand states: "FOR YOUR PROTECTION A CONFIDENTIAL FILM RECORD IS BEING MADE OF YOU AND THIS TRANSACTION."

At least thirty supermarket chains now use this camera. The A&P supermarkets have more than 1000 cameras of this type in stores across the country. And such department stores as Carson Pirie Scott in Chicago, Sam's in Detroit, Titche Goettinger in Dallas, and Shillito's in Cincinnati use them. Some department stores—Macy's of New York included—also use them to photograph all people seeking refunds for merchandise being returned. (Many shoplifters often bring stolen merchandise back to convert it into something they desire more—cash.)

Banks have developed a number of uses for motion picture cameras and closed-circuit TV, with customers usually not aware of the cameras. Mosler has sold several hundred photoguard cameras, which can make a short motion picture record of any suspicious-looking person entering the bank. Then if an attempted holdup occurs any official can press a button to activate the camera and get a complete record of the robbery. Mr. Ward of Mosler contends that motion pictures are more valuable than still photographs for apprehending holdup men because the still photo "may miss many important things, such as mannerisms, limp, or whether the man is left-handed or not."

The First National Bank of Miami boasts that it has seven TV cameras placed strategically about its building, with a security officer at a panel of monitors. He can thus have a "bird's-eye view of every important part of the bank at every moment during the day."

A few banks have started handling the teller-customer relationship by remote pushbutton control with the help of closed-circuit television. A person who wishes to cash a check steps up to a drive-in window and may be instructed by a voice to lay the check in a designated spot. The check is being photographed. He is being photographed. The check disappears. In a moment the cash appears. It is all nice and friendly.

Mr. Lee Bunting, the head of Bell Television, predicted: "The banks of the future may be in lofts some distance from where the customer comes, so that a stick-up in the old sense becomes impossible." Then perhaps the robbers, straining to keep up with technology, will apply their ingenuity to locating and robbing the lofts!

5. Where Is All the Distrust of Jobholders Leading?

"I can tell you unequivocally that the lie detector is my most trusted and faithful 'employee.'"—An employer quoted in *Printing Impressions*, May 1962

The employee who has run a gantlet of questioners and questionnaires regarding his honesty, his life history, his health, and his psyche in order to get his job initially usually has not seen the end of his brash interrogators.

Consider, for example, industry's growing infatuation with the use of the lie detector on people already employed. The polygraph examiner with his portable box of dials drops into offices or plants and runs spot checks or better still—from his viewpoint, since he may be charging $25 a head—makes an across-the-board survey. Such surveys, he may argue, are more impersonal and so less apt to influence morale adversely. Many hundreds of companies use the lie detector for across-the-board checks. Or they use periodic spot checks. Or they simply check any group of employees that they suspect may include one or more rotten apples.

The Dale System with its 4500 investigators in various cities advertises its polygraph service with the words: "Reduce losses from employee abuses—pinpoint responsibilities." A spokesman explains that you can cut pilferage by employees not only by investigating an actual loss but also by "periodic checks of employees." There is no law to prevent employers from demanding that their workers take such a test.

An official of the William J. Burns International Detective Agency, in speaking of its polygraph service, advised me: "Frequently we go into a company periodically to screen the employees, maybe every eight or ten months—to keep the honest people honest—and we do this across the board so that there is no personal affront."

The Harvard and MIT investigators studying the polygraph's uses reported a particularly interesting use of a polygraph examiner by a client. After he had screened all workers in a large supermarket he "was retained by the company simply to walk around the store every six months, saying 'hello' to all the employees."

A bank that had a polygraph operator periodically check all personnel handling money found that a vice-president sent the polygraph needles soaring on the question: "Have you ever stolen any money from the bank or its customers?" An audit couldn't find any losses. He was retested several times, and each time the needles soared on that question. The man was almost fired, but the president refused to do so because he liked the man and because no audits could uncover losses attributable to him. The man was turned over to psychiatrists who subsequently contended the man had been giving a "false positive" response to that particular question because it made him think of his wife and mother, whom he loathed. They were both customers of the bank who might be hit by any large embezzlement.

But neither the questionable validity nor the morality of using lie detectors on captive employees seems to disturb some entrepreneurs unduly. *Printing Impressions* carried an article pointing out that companies using lie detectors were sullying their reputations and were even guilty of trespassing on the dignity and privacy of their employees. Later the journal printed a blistering rebuttal by a businessman in the graphic arts industry who reported:

"Any businessman—or outside do-gooder—who shuns the lie detector on moral grounds just isn't being realistic, in my opinion." To defend his viewpoint he cited an instance: at one of his branches his checks of inventory showed a profit drain. The checking narrowed "the guilt down to one of four people."

He couldn't tell which was the culprit so he brought in the poly-graph operator and let him try to finger the guilty one. He asked: "Would I have been on firmer moral grounds in this case if I had fired all four suspects just to make certain of getting the guilty one?"

He says his employees now "have the message. They know that if there's any hanky-panky at any branch each person at that location will be required to take a test. Refusal means dismissal. True, it's a rotten way to have to run a business."

At the managerial level a serious question of privacy invasion has arisen in the widespread expectation that the individual will permit the company to make a periodic assessment of his physical and mental health. In the executive dining room of Sterling Drug, Inc., there are scales. And at least once a week each executive is expected to mount the scales and record his weight. If he gains more than five pounds above what was his earlier norm, he is banned from the dining room until he gets his weight back near the norm.

Management Review reported on a nationwide survey of the policies of 400 companies in checking on the health of their executives.[1] It carried shocking implications. Consider these reported facts:

—Nearly half of the companies either required executives to take periodic health examinations or made a point of urging them to do so.

—Only one firm in ten permitted the executive to go to a doctor or clinic of his own choice.

—Nearly half of the companies required that the company receive as a routine a copy of the doctor's report. In sixteen instances a copy of the report went only to the company, not to the executive.

For doctors engaged in such mandatory or semi-mandatory health checks the ethical issue was troublesome. For one thing, they were finding that men were reticent about revealing disquieting symptoms. For another, the whole idea of reporting on a man's health to an outsider disturbed them because it was a violation of the traditional doctor-patient relationship.

Until recently, at least, psychologists who are retained by corporations to "audit" or "assess" the company's on-the-job managers at regular intervals have generally been notably less squeamish about revealing their findings to managements. After all, management pays the bills. And many of the psychologists have not had as long a tradition as medical doctors in regarding the professional patient relationship as inviolate. The psychologist's report—or a summary of his conclusions that pertain to the man's ability on the job— usually goes into the subject's personnel file at the company. If the psychologist tells the man anything about his conclusions, he is likely to state his critical findings in gentle terms in order not to inflict lasting psychological damage upon the individual. In his report to management, however, the psychologist is likely to show no such tendency to be gentle. He'll cite his opinion of the man's strengths and weaknesses, perhaps in parallel columns.

An evaluation of a man's personality—even if at least partially valid at the time it is made—becomes less and less valid with each passing year, because personalities do change. Yet at many companies the personnel folders on managerial personnel contain psychological assessments that were made years ago. Dr. Harry Levinson of the Menninger Foundation has offered some scorching comments on the way personnel files are handled. He told of visiting a company after it had been swallowed up in a merger with a larger corporation whose headquarters were thousands of miles away. The executives at the faraway headquarters called for the files of middle managers of this smaller company whom they had acquired in the merger. In each man's file was an assessment made by a psychological consulting firm. Levinson said that even in the first place the assessments had been "superficial." But now these partially obsolete psychological-test reports were being used by a management far removed from the scene to make some quick decisions about what to do with each of the new managers it had acquired.

Some of the psychological consulting firms feel they can offer their best service not by testing but by periodically interviewing and observing each manager. An officer of one such major consulting firm told me his office likes to assign a psychologist to stick with a manager over the years, to see him every few weeks, chat with him both on the job and off. This service is offered with the best intentions of helping the man be a more effective manager for the company that is paying the bill. And such friendly consulting by competent psychologists can be very helpful to a man if he knows it is a completely confidential relationship. But such uses of psychologists can have Big Brotherish possibilities. If the psychological consulting firm is invited to advise the corporation on whom to choose for an important opening, the firm may—unless sound ground rules have been established regarding confidentiality—confer with its various psychologists assigned to various executives before making a recommendation.

The harshest words yet addressed to the multitude of psychologists who work for managements assessing men on the job and screening applicants came from Dr. Jay L. Otis, director of the Psychological Research Service at Western Reserve and onetime president of the Division of Consulting Psychology of the American Psychological Association. Dr. Otis kindly supplied me with a copy of the scalding remarks he addressed to his colleagues a few years aso on the occasion of turning over his presidential gavel. His talk was entitled "Psychological Espionage." He said he chose that title because the trend in consulting work had made him pause and wonder. The phrase "psychological espionage," he conceded, "is not a nice phrase; yet it does characterize some of the work we are doing and describes the attitude of some of our examinees and clients toward us." He observed: "We are professional practitioners with very complicated professional obligations."

He singled out aspects of the work done by psychological consultants when working for industry that were of particular concern to the conscientious professional:

1. The use of disguised tests. He explained that the person being examined may feel safe until "he is faced with certain psychological measures he does not understand. Without telling him the ultimate implications of his remarks, we show him some ink blots and proceed to help or harm him by interpreting remarks such as cat, insides of person, branches, sweet peas, sunset, and crab in terms of introversion-extroversion, adjustment, inferiority, and insecurity. Do we as psychologists have the right to subject a captive examinee to an examination without a full explanation of what the real purpose of the examination is?"

2. The role of the psychologist in making attitude surveys. Examinees are often invited to check any negative statements that they feel may apply to colleagues, bosses, or the company and to check statements reflecting their opinion on controversial subjects. "It is amazing to observe the tremendous amount of information obtained through attitude surveys," he said. And he added that it was often difficult to make sure no harm would be done in revealing to management responses made by employees concerning their "opinions and attitudes about people, policies, practices and working conditions. One set of survey results not too long ago could have resulted in great harm to a few individuals if care had not been exercised in reporting the findings."

3. The dual role of serving an industrial firm and serving the individual sent by that firm. Dr. Otis invited his listeners to put themselves in the position of a man or woman sent into a psychological service for an audit. "The receptionist who greets you, the psychologist who interviews you, the psychometrist who administers the tests, are all attempting to secure information, some of which will reveal your best qualities and some your poorest." The man across from you "is one who watches, views, inspects and examines secretly, as a scout (and this is a major professional

problem)....Is he trying to save [you] or the company from making a mistake?" And he added: "I wonder how infallible we think we are when we make a recommendation, after a day or two of observation, that may affect the lifetime career of an employee."

He also wondered if such psychologists should not resolve this dual role "by refusing to accept it.... I believe we can accept but one role, that of a genuine interest in the human being we are working with so that from his point of view he will obtain maximum adjustment under present and long-range conditions."

That was a finely stated recommendation. But still there is the awkward fact that the managements are paying the bills. And until the consciences of managements are aroused, or until the psychologists develop new ground rules for cooperation, the managements probably will be satisfied with nothing less than getting a report, with neat percentage charts, purportedly giving the lowdown on the employee in question. In view of the damage they can do to a man, perhaps it is time the psychologists adopted their own solemnly attested oath comparable to the physician's Hippocratic Oath.

The total ultimate impact of all this managerial reliance upon psychological spies, lie detectors, hidden cameras, undercover agents, bugging, health reports, controls, police dogs, and fingerprinting is appalling to contemplate.

First there is the ethical tone being set for a large part of the U.S. society, which might best be described as moral squalor.

Then we must surmise what impact all this surveillance and distrust has on the people who feel themselves victims of it. Clearly millions of people are receiving psychic scars that will influence their behavior and aspirations for many years.

Finally there is the question of the well-being for the long run of the companies that demonstrate such distrust and callousness. They have been lured into the trap of accepting archaic assumptions about employees that are not only being discredited but are crippling their efforts to have a fully effective workforce.

The archaic assumptions that have dominated management thinking in recent decades are that the average employee, while well-meaning, is prone to be irresponsible, a bit lazy if given a chance, and more than a little dishonest about company property if not watched. The management that follows the logic of these assumptions knows that, while it must humor the employee, it must also accept his irresponsibility and keep a sharp eye on him.

These assumptions fly in the face of all that behavioral scientists and other careful investigators who study employee behavior are learning about what motivates people to superior performance.

I refer to such distinguished investigators as Chris Argyris of Yale, Douglas McGregor and Charles A. Myers at MIT, Abraham Maslow at Brandeis, Frederick Herzberg at Western Reserve, and Rensis Likert at the University of Michigan.

Their findings in general support the view that many managements have been digging themselves into a deeper and deeper hole by their suspiciousness, their careful splintering of responsibility, and their devising of ever-tighter controls on the individual employee, whether he is a line worker or an accountant or a middle manager.

The employees have been profoundly insulted and alienated by the feeling of impoverishment in their main life roles. They have fought back the best way they could: by restricting their output, by making a game of pilfering, by adopting a facade of indifference.

A team of investigators led by Frederick Herzberg asked 200 subjects, mostly accountants and engineers, to describe critical events in their careers that made them feel exceptionally good or bad about their jobs. One finding that stood out was that being given "responsibility" produced the greatest of all long-term satisfactions. The team concluded that a "feeling of growth in stature and responsibility is still the most exciting thing that can happen to someone in our society."[2]

Dr. Argyris has demonstrated in experiments that the output

and dedication of girls on an assembly line shot up when they were put completely in charge of making the entire electronic product themselves and the controls over their work by the foreman, inspector, and industrial engineer were eliminated. Dr. Argyris stresses the finding that one of the most powerful motivators of constructive human conduct is simple trust. I mentioned to him the widespread evidence of mistrust I had encountered in this research. He suggested that a "causal chain" along the following lines seems to develop in many organizations:

1. The employee comes into the organization with honest, earnest motives.

2. He experiences the frustration that comes from a feeling of failure because he is given little feeling that he is trusted and little responsibility.

3. He reacts by feeling less responsibility for the wellbeing and success of the organization. He also may gradually respond to his feeling of failure in a number of active ways, including stealing. Partly he steals because it is a safe way to express his aggression. In a deeper sense "he steals from a company which has helped to alienate him from feeling responsibility, commitment, and trust."

4. Once the stealing occurs, management tightens up the very factors that caused the original stealings.

5. Now the distrust of the workers is out in the open. They begin to feel, "Okay, if they think I cannot be trusted, I will act as if I cannot." Dr. Argyris has found in his studies that distrust is not confined to the lower-level employees. "In my opinion there is a lot of distrust at the upper levels," he states. He documents this impressively in one of his latest works.[3]

Perhaps the most revolutionary firm in the country is a rapidly growing, highly successful electronics firm near San Diego, Non-Linear Systems, Inc., which makes digital computers costing from $1000 to $6000 each. A few years ago this company threw out its assembly lines, broke the entire company up into small teams charged with running their own small businesses. There are no time clocks, no need to explain either absence or lateness. A woman in an assembly group may have entire responsibility for constructing an instrument herself, based on her own planning and programming. She tests as she goes along, packs it, and is responsible for correcting any malfunction that ever develops while a client is using it. Man-hours devoted to building each instrument have been cut in half; complaints of trouble from clients have dropped 90 per cent in two years.

Non-Linear's philosophy of trust in the individual who is given responsibility shows up dramatically in its attitude toward money. Some supermarket chains will not permit a manager of a store doing a million-dollar annual business to spend more than $25 without getting authorization from headquarters. At Non-Linear any project manager in engineering can, without consulting any higher official, spend up to $2500 for a piece of needed equipment on his own signature.

Sales representatives at the company's nineteen branch offices are given a monthly allowance sufficient to cover all reasonably conceivable expenses, including entertaining and buying a new car every couple of years. No accounting to the company is required. If by prudence the man can get by on less, he is free to pocket the savings. The only check is on results. An official advises: "Responses have been extremely favorable to this approach. We know of no abuses nor have we any reason to believe that there will be."

This company, then, has by assigning large responsibilities and demonstrating genuine trust achieved a spectacular showing of commitment by individuals to their jobs. As for the possibility that the display of trust would inspire some slippery employees to take advantage of the company, a spokesman had this to say:

"We have had no problems with stealing or pilferage . . . we have found that people in our plant seem to become more trustworthy as we place trust in them."

6. The Very Public Lives of Public Servants

> " ... more than 5,000 gadgets to permit telephone eaves-dropping still are attached to Government telephones in the Washington area alone."—From report by House Committee on Government Operations, 1962

"Every poor devil who wants to get a job in the federal government must fill out a Form 57," commented attorney Joseph L. Rauh, Jr., a much-decorated former lieutenant colonel. The tall, rugged Mr. Rauh has spent a considerable part of the time since he shed his uniform leading battles along the Potomac against the fattest, most-tentacled bureaucracy in history on behalf of individuals he feels have been treated roughly by this bureaucracy.

Form 57 is Washington's version of "This Is Your Life." It runs six pages. You are instructed to reveal your salary at each of your last three jobs and reasons for leaving. You must list every foreign country you have ever visited with an explanation of what you did while there. You must disclose any physical disabilities or handicaps. And you must answer the question "Have you ever been discharged from employment for any reason?" (I was first fired from a job at the age of eleven for thoughtlessly leaving in my boss's office a mop and bucket I had been using.)

Two of the most troublesome questions on Form 57 for a great many thousand loyal, law-abiding citizens who want to serve their country are numbers 27 and 37. Question 27 asks if you now belong or *ever* belonged to a subversive organization. (The actual question runs 79 words.) A footnote explains that for guidance in deciding whether you ever belonged to such an organization you might check the so-called Attorney General's list available at federal employment offices. But it adds: "Your use of this list does not release you from the responsibility of listing your past or present membership in any other organization which you have reason to believe comes within the meaning of the question." If you decide that perhaps you did once belong to some such organization you must write a complete explanation on a separate sheet.

Mr. Rauh pointed out that fifteen years ago a bookshop association was on the Attorney General's list as a "front" organization. It had been peddling Communist propaganda, mostly to people who were more interested in discounts on books, records, and the like. If you acknowledge having once—fifteen years ago—been affiliated with this bookish group, Mr. Rauh said, "You are in trouble." If they really need you for a job they'll ignore such associations that are clearly interests of another era, Mr. Rauh explained, but the run- of-the-mill bureaucrat "never takes a risk if he can help it. He's a bland guy and likes to pick bland guys."

The other question, 37, reads: "Have you ever been arrested, taken into custody, held for investigation or questioning, or charged by any law enforcement authority?" (It generously allows you to omit minor traffic violations or incidents before the age of sixteen.) But it stresses that "All other incidents must be included, even though they were dismissed...."

The police in many U.S. cities—as we'll see—have fallen into the highly questionable practice of throwing out a dragnet when a well-publicized crime occurs and holding for questioning—without charge and perhaps without technical "arrest"—dozens of people who might conceivably be associated with, or know something about, the crime. All caught up in such a dragnet would have to answer "yes."

Or perhaps the job applicant has to give a "yes" answer to this question because he was once taken into custody for participating in a demonstration against nuclear testing, or demonstrating in opposition to racial segregation, or handing out pro- or anti-union literature.

The American Civil Liberties Union, in protesting the unreasonableness of this question, pointed out that hundreds of college students were arrested or taken into custody temporarily in certain Southern states for being Freedom Riders. This detention will have to be listed if they ever apply for jobs with the government or, for that matter, with many corporations. Large bureaucracies, whether public or private, are tending more and more automatically to eliminate from consideration all people who have ever had a brush with the law rather than bother to assess the incident or each individual's merits in terms of his total pertinent life experiences. They often don't even bother to inquire whether the charges were dismissed. In most cities it is difficult to obtain the return of an arrest record, if the person has been released without charge, and even if the record can be obtained, that does not change the requirement that a "yes" answer must be given to question number 37. It would be much fairer, in view of the above practices, to require people to list only criminal convictions, or at least only indictments and convictions.

The seriousness for society of this indiscriminate wariness of people with "records" of detention can be seen in the fact that in recent years many thousands of the best-educated, most articulate, or most promising young American Negroes have been taken into custody somewhere for participating in demonstrations over civil rights.

Each of the federal government's 2,500,000 civilian employees must fill out this Form 57 whether he or she hopes to be a stenographer in Colorado for the park service or a confidential aide who works thirty feet from the President. Further, he or she may be checked out specifically to make certain his or her employment is "clearly consistent with the interest of the national security," pursuant to Executive Order 10450. If the job is more sensitive, requiring security clearance, the person's life history is likely to be reconstructed bit by bit with a "full field" investigation. At the State Department, where every job is "sensitive," it has been common-place to check not only neighbors and former teachers of an employee but also his or her hairdresser, barber, or grocer.

An official of Security Planning and Programs for the Department of Defense advised me that the department currently has approximately 600,000 civilian employees who have undergone the more thorough scrutiny required for security clearance.

Like private industry, the federal government has become enchanted with the marvelous new ways of maintaining surveillance over employees that are offered by advances in electronic devices. In fact, as we have seen, many of these advances came in response to federal demand. In the late 1950s it was discovered that the General Services Administration had included on its price list of office supplies circulated to all federal agencies bugging equipment that could be concealed under one's garments. Inquiry disclosed that in one three-year period federal agencies had spent $141,136 for a single brand of concealable wire recorders, Minifon.

One of the more startling—and useful—investigations undertaken by a congressional committee in recent years was that made of telephone monitoring practices in the federal government. We are indebted to the Special Government Information Subcommittee of the Committee on Government Operations, chaired by Representative John E. Moss, for its findings. In the course of the study the staff investigators discovered that some of their own investigative calls were being routinely monitored in the offices of the officials being called.

A call is monitored by putting either a tape recorder or a secretary with note pad on an extension line. The monitoring is facilitated by the installation of a "snooper button"—to activate either a cutoff switch or a listening-in circuit so that the monitoring device or person can hear but not be heard humming or breathing.

The investigators, under staff administrator Samuel J.

Archibald, discovered that thirty-three of the thirty-seven federal agencies that were queried permitted telephone monitoring! Most of the thirty-three had no regulations whatever controlling the practice, and most of them did not always require the other party to be warned that the call was being monitored.

Most shocking, it turned out that the Federal Communications Commission itself had no regulations controlling telephone monitoring by its personnel. The FCC is charged by law with the duty of regulating interstate and foreign commerce in communication. Its chairman admitted that monitoring went on there without notifying the caller that he was being monitored.

The investigators also found that the General Services Administration had 876 cutoff devices on the switchboard it was operating in Washington. Altogether, the investigators found many thousands of snooper buttons in use in federal offices in Washington. The full committee in its first report observed that the discoveries indicated "a dangerous drift toward a huge bureaucracy peering over the shoulder of the citizen" (whether the citizen is in or out of government). It recommended that the federal agencies get busy and set up regulations banning telephone eavesdropping. A good many agencies did draw up regulations as a result of the committee's report. But by the next year, 1962, close to 5000 snooper buttons were still in use. And in at least fifteen agencies there was no clear requirement that the caller be notified that his words were being recorded by machine or stenographer. Two of the agencies that declined to acknowledge drawing up any written regulations whatever on monitoring were the Department of Justice and the Central Intelligence Agency. On the other hand the Defense Department, which has at least as much reason to be security conscious, drew up a stern prohibition on all unannounced monitoring.

Mr. Archibald and his investigators have now turned their attention to an even smellier kettle of fish—the use of lie detectors in the federal government. The subcommittee's interest was piqued by a report that the U.S. military agencies owned 440 lie detectors, had 560 polygraph examiners on the federal payroll, and operated a special eight-week school for training 100 new polygraph examiners each year at Fort Gordon, Georgia. There were indications of widespread use of the lie detector in many agencies. The CIA gives virtually every applicant for a job a lie-detector test. The National Security Agency uses it on everybody—typists, secretaries, plumbers. On the other hand, the FBI does not use it in personnel evaluations and only uses it occasionally in investigations.

Apparently the military intelligence agencies use the lie detector to try to smoke out not only subversives and homosexuals but any so-called psychological deviates. The Internal Revenue Service has used it but apparently, so far, not on taxpayers. One reported use was to try to find who in the Revenue Service had been leaking information to a U.S. senator.

Official Washington's new proneness to strap public servants into chairs and subject them to the mental intimidation of the polygraph came ludicrously into view during the investigation of the leak over the TFX plane contract. The Pentagon was trying to get to the bottom of an embarrassing matter that did not even involve security. It was simply trying to discover who had leaked to a newspaper an Air Force memorandum critical of a Senate committee's tactics. In the process of trying to find the answer, investigators for the Air Force Inspector General grilled 120 people in the Pentagon and induced the 120 people to sign sworn statements agreeing to take the lie-detector test. The people who were induced to agree included office girls, the Secretary of the Navy, the Secretary of the Air Force, and the Deputy Secretary of Defense! A spokesman for the department referred to the lie-detector test—whose validity has been challenged, as we've seen—as part of the "regular technique" of military investigations.

Happily in this instance news reports of the mass inquisition inspired the President to call off the whole thing as a "mistake."

But the *New York Herald Tribune* offered a highly pertinent editorial afterthought when it said: "We would hate to think of the possibilities of government by lie detector if every department turned to this device to check on suspects within its fold."

The hidden microphone is also evidently another "regular technique" of military investigations. A good many public servants working in the military have from experience come to assume there may quite possibly be a bug in their offices or a tap on their phones. Writer Ben H. Bagdikian, after talking with a good many people who work in, or deal with, the Pentagon, reported that "A surprising number of Pentagon officials take for granted that their offices are 'bugged'—monitored by hidden microphones. Almost every defense correspondent I talked to assumed his telephones, office and home, are tapped by some government agency." The editor of *Aviation Week and Space Technology* commented in regard to his downtown office: "I assume they have these phones bugged."

In the furor that developed at the State Department in late 1963 concerning charges that its chief security evaluations officer, Otto F. Otepka, had been transmitting classified documents to a Senate committee, there was an interesting sidelight. It turned out that three of his associates in the department's security office had planted an eavesdropping device inside *his* office to try to pick up his conversations. It was placed in his telephone. A *New York Times* reporter quoted State Department officials as saying "they were uncertain about the legality of various forms of eavesdropping in their offices." (As this was being written, incidentally, a tremendous row had broken out in Holland about telephone tapping by government agencies.)

Congressmen have always found it easier to vote for more rather than fewer security measures, and in some instances have been chagrined by their own zealousness. Six congressmen professed to be shocked when they learned that investigators for the Civil Service Commission had been checking quite thoroughly into their backgrounds, and after comparing notes they demanded an explanation. It turned out there was a simple explanation. They were going to Minneapolis, Minnesota, U.S.A., as delegates to a meeting of the World Health Organization. Under a law several of them had helped pass, any American designated to work with an international organization had to undergo a security check.

The quickness of members of the House of Representatives to authorize the military establishment to deal arbitrarily with the individual was demonstrated, as on many previous occasions, in mid-1963. By a margin of 340-40 it voted to give the Secretary of Defense the right to fire any employee of the National Security Agency without hearing, without any explanation, or without any right to appeal, if the Secretary decides the employee is a security risk. A badge of infamy, to use Mr. Justice Tom Clark's phrase, can be hung on the employee without his ever knowing why it was hung there. The *Washington Post* commented, when the same measure was under consideration earlier, that it would put everyone working for the agency "at the mercy of any mischiefmaker or malcontent or personal enemy who might call him a subversive or a homosexual or an alcoholic."

The military mind, even more than the corporate mind or the civilian bureaucratic mind, seems prone to assume that the individual should adjust his off-duty life and his private thoughts to the patterns esteemed by the organization. Navy officials are particularly inclined to enforce this subordination of the individual. Perhaps this is because they have long been indoctrinated to idealize the tight ship—even though tens of thousands of people on Navy payrolls rarely set foot on a ship.

Navy officials have frequently assumed the right to approve or disapprove any marital partner a Navy man or woman chooses. A Navy fireman apprentice was court-martialed for failing to get written permission from his commander before marrying in the Philippines. When this case came before the U.S. Court of Military Appeals, the chief judge indicated that a commander's right to control marriages was *not necessarily* confined to foreign areas. He said: "A military commander may, at least in foreign areas, impose reasonable restrictions on the right of military personnel of his command to marry." Judge Homer Ferguson, in dissenting, declared that any order requiring a commander's permission to marry was "illegal on its face."

Even the Navy withdrew under fire when the naval-mind-at-work concerning marriage broke into the news in 1962. At issue was a new fitness form for assessing junior officers. It contained a section on the officer and his wife as a "team." The form invited the reporting officer to comment "on the officer-wife team as to their suitability and desirability as representatives of their country and their Navy. . . . Do you consider them to be: particularly suitable? suitable? not observed or not applicable?" There was also space for "comment if appropriate."

The Navy wife has often played an important part, informally, in her husband's progress or lack of it; but a good many wives were upset by the idea that the fitness of their marriage was subject to official assessment. An Associated Press reporter got an earful when he queried officers' wives at the Norfolk, Virginia, headquarters for the Atlantic Fleet. They not only decried the invasion of privacy involved but voiced strong suspicions that their husbands' superiors would consult their own wives in making any evaluation. One commander's wife declared: "Suppose you're the kind of person who doesn't want to go running around to teas and luncheons all day? So then your commanding officer's wife doesn't know you—or, if she's the clubby type, she doesn't like you—and what kind of a fitness report do you think you'd get then?" Another wife predicted: "This same type of mind is going to produce a fitness report on the children one of these days. After all, the children represent the Navy, too, if you want to look at it that way—which I don't."

The combination of the wives' ire plus the role of the American newspapers in airing the controversy forced the

Navy to retreat. The Secretary said: "I have concluded that the proposed report will not produce the information needed and may unnecessarily hurt the promotion chances of some officers who are exceptionally well qualified for sea and other duties not requiring special attention to the suitability of dependents for such assignments."

But at approximately the same time that the Navy was retreating on the issue of officers' wives it was moving to strengthen its control over the private thoughts and friendship patterns of Navy civilian employees. In this quotation from *OPNAV, Civilian Personnel Newsletter*, note the ominous use of the word "appraisal" in the Navy's admonition: "A number of our citizens unwittingly expose themselves to unfavorable or suspicious appraisal which they can and should avoid. This may take the form of an indiscreet remark; an unwise selection of friends or associates; membership in an organization whose true objectives are concealed behind a popular and innocuous title; attendance at and participation in the meetings and functions of such organizations even though not an official member. . . .

"It is advisable to study and seek wise and mature counsel prior to association with persons or organizations of any political or civic nature. . ."

Apparently some naval civilian was sufficiently disturbed by the implications of this intrusion into his private life to forward it to the American Civil Liberties Union. An official of the ACLU, in showing this admonition to me, quite properly characterized it as "shocking."

Thus far we've confined our exploration to the scrutiny of the private lives of federal personnel. We should note, however, that heavy-handedness in intruding into the private lives of public employees has also spread to the city level.

The acceptance of the lie detector as a general screening and surveillance device is perhaps as good an indicator as any of this heavy-handedness. Los Angeles, Dallas, San Antonio, and Detroit now make general use of the lie detector in assessing applicants for a variety of municipal jobs. And a great many other cities—including Kansas City, St. Louis, Phoenix, and Wichita—are starting to use the lie detector specifically in assessing candidates for jobs on the police force.

Public Personnel Review in July 1962 presented an account of the growing use of the lie detector at the city level. The author was George Washnis, the personnel director of Evanston, Illinois. And his glowing article was subtitled: "How the lie-detector helps to spot the 'rotten apples' and cuts down selection time and costs." (Here once again we see the exaltation of no-fuss-and-no-bother efficiency over the older-fashioned methods of getting to know a man personally.)

He said that he and his associates first started using the polygraph on certain municipal parking-lot attendants in 1959 when they suspected that every nickel was not getting to the city treasury. They were pleased with the results— and they then began to strap every parking-lot attendant into the lie-detector chair every three months. And, thereafter, they induced the Civil Service Commission and Administrative Staff to start strapping down the seriously considered applicants for firemen's and policemen's jobs, and "certain other appropriate classes of employees."

One of the questions thrown at a police candidate is whether he lied in answering any of the 150 probing questions asked of him on the application form. The questioning by the polygraph examiner covers the man's drinking and gambling habits and often apparently gets into the man's personal finances. Mr. Washnis said the polygraph examiner had discovered several candidates "who were in serious debt troubles not yet brought to the attention of the various credit bureaus." One of the more fascinating discoveries in Evanston was a police applicant who "admitted to Communist sympathies." This man, instead of being tossed out, was turned over to "our psychologist and psychiatrist" (as are all "questionable" cases) for a checkout on this angle. The result offers an interesting commentary on the city's assessment of what it takes to be a good cop. Mr. Washnis reported: "The psychiatric interview revealed that this applicant did not have the intellectual capacity to understand what it was to be a Communist, and for our purposes he was an acceptable candidate."

The city of Evanston is so pleased with the results achieved in sorting people by use of the polygraph confessional chamber that it has started making periodic rechecks of all policemen who submit to the polygraph in order to get a job in the first place.

Mr. Washnis said that without question the polygraph "should not be used to pry into the private lives of individuals or their thoughts or philosophies." But what is left of one's private life and thoughts after he has been worked over by a good tough polygraph examiner?

7. The Watch Over the Teachers

"A nation that cannot trust its intellectuals cannot trust itself."—A. Whitney Griswold, late president of Yale University

At the Houston office of the William J. Burns International Detective Agency someone had a dandy idea for adding to his office's volume of assignments. He had undoubtedly read about all the controversial professors in Texas and the strenuous efforts of various superheated conservative groups to root them out. This seemed like a natural challenge for Burns's fast-growing "confidential survey" operation. So he dispatched letters to six college presidents in Texas. Possibly with some exaggeration he began:

"Many colleges and universities have found that our services can be very beneficial and informative.... This same system which has saved countless dollars in business can be used in your institution to give you an inside, on-the-scene report concerning any practices detrimental to the institution's character and reputation.

"Teaching practices can be viewed with information from a 'student' who is trained to report objectively on what he or she sees or hears from the classroom. Almost every department has its controversial faculty member. These departments invariably are: religion, philosophy, psychology, English (literature), biology, history, government, journalism, speech and drama.

"A 'student' trained in his duties as a Burns operative can enroll ... obtain his class schedule ... attend class and send daily, confidential reports to the Agency...."[1]

Someone publicized the letter, and it brought a quick reaction. One of the many educators who were outraged was

William P. Fidler, general secretary of the American Association of University Professors. He shot off a letter expressing "deep concern and vigorous objection" to W. Sherman Burns, the agency's president. The reported proposal, he said, was "entirely inconsistent with every concept of academic freedom and academic due process," and added, "In all frankness, I can also tell you that we cannot particularly appreciate the whole concept of an undercover system." He called for "prompt action" by the agency to discontinue this type of activity.

Mr. Burns in his response blamed the letters on an employee impelled more by "sales enthusiasm" than "mature thought." He asserted that the letters hadn't been approved by the local manager and that "steps have been taken to correct this and see that there is no recurrence of it."

Unfortunately the episode was simply a symptom of the growing assault upon the freedom of both educators and students to express provocative ideas in our schools and colleges. The many drives to ban books from public-school libraries are also symptomatic. Mr. Fidler advised me that invasions of privacy as well as attacks upon academic freedom have been increasing in the academic community.

Parents have a wholly legitimate right to know, and be deeply curious about, the caliber of teachers and methods of instruction that are influencing the intellectual growth of their youngsters. Our schools would be better, and the caliber of our educators would be higher, if parents showed more genuine curiosity than they do.

But the watchers over the nation's schools who cause the most commotion and are the most intrusive are not parents or parent groups as such. They are the chronically "anti," chronically suspicious groups whose attitude toward education is often one of generalized hostility and whose attitude toward society is one of generalized anxiety, or they exploit such hostility and anxiety in others. Among the more conspicuous are the veterans' groups, the "radical right" groups, the segregationist groups, the let's-cut-taxes groups, and politicians looking for publicity or the support of these groups.

Although the surveillance and the attacks upon academic freedom have been most intensive in the South, Southwest, and West, they have occurred in many areas. One episode that deeply disturbed Mr. Fidler occurred in Brockport, New York.

A few faculty members at the State University College of Education at Brockport sent a petition to their congressman urging that he vote for the elimination of a congressional committee. The committee in question was the highly controversial House Un-American Activities Committee. Their petition seems to be one that fair-minded taxpayers might reasonably make for economic if not philosophic reasons. The committee in question has served virtually no legislative purpose in a decade despite the fact that millions of dollars have been appropriated to it in this period.

Soon after the professors dispatched their petition, the New York State Bureau of Criminal Intelligence invaded the campus. One report indicates that an American Legion unit had brought complaints. At any rate the startled president of the university was interrogated at length by the police, who also demanded, and dispatched to Albany, the personnel files of all the faculty members who had signed the petition.

The police closed the case upon finding that "no violation of law had been committed." Presumably police records on all the professors involved are now filed somewhere, subject to possible misinterpretation or distortion at a future date. Mr. Fidler protested to New York's Governor Nelson Rockefeller. He contended that the invasion of the campus was "inconsistent with our American traditions of fairness, decent tolerance for the opinions of others," was a threat to academic freedom and had an "intimidating" effect upon faculty members and educational administrators throughout the state. In reply an aide to the governor sought to make light of a closed matter and endeavored to justify whatever inquisition had occurred on the basis that the professors had drawn up the petition on college stationery. Mr. Fidler suggested tartly that such use of institutional letterheads was a common practice and that any investigation of misuse of stationery should have been referred to the college administration, not the State Bureau of Criminal Intelligence. (I have in my files many hundreds of letters from professors written on their office stationery, and it has never occurred to me to assume they were speaking for their college or university. Use of office stationery by professors simply reflects a minor desire for perquisites and offers a money saving to a generally underpaid profession.)

Perhaps the most relentless inquisition of educators in the last few years occurred at the University of Florida in Gainesville. A gubernatorial candidate who happened also to head a committee of the state legislature moved his committee to Gainesville and for seven months conducted his investigation on the campus. Yale historian C. Vann Woodward, in reporting on the affair, related: "With the aid of lawyers, police, detectives, and paid informers, the committee dragged in hundreds of witnesses, mainly students, to testify against professors. Disclosures of political heresies were disappointing, but sexual deviations supplied headlines."[2]

A new and delicate problem involving possible invasion of privacy has arisen from the fact that many thousands of college and high school students now possess portable tape recorders. When I asked a student at the University of California in Los Angeles, who was driving me to another campus, if he was not missing an important class, he replied: "Oh, I'm being covered on tape. I'll have a transcript of the lecture and discussion tomorrow." It turned out that twenty of the hundred and fifty members of his political science class owned tape recorders. Some display them openly on their desks, others keep them concealed in briefcases. He said a few professors had been fussing about the growing use of recorders and were demanding that their permission be obtained before recorders were used. Others didn't seem to care.

Obviously a recorder can be a convenience to students, particularly for those choosing to sleep through early morning classes. Perhaps also there should be little objection to the use of recorders in the large introductory lecture courses at universities that may have 1500 members in the "class." Such a lecture is virtually a broadcast.

But a true classroom is not a public proceeding and should not be viewed as such. It is here that there is an exciting exploration of ideas. The good teacher will often use the Socratic method of raising questions about novel possibilities. And he may, to stimulate the interchange of ideas, take the position of the devil's advocate. The students in response may express unconventional ideas either after serious reflection or simply out of postadolescent rebelliousness. Several years of such interchanges will, hopefully, result in increased wisdom and discernment for the student. Dr. Clark Kerr of the University of California has observed that "The university is not engaged in making ideas safe for students. It is engaged in making students safe for ideas."

The free flow of such ideas in seminars and other intimate classroom discussions is certainly inhibited if students or teacher know—or wonder whether—they are broadcasting to unknown outsiders. A professor in San Diego found that a tape of one of his classroom discussions was being broadcast by a local radio station engaged in a campaign to try to discredit professors whom the station's management considered to be too liberal. In San Antonio, Texas, a high-school teacher was fired after a student turned over to the trustees a tape recording in which the teacher had tried to surmise how certain Cold War issues must look from the Russians' viewpoint.

And then there was the celebrated case, dramatically photographed by Bill Ray for *Life*, of a high school student in Paradise, California, who was trying to get the goods on his social-science teacher.[3] He and his dad had built a tape recorder into his textbook. The teacher—with the support of the school administration—had won the enmity of the local American Legion post, some local John Birchers, and other townspeople for exposing youngsters to widely divergent points of view from the radical left to the radical right.

The teacher had won an award from the respected Freedom Foundation for her outstanding work in helping youngsters understand and cherish "The American Credo." Among her most emphatic critics pictured in the article were two retired Los Angeles policemen and a retired major who posed with his rifle at the ready.

The student was caught with his concealed recorder after he unsuccessfully tried to provoke the teacher into making a comment that might be interpreted as irreverent. Partly as a result of the storm raised by this episode, the Speaker of the California State Assembly introduced a bill to ban all monitoring devices from school classrooms unless the consent of both teacher and principal is obtained.

Three students were expelled from Groton School a couple of years ago when it was discovered that they had bugged their housemaster's home, and quite thoroughly. They had concealed listening devices in his desk, chair, office, room, and other places.

U.S. teachers in the first twelve grades have traditionally been subjected to a good deal of community scrutiny. Quite recently the school board in Pasadena, California, transferred a teacher to a less desirable position because he refused to shave his very handsome, well-trimmed beard. He taught in the John Muir school, named after a man who had worn a beard.

Today, however, new factors are bringing college professors, too, under more and more surveillance. At a number of the larger universities there is a Central Intelligence Agency representative in residence to make the necessary checks on professors authorized to attend the increasing number of international conferences being held today. And there are various federal inspectors checking out academic researchers involved in space or defense or other projects classified as secret.

What is most disconcerting, however, is the power of the Department of Defense to call upon colleges to turn over reports on many thousands of professors.

Hundreds of colleges and universities have accepted contracts from the Defense Department. Under the contracts certain staff members, as part of their duties, conduct research of interest to the Department of Defense. In the Defense Department's view the college is just another contractor and comes under the rules that apply to industrial contractors. These rules are laid down in the *Industrial Security* Manual.

The only cheering thing that can be said about the manual is that now it is not as frighteningly all-enveloping in its phrasing as it was in the mid-fifties. In 1955 the manual stated: "The *contractor shall submit* immediately to the security office of the cognizant Military Department . . . [when] requested . . . and [when] stated to be needed in connection with an official investigation . . . *information available to the contractor concerning any of his employees working in any of his plants, factories, or sites* at which work for a Military Department is being performed." (Italics supplied.)

A college is a site. This meant then that the Department of Defense if it chose could call for all file information the college had on any member of its faculty! And furthermore the faculty member quite probably would not be advised that his file had been sent to Washington.

The battle to get this phrasing modified has been vividly related by one of the participants, Louis Joughin, who was then with American Civil Liberties Union and now is with the American Association of University Professors.[4]

A spokesman for the Defense Department contended mildly that while the department did indeed have these dragnet powers it was using them with discretion and reasonableness. The ACLU retorted: ". . .the legitimate concern of the government with national security does not give it the right to know anything it may want to know about anyone. . . . Americans are accustomed to a government of law, not of men and not of discretion."

Subsequently the Defense Department's director of Personnel Security Police met with ACLU and AAUP representatives and some months later the manual was revised. It now stated that a "report" on a man—rather than a man's entire file—could be demanded. And it provided that such a report could be demanded only in connection with an official investigation "*of possible or probable compromise of classified information.*" (Italics supplied.) Further exchanges brought written assurance that any requested "report" need not include information not relevant to security.

The situation thus was considerably improved even though the word "possible" in front of "compromise" was lamentably vague. And despite the improved language, reports on thousands of academic scientists are delivered to security officers in Washington without the scientists' knowledge.

What is perhaps most disheartening is that this massive intrusion of the military into the academic world has served to denigrate the faculties vis-i-vis the colleges' administrators. Traditionally in a strong school the faculty has been the power center of the educational and research functions. But the businesslike Department of Defense deals with the college administration, considering faculty members to be employees.

Aside from governmental probers, there at many colleges and public schools intrusive questionnaires, political screenings, and other acts singling out teachers as potentially dangerous characters who require watching. Teachers in Montgomery County, Maryland, have been requested to submit to fingerprinting, and such a proposal for teachers in at least one major city is being pressed. The efforts to keep teachers under close watch are aimed at intimidating or weeding out the "controversial" members. Mostly this process is a legacy from the era of Senator Joseph McCarthy when suspiciousness of the intellectual was particularly virulent; it is also a facet of the more recent battles to silence critics of racial segregation.

Anyone hoping to get a teaching job in California's public schools must expect to be screened by a staff of security officers employed by the state Department of Education. In 1958 the state of Arkansas enacted a law requiring all teachers in publicly supported schools and colleges to file affidavits listing all organizations to which they had belonged or contributed in the preceding five years. Presumably it was aimed primarily at smoking out teachers sympathetic to work of the National Association for the Advancement of Colored People. Its wording, in any case, embraced all kinds of organizations, political, social, religious, or professional.

Five professors at the University of Arkansas and one at Arkansas Polytechnic College refused to sign on the grounds of conscience and because it was an unwarranted invasion of privacy. Their contracts were canceled. The AAUP was instrumental in getting a challenge of this law up to the Supreme Court, which in late 1960 declared it unconstitutional. The state of Mississippi has had a virtually identical law and has chosen to ignore the Supreme Court's verdict. In 1963 the legislature of Alabama was considering a comparable requirement for its educators.

The rash of test oaths that have appeared as a requirement for employment has likewise troubled many educators. The oaths are usually aimed at ferreting out private beliefs that may be contrary to those of the politicians who frame them.

One of the nation's most distinguished scientists, Professor Bentley Glass of Johns Hopkins, accepted appointment to Maryland's Radiation Control Advisory Board. Then he learned that a state law passed a few years earlier required him to take a test oath under the state's Subversive Activities Act. Professor Glass finally declined the appointment, on grounds of conscience, because of the requirement. He offered an eloquent explanation to the governor. In part he said:

"I have of course as a citizen of this country on numerous occasions taken the oath of allegiance, and will never hesitate to do so. Loyalty, like love, is a positive thing. But to be forced to swear that one is not disloyal or subversive to one's country is like being forced to swear that one is not disloyal in marriage. For that the loyal need no oath; the disloyal swear anyway..."

The singling out of teachers and students for such negatively phrased affidavits has struck many of them as odious. Without doubt the requirement that produced the most widespread concern and irritation was the provision of the National Defense Education Act of 1958 specifying that all students and graduate students (who often serve as instructors) applying for loans under the program sign a disclaimer affidavit. The applicant had to swear under oath that he "does not believe in, and is not a member of, and does not support any organization that believes in or teaches the overthrow of the United States Government by force or violence..."

Many in the educational world were deeply offended not only by the negativism of the oath but the discriminatory nature of it. Many kinds of citizens—farmers, small-business operators, the unemployed, transport operators—regularly get federal help without having to sign disclaimer affidavits. The storm spilled onto the floor of Congress, where the first recorded debate on academic freedom in the history of the Congress was finally held. Thirty-two colleges and universities—including a number of the nation's finest—withdrew entirely from the federal program rather than ask needy scholars to sign the disclaimer.

Finally in 1962 Congress, in its wisdom, discreetly negotiated a compromise that struck out the disclaimer affidavit. It simply made it a crime punishable by fine up to $10,000 and prison up to five years for any member of a Communist organization even to apply for a loan under the act! And the government still retained the right to deny or revoke any graduate fellowship under the program if such action seemed to be "in the best interests of the

United States." That is hardly a lucid guideline. But we should note with interest that Congress, in eliminating the disclaimer, did something that politicians rarely have had the courage to do. This is believed to be the first time in history that Congress has seen fit to backtrack on requiring a declaration of patriotism.

Thus far we've been primarily concerned with the unreasonable scrutiny of teachers. Now let us turn to evidences of seemingly unreasonable scrutiny of the students.

8. Are We Conditioning Students to Police State Tactics?

"I am ashamed of my father's job."—Statement No. 184 of a student inventory which several hundred thousand school children in the U.S.A. have been instructed to check if they feel the statement applies to them

In the last few years the surveillance of students and the invasion of the privacy of their thoughts, anxieties, opinions, and home life have in some areas reached disturbing proportions. The events have raised perplexing questions about where lines should reasonably be drawn. At issue are questions of privacy invasion that affect not only college students but high-school and junior-high-school students as well.

Consider as a rather flagrant example a disclosure involving students at a high school in California.

The authorities at this school were troubled by students smoking in the toilets and by vandalism. In constructing a new school facility they took steps to eliminate the problems. They installed one-way viewing mirrors in both the boys' and girls' toilets.

A local newspaper exposed this as a seemingly unreasonable invasion of privacy. But the report didn't create much of a public stir. The people of California, as we've seen, are used to being watched. Youngsters are getting the message from such episodes that it is okay for authorities, including the police, to practice surveillance. And if you want to smoke or commit vandalism you just figure out a new way to go about it. This philosophy is impelling the forces of order in schools and elsewhere to engage in more spying and checking and thus adding to the erosion of privacy.

Unfortunately school authorities fall into some of the same surveillance patterns that are practiced in business and in government as they try to cope with the increasing numbers of students placed in their charge. And this applies to higher institutions of learning.

During the Christmas holiday two years ago the security police of Miami University in Ohio searched all residence rooms for pilfered goods, according to a report in the *Miami Student*. Apparently the police came upon a great deal of material that they presumed to have been illicitly obtained, including street signs. The student newspaper observed editorially that quite a few students didn't seem to have "the vaguest conception of what honesty is."

But the larger issue was the ethics, at least, of such a dragnet search of rooms by "security" police. Granted, the buildings are owned by the university. And where you have private residential groupings of people, you commonly have rules and inspections to see that rules are enforced. Miami had such a regulation authorizing inspection of student rooms. But on most campuses this is assumed to mean that inspection may be made to see that there are no infractions of house rules. Most of the students were paying room rent. If a student pays rent for the exclusive right to a room (or half a room), is not that space his castle—subject to published rules—just as much as a rented apartment would be? And isn't he entitled—under the Fourth Amendment of the Constitution—to expect that he will be presented with a properly drawn search warrant before his pad is subjected to a thorough search and perhaps seizure of possessions? The editor felt that "no one should have the right to search desk drawers or personal luggage which contains the private property of the student" without a search warrant or unless the student is present. He was a little uncertain about whether the police had a legal right to barge into the room itself, but he felt the police certainly had infringed "on the right of every person at Miami to maintain his privacy."

The promise of "efficiency," alas, has so appealed to the administrators of some schools for advanced training that they have been lured into studying the use of modern surveillance techniques for what they feel to be worthy educational purposes. A proposal has been made that a school of social work at a Western university start using one-way mirrors and tape recorders to permit students to observe more advanced social workers as they interview patients. It is not clear whether the people being observed would be notified that they were under observation. Quite possibly they would not be, since such notice would obviously destroy the spontaneity of the interpersonal exchange.

A far more ambitious project for the obviously worthy purpose of promoting efficiency in nursing instruction is being tried out by the U.S. Public Health Service at a large hospital in the Bronx, New York. Closed-circuit TV cameras have been introduced to train nurses in the third year when they are ready to start treating patients. In the past the practice has been for one supervisor to be in charge of six or seven girls. Mr. Max Kanter, whose company, ITV, made the installation, explained: "This supervisor has gone crazy running from room to room to make sure the girls are not killing the patients." Now, with TV, the supervisor has fifteen girls under her supervision. She sits in a TV control room, keeping an eye and ear on all fifteen by cameras and microphones mounted on the wall in each hospital room in which a girl is working. The girls all have earphones. The supervisor doesn't need fifteen monitors to follow the fifteen girls. That would drive her crazy. Instead she has just two monitors. The scene on the left monitor changes from room to room every eight seconds. The right one can hold on any trainee who the supervising nurse feels is in need of criticism or help.

The Public Health Service's brochure selling the TV idea to patients and trainees stresses the fact that a "tally light" goes on when the camera is operating. (Otherwise, I would imagine, patients would think twice before reaching for a bedpan.) And the brochure also carefully explains that the microphone will pick up voices only when the tally light is on. Apparently patients and trainees are accepting the presence of the cameras and microphones calmly. And the Public Health Service talks hopefully of installing them in 1100 other programs for nursing education.

Since the pilot project at this hospital is functioning with scrupulous emphasis upon the notice provided by the tally light, and the careful published explanations provided to both trainees and patients, nearly everyone, I would imagine, would applaud this more efficient way to train nurses. But what of the future when there may well be cameras and microphones in thousands of hospital rooms across the land? It is going to take a lot of scrupulous people and a lot of enforcement of tough regulations to make certain the tally lights are installed to signal the use of both camera and microphone and that they are always in functioning, tamper-proof order. Otherwise the possibilities for surveillance, voyeurism, eavesdropping, and practical joking become frightening to contemplate.

A perplexing problem has arisen in thousands of schools, particularly colleges, as to the kinds of information a teacher can properly give out to prospective employers about ex-students or graduating seniors. The problem has become acute at the college level because both corporate and government investigators, including FBI agents, have tended to become ever more probing in their questioning. And, to further complicate the matter, increasing thousands of graduates are being considered for "sensitive" jobs in government, industry, or military service; and their professors are approached by investigators making loyalty-security inquiries. The Department of Defense spells out the approach that should be made in its Directive 5210.8 if a "Background Investigation" is being conducted on someone among the department's personnel who is to have access to classified information. The investigators, it states, should not only examine school records but interview at the subject's school "persons in a position to know the individual's activities," if available.

Meanwhile we have the harsh fact that bureaucratic hiring officials in general—whether private or public—tend to be wary of anyone with a "controversial" air about him.

What is a teacher's responsibility in dealing with such investigators? Unfortunately the schools have offered the teachers virtually no guidance. When I asked one professor in the Chicago area how he responded to personal questions relating to the students' views, attitudes, and activities, he said: "Why, I tell them everything I know about the fellow . . . otherwise they could subpoena me." Fortunately for our society, he was misinformed on the last point. A report by the Committee on Academic Freedom of the faculty at the University of California at Berkeley has stated that no prospective employer has a right to demand even *relevant* information about a student or former student and "even when the inquiry comes from the Civil Service, Military Intelligence, or the FBI there is no legal obligation . . . to provide answers."[1]

A few years ago a number of faculty members at the University of California became upset by the kinds of intrusive questions about students or former students being put to them. In one case a man from the Civil Service Commission asked a professor about an individual the professor had had as a student nine years earlier. Besides the usual questions, the investigator wanted to know about the man's associations and loyalty and whether the professor "remembered any discussions in class with the investigatee." The investigator said he understood class discussion often became quite heated at U. Cal. The professor answered that he remembered no discussions with the man. The investigator "then asked if I could remember even whether the investigatee's responses were generally conservative or liberal," the professor related.

Another professor revealed that an investigator for Army Intelligence had asked about one of his current students: "How about his political thinking?"

The University of California's Committee on Academic Freedom (chaired by Dean Frank C. Newman of the School of Law) was instructed to investigate the possibility of providing a guideline for the faculty. In its report the committee stressed that teachers "should regard as a part of their University assignment the supplying of information as to the ability, character, and promise of students and former students." But it felt they should as a matter of general policy not supply information about the person's "beliefs, attitudes, activities, and associations." Otherwise their school would not be a "free university." The committee offered this observation:

"If it were generally known by students that their political and religious freedom to disclose beliefs, to express attitudes, to recount activities, and to refer to associations did *not* protect them from faculty response to loyalty-security inquiries, many students, in the classroom and in academic consultations, would apply rules of caution differing markedly from the rules of free inquiry we now tend to take for granted." The committee noted with concern reports that students in many parts of the country were starting to be overcautious in expressing views that someone might consider unpopular.

It also noted that in Britain the Council of the Association of University Teachers had adopted a form notice that states: "The Association of University Teachers has expressed its disapproval of questions concerning the political or religious beliefs, activities, or associations of students. I share this view, and am not prepared to answer such questions." (Signature.)

Dean Newman's committee recommended to the Representative Assembly of the faculty the adoption of the following resolution: "This Faculty asserts that freedom of discussion in the classroom and in academic consultation is fundamental to higher education. The essential freedom of a university can be seriously jeopardized if argument and expression of opinion are inhibited, particularly in those subjects which are held controversial in some quarters and at some moments in history. Therefore, reports by a teacher concerning the beliefs, attitudes, activities, and associations of a student regarding religion, politics, and public affairs in general are not permissible when the reports are based on information acquired by the teacher in the course of instruction or in the course of other student-teacher relations that involve the student's academic program."

The resolution was passed. If the decision had stood, faculty members would have been able simply to hand out a copy of the resolution to too nosy inquirers and thus they would not appear to be trying to avoid making revelations about any particular student or former student. Unfortunately the university's legal counsel held that under the Regents' rules of that particular university the action of the Representative Assembly was not legal. Dean Newman advises me that while a few colleges such as Haverford and Swarthmore have produced some rules about how to respond to inquiries, he knows of no university that has adopted a rule with the strength that California's statement would have had.

Meanwhile the ACLU took up the issue, and in 1961 its national Board of Directors sought to cope with "this proliferating process of interrogation and response." The board approved a statement that set up guidelines for professors. It stated: "Ordinarily, questions relating to what the student has demonstrated as a student—for example the ability to write in a certain way, to solve problems . . . to reason consistently, to direct personnel or projects—pose no threat to educational privacy. But questions relating to the student's loyalty and patriotism, his political or religious or moral or social beliefs and attitudes, his general outlook, his private life, may well jeopardize the teacher-student relation."

The ACLU statement also considered the hazard that questions might rise in the mind of an investigator if he received a simple refusal to answer too intrusive questions about a specific student or ex-student. It suggested that teachers preface each questionnaire or interrogation with a brief form statement "to the effect that the academic policy to which they subscribe makes it inadvisable to answer certain types of questions, no matter who the individual student may be." [2]

The American Association of University Professors has set up a Committee on Faculty Responsibility for Academic Freedom of Students. I am advised at this writing it is wrestling with the problem of developing a statement that can serve as a guide to teachers. Meanwhile I have just seen a report that the Student Council of City College in New York has protested the college's policy of turning over to the FBI on request information from the students' personnel files. Many of these files list membership in student organizations, including political groups.

Undoubtedly, however, the most perplexing question relating to a student's right to privacy arises from the widespread intrusion into the student's private world by his own school authorities. I refer specifically to the rapidly growing use of "personality" tests and family-background inventories used on public-school children. I am not about to launch an assault upon all psychological testing: testing for mental ability and aptitude—and in fact all methods for determining a student's capacity by guidance teachers and school psychologists—should in my opinion be supported and applauded. The "personality" tests and family-background inventories, however, are quite a different matter.

Nearly half of the nation's public high schools use these "personality" test instruments on certain of their students, and about a quarter of the schools use them at some time on all the students. For the most part, parents are not informed when these tests are being given on a wholesale basis and usually are not advised until afterwards, if at all, when the tests are used individually in connection with counseling a child who may seem, to school authorities, to be emotionally disturbed.

I am aware as I write this that some pages ago I admiringly cited the late A. Whitney Griswold as saying, "A nation that cannot trust its intellectuals cannot trust itself." And I am acutely aware that some of the most vehement criticism of non-academic school testing is coming from individuals and groups that appear to have a generalized distrust of intellectuals.

Perhaps I could escape this seeming contradiction in my viewpoint by mentioning that many leading intellectuals among the nation's psychologists doubt the validity of these instruments. But our primary concern here is with invasion, not validity.

Perhaps I could also try to escape by pointing out that I've been inside a number of the test-making factories that sell these tests to schools—some of them multimillion-dollar enterprises—and have sensed that the atmosphere in most of them is more entrepreneurial than professional. Some are all-out hucksters. But in truth it must be acknowledged that quite a few of the actual test designers command the respect of many of their academic colleagues.

I do feel, however, that two valid points can be made. First of all—and this is too often forgotten—the public schools are dealing with an essentially captive audience. The law requires that parents send their children to school; and most parents can't afford to express disapproval by withdrawing their children from public schools and sending them to private schools. Thus we are talking about the use of devices that probe into the private world of the student by government-operated institutions that require compulsory attendance.

As for the question of trusting my children to intellectuals, it seems to me that one exception can validly be made without putting myself in the ranks of those with generalized distrust of intellectuals. I am gratified by the opportunity to have my children exposed to all the insights that intellectuals can impart to them. And I am confident that the more provocative the thinking of these intellectuals the wiser my children will be in the end. I know from my children's comments that they are already quite competent to distinguish scholars from screwballs. On the other hand, I would be less trusting if I heard that public school authorities were arbitrarily using probing test instruments to try to extract information and insights from my child about his home life or inner world instead of imparting knowledge and insights to him. The test makers have been carried away by their own curiosity and virtuosity. They have plunged into areas of a child's life that they have no business probing, unless permitted to do so by the child's parents. Our society should recognize that thou-sands of well-intentioned persons are getting a vested interest in constructing, selling, or administering "personality" tests. And it should recognize that too many harried school authorities, faced with mounting attendance rolls and floods of new student transfers, have been overeager to embrace sorting tools promising to identify "problem" children and purportedly profile the emotional make-up of all children, tools that offer quick answers in percentiles.

Among the more popular or controversial "personality" probing tools used in the public schools are the Minnesota Counseling Inventory, the Junior Inventory distributed by Science Research Associates, Kansas Junior High School Student Survey, the Moody Problem Check List, "The Wishing Well" produced by Ohio State's Bureau of Educational Research, the California Test of Personality, and the "Blacky Test" produced by the Psychological Corporation. From a privacy-invasion viewpoint some are quite intrusive. Parents or parent-teacher groups should be given an opportunity to inspect any non-academic testing tools being used in their schools upon their children. Let us note a few examples; they come from nine different inventories or tests. Large numbers of school children of varying ages have been asked to indicate by check or comment whether these problems applied to them.

Regarding the youngsters' private anxieties and self-doubts
—"I'm too short..."
—"I'm not popular with (boys) (girls)."
—"My nose is ugly."

—"I wish I knew how you can make a lot of money and still be a very good citizen."

—"People dislike my race or nationality."

—"I feel I'm not as smart as other people."

Regarding youngsters' worries about health

—"I am bothered by menstrual disorders."

—"I have sores between my toes."

—"It hurts when I go to the toilet."

—"I want to get rid of pimples."

—"What can I do about bad breath?"

—"I have to pick my nose a lot."

—"Do you bathe every day?"

Regarding life at home

—"I wish my daddy was home more."

—"There has been a lack of real affection and love in my home."

—"Do you eat together as a family?"

—"Do you prefer to keep your friends away from home because it is not attractive?"

—"Have your parents slapped you . . . ?"

—"Are your parents happy together?"

—"I wish my parents did things that would make me feel more love toward them."

—"I am ashamed of my parents' dress and manners."

—"My parents don't trust me."

—"My parents avoid discussing sex with me."

Regarding their religious beliefs

—"I'm losing faith in religion."

—"Is it wrong to deny the existence of God?"

—"I'm confused in my religious beliefs."

—"I'm bothered by thoughts of heaven and hell."

Regarding their thoughts about sex
—"I wonder if I am normal in my sexual development."
 —"I wish I were not bothered by thoughts of sex."
—"Many of my dreams are about sex matters."
—"I think about sex a good deal of the time."
—"Must I neck to be popular?"

Admittedly these items are among the more intrusive I encountered; but every question has been asked of hundreds of youngsters and some of them have been asked of hundreds of thousands. I am grateful that my own daughter and two sons have attended a public school system—and a good one—that has never used such "personality"-probing devices on them.

Questions such as the above seem open to criticism not only because they invade the student's privacy but because they plant ideas and doubts in his head where none may have existed. They can generate pity within himself and hostility toward his or her parents.

In some schools the youngster's sexual development is also probed by the Guilford-Zimmerman Temperament Survey, which has been actively marketed to high schools. One of the dimensions it measures, we'll recall, is "masculinity- femininity."

In addition to check lists, children in some schools are subjected to projective tests in which they look at pictures and then purportedly reveal their inner dynamics. These are most often used with children who seem to have special problems. One of the controversial probing devices of this type is the Blacky Pictures. The accompanying manual of instructions states that it represents an attempt "to get at the deeper recesses of personality. ..." It explains that cartoons of dogs rather than humans are used to "facilitate freedom of personal expression in situations where human figures might provoke an unduly inhibitory resistance as being too close to home." The Blacky Test has turned up at schools in Minnesota, the state of Washington, on Long Island, and presumably many other places. It was used with nineteen students in a Long Island public school, without the knowledge of the School Board or the superintendent of schools.

The Blacky Pictures consist of eleven cartoons portraying the adventures of a dog named Blacky. The cast of characters includes Blacky, Mama, Papa, and Tippy, who is "a sibling figure of unspecified age and sex." The manual states that each cartoon is designed to "depict either a stage of psychosexual development or a type of object relationship within that development." The tester introduces each cartoon with a comment. Here are some of the introductory comments and the "dimension" being tested by the students' responses to the pictures:

Cartoon I—"Here is Blacky with Mama. . ."
—Oral Eroticism.

Cartoon III—"Here Blacky is relieving himself (herself). . ."
—Anal Sadism.

Cartoon IV—"Here is Blacky watching Mama and Papa. . ."
—Oedipal Intensity.

Cartoon V—"Here Blacky is discovering sex. . . ."
—Masturbation Guilt.

Cartoon VI—"Here Blacky is watching Tippy. . . ."
— Castration Anxiety (M) or Penis Envy (F).

The youngster at school who is being given the Blacky test is told by the tester, if instructions are followed, that "this is sort of a test of how good your imagination can be. . ." The "dynamics" of the subject actually being investigated are such factors as "Intensity of anal expulsive needs," "Intensity of masturbation guilt," "Intensity of castration anxiety," "Intensity of penis envy," "Intensity of sibling rivalry," etc.

When a man who was running for the School Board in the same Long Island town made a campaign issue of the use of these

Blacky Pictures on the school's children, a local psychological association defended Blacky. Its president insisted to *Newsday* that children "do not see any overt sexual implications in the pictures." And he complained that "If lay people try to force their own particular bias on the educational system in such a manner as attempting to eliminate an accepted and legitimate psychological technique it is but a short step to eliminating a textbook...." (The man running for the School Board, a "conservative," won—and then, alas, proceeded to try to eliminate from the school district's libraries all books "that do not promote the American cause"!)

Our concern here, however, is with the arguments advanced to justify Blacky by the president of the local psychological association. He contended that censoring the use of psychoanalytic probing tools on children was just about as reprehensible as censoring their textbooks. I believe he ignores an important distinction. A textbook imparts information to a child: the testing tool extracts information or presumed insights from the child. It is true that the extracted information may be used later in an effort to help the child or to decide what to do about him; but you still have the disturbing fact that the extraction was based on a compulsory invasion of the child's personality by a government-operated institution.

It is quite possible that this psychological spokesman was entirely correct in describing the Blacky test as a "legitimate psychological technique." I question, however, whether its mere legitimacy qualifies it as an appropriate tool to use in the usual captive setting of a public school. Any use of it should be made only after consultation with the child's parents—and by people clearly qualified by training to interpret the results.

Many children badly need more understanding. And a better knowledge of the child's inner world and family situation can contribute to that understanding. But the use of some of the probing tools I have been describing clearly involves trespass and so should be used only with parental consent and preferably by a trained consultant outside the school system so that the results do not go into the child's cumulative school file, where they might serve to stigmatize him years later. The outside consultant could, with parental permission, make a verbal report to the appropriate school authorities.

Parents should show a greater interest in whether personality-probing tools and family-background questionnaires are being used arbitrarily on their children. And educators should show greater awareness that they are treading in a sensitive area where privacy rights are involved when they use many of these tools. In a few communities, groups of parents have sought to eliminate all personality testing done without the parents' consent. Such groups have been active in Kern County, California, in East Hampton and Levittown, New York (Island Trees Public Schools). Protests from parents played a part in inducing this last school system to drop an inventory that probed junior-high-school students in their attitudes toward sex, home, religion, etc. It is questionable, however, whether the superintendent of schools there has undergone any significant change of heart. He stiffly informed me the whole matter had been a "minor problem" involving a "few parents" but that it had got blown up by outside troublemakers opposing "this type of evaluation."

The most persistent and perhaps dramatic battle by a parent against personality probing centered on a parent's insistence that he had a legitimate right to see the personal file kept on his youngster at the school. This struggle took place at East Meadow, Long Island, where an angry father demanded to see the psychological records maintained on his seventh-grade son. The school had offered to "interpret" the records for the father but not let him see them. The father, Edward J. Van Allen, had been a court stenographer and was managing editor of the local newspaper, the *Kernel*, both of which roles made him a rugged adversary. He sued the School Board and carried on a running campaign in the newspaper to arouse public opinion with such headlines as ARE PUBLICLY PAID SCHOOL PSYCHOLGISTS BURYING THEIR OWN MISTAKES? This was based on the plea in the court proceeding by a spokesman for the New York State Psychological Association that if psychological records were opened to parental inspection a psychologist might be sued if he had reached any "dubious" opinions.

Nassau County Supreme Court Justice William Brennan, Jr., found the state constitution "silent" on the question of the parents' rights to see their own children's public-school records. He concluded that the father's rights stem "from his relationship with the school authorities as a parent who under compulsory education has *delegated* to them the educational authority over his child." (Italics supplied.) Justice Brennan held in favor of the father's right to see the records.

When Mr. Van Allen appeared at the school to see the records he was shown an unbound folder that contained papers showing IQ scores, achievement scores, some teachers' notes, etc. But conspicuously missing, Van Allen contended, were the results of the special psychological tests that he contended had been given to his son without written permission from either parent. A school official reportedly explained that the school's psychologist kept the tests "in her head."

Mr. Van Allen marched back to court and promptly had a legal notice served on every member of the board and the superintendent. The next time he returned, the psychological records were produced for his inspection.

Largely as a result of this decision the New York State Commissioner of Education issued a ruling that parents could be shown only "official" school records, not all the file information the school might have on a student. A committee of the Medical Society of the County of New York had, during the controversy, urged that "school psychological reports be viewed and treated as medical records. . . ." Parents frequently are shown only carefully interpreted "information" about medical records. This argument that a school's psychological report be treated in the same manner as a medical report suggests an interesting parallel. Should not psychological treatment of school children be approached with the same circumspection that is shown before *medical treatment* is rendered in schools?

An outspoken critic of testing, Martin Gross, has pointed out: "While Johnny's parents must usually sign a legal release before school authorities feel confident enough to have a licensed doctor jab him with a hypodermic, no one feels obligated to ask or inform the parents that pseudomedical experiments are being conducted on his mind."[3] And in some states, he finds, a doctor can't even give a child an aspirin without parental permission. In New York State, I am advised, public-school authorities can lawfully subject a child to physical examination by a school physician only if the parents fail to have the child examined by a physician of their own choice. It seems reasonable that parents should have the same right with respect to examination for emotional disorders or personality problems.

The battle goes on. Two different parent groups have been pressing for enactment of a bill introduced at the 1962 session of the New York State legislature. It would provide that "Tests of a student for anything other than mental ability and proficiency in basic skills and subject matter of the curriculum shall be given in the Public Schools of New York State only after notice to the parent and receipt of parental permission." In Washington, D.C., Congressman John M. Ashbrook of Ohio was pressing again in 1963 his bill H.R. 10508. It would prohibit use of any funds of the Department of Health, Education and Welfare for examinations in elementary or secondary school of a student's "personality, environment, home life, parental or family relationships, economic status, religious beliefs, patriotism, sexual behavior or attitudes, or sociological or psychological problems" without the approval of the student's parents.

But the battle is likely to become more discouraging to those fighting for greater respect for individual privacy. At the 1962 Invitational Conference on Testing Problems one of the most esteemed figures in educational testing, President Henry Chauncey of the Educational Testing Service, predicted that mass personality testing "will be common in every institution of higher learning and high schools as well."[4]

The College Entrance Examination Board reports that tremendous interest is being shown by colleges in finding non-academic "personality" tests that will help them decide whom to admit. The Board itself has financed several research projects aimed at finding such a handy sorting tool. It suggests that in a few years such tools may be at hand. But it adds that "no existing personality test known to the Board seems to have been sufficiently studied to warrant the acceptance of the very serious risks that would certainly attend the actual use of such tests in making admission decisions."

And it also acknowledges the awkward fact that "personality scales require students to report rather than exhibit behavior, and therefore to make hard choices between lying and informing on themselves to their own disadvantage. The tests put information which in some cases can be considered personal and private into the hands of authorities in school and college." It adds that this consideration may raise "insurmountable difficulties even with complete knowledge of the scales."

Let us hope that this concern about invasion of privacy permeates to the multitudes of college admissions officers seeking a handy sorting tool!

9. How Safe Is Thy Castle?

"A sane, decent, civilized society must provide some . . . oasis, some shelter from public scrutiny, some insulated enclosure, some enclave, some inviolate place which is a man's castle."—Judge Jerome Frank

Judge Frank contended that some such "inviolate place" is "still a sizable hunk of liberty—worth protecting from encroachment." He was dissenting from a majority decision of a U.S. Court of Appeals that permitted the use of evidence gained by electronic eavesdropping within the walls of the defendant's private property.[1]

As enclosures for the privacy-cherishing individual, modern castles, alas, are much less protective in a number of ways than they were a few decades ago. Living space for the average citizen has shrunk. This is true in several parts of the world, but particularly in the U.S.A. Not only are the castles being pushed closer and closer to each other but there is the ever present matter of sounds intruding into the home. The U.S. is one of the few major countries that has not started to require building codes to limit the amount of noise that can emanate from structures in heavily developed areas.

Speculative builders have been applying much of their ingenuity to find ways of making walls and floors ever thinner, and the ceilings of apartments ever lower. In order to reduce piping costs bathrooms of neighboring apartments are placed back to back—and above and below each other.

Dwellers in most of the newer apartment houses learn a great deal, reeardless of whether or not they want to, about their neighbors' love-making and bathroom habits, quarrels, visitors, and the hours at which their children cry themselves to sleep. A New York friend who works at home and whose study is next to that of a psychiatrist (with a thin wall between) has never seen the psychiatrist but, perforce, knows a great deal about the doctor's patients. The continuing problem of one lady patient, he relates, is that her husband's amatory advances cause her to have a gastrointestinal upset the following morning.

Not only are the walls thin, but inside our castles there are fewer walls, again perhaps for economy reasons. Modern architects have promoted the idea that living space should "flow" and that partitions are to be indicated simply by screens or bookcases. This helps to disguise the fact that the family dining room has virtually disappeared. In suburban developments there is often the continual flow—from 10 A.M. on—of neighbors popping in and out, often without knocking.

All the noise and clutter may be producing a new kind of longing in many Americans. At any rate when a Dallas development builder advertised "The Quiet House" he was swamped with 3400 visitors in one weekend. It was the largest turnout he had seen in many years.

The lack of privacy at home is driving increasing numbers of teenagers into pack-running and finding privacy in the family car. And this condition causes them at ever younger ages to cross what David Riesman has called the last frontier of privacy: sex. After a long study of teen-age habits Grace and Fred Hechinger reported: "For many teen-agers, reared in the no-privacy layout of the modern home's 'family living area,' the car is almost the only enclosed means of escape from togetherness. It has replaced the screened back-porch and the parlor—the traditional, semiprivate courting spaces."[2]

Not only are modern homes physically less private, but modern electronics are making it possible for parents to keep an eye on their children in other areas of the house—and for children to keep an ear on their parents. The head of a closed-circuit TV company reports that he has sold TV cameras to families in such cities as Miami and New York for watching not only babies and the swimming pool, but also the older children in the playroom and the "clubhouse."

Children have their electronic allies, too, as a visit to a Toy Fair or a sampling of pre-Christmas TV commercials will reveal. One of the most requested toys in 1962 was Little Miss Echo, the cute doll with a battery-powered tape recorder hidden in her tummy. (About $25.) It is fine for leaving around when family secrets are being discussed.

If Junior suspects Pop of fibbing about why he wasn't home for dinner last night, there is now available to him (at $12.95) Lie Detector, the "New Polygraph Scientific Game." An electrified band is fitted around one hand and the machine measures the amount of perspiration brought on by questions. An indicator on the dial moves from a response marked "Could Be" to one marked "Big Whopper." In its annual report on Christmas toys, *The New Yorker* (December 7, 1963) commented: "Among the suggested questions are 'Do you like to go to school?' but we imagine someone will think of others."

Or if the modern Jack and Jill desire, they can now listen to what Daddy and Mommy are doing or saying in the bedroom, or anywhere else in the house, and what Brother and Sister are saying. The Futura Line of Bell Products of St. Louis, a subdivision of Gabriel Industries in New York, has been featuring "precision electronic products for the entire family." One of its items heavily promoted for at least the past two years is the Big Ear (about $18), a small transistorized parabolic mike that "Picks up voices too distant for you to hear." One radio commercial for it, I am advised, suggested it could hear whispers nearly forty feet away. Its colorful brochure shows a boy and girl listening to a distant group with stethoscope-type earphones. The brochure promises: "Aim it at a group of friends a block away and hear every word." A spokesman for Gabriel tells me its greatest appeal has proved to be "to the eight-to-fourteen-year group and principally to boys."

Possibly the company's promise of performance is on the enthusiastic side—if one is to believe what the technicians report about the capabilities of much larger and more expensive parabolic devices—but at the least its makers are promoting among the young the idea that electronic eavesdropping is fun. A bright young engineering student living about a third of a mile from my house built his own seven-foot-high parabolic mike and demonstrated to me that it greatly enhanced distant conversations.

When a man and woman who have been living together have a falling out—or become suspicious of each other— they may find individual privacy harder to come by than in the past, thanks to the marvels of electronics. A husband who suspected his wife had been unfaithful on several occasions insisted she take a lie-detector test. This was gladly arranged by the lie-detector division of the giant Wackenhut Corporation of Miami. The operator of the machine wasn't willing to give her a clean report after the testing: but the husband seemed to feel the situation was not as bad as he had suspected (and perhaps was satisfied that he had forced her to undergo what must have been a humiliating experience). At any rate he reportedly accepted her back to his bed and board.

Investigators for a New York State legislative committee uncovered a number of instances involving separated couples in which one arranged to have a microphone and transmitter hidden in the bedroom of the other. (New York's divorce law, which requires evidence of adultery, has encouraged a vast amount of eavesdropping.) There have been published reports that when the late Serge Rubinstein, notorious financier, took a business trip from New York to California he arranged for a microphone to be placed under the bed of his current girlfriend. This mike could pick up every sound made in her room. The New York legislative investigators were able to verify that there was a transmitter hidden somewhere in her apartment.

For the first seven years of the 1950s professional wiretappers in New York were permitted to offer their services openly to quarreling spouses because of a controlling court decision in the so-called Appelbaum case. Mr. Appelbaum was upheld in his right to have his own telephone tapped and his wife's phone conversations recorded because the right to privacy of telephonic conversation was termed subordinate to a "paramount right" of a subscriber to see that his phone is not used to damage his business, household, or marital status.

This was obviously unfair to wives, since the phone is commonly listed in the husband's name. The ludicrousness of the situation was emphasized when a couple whom I'll call Mr. and Mrs. Wilson took out after each other electronically. Mr. Wilson smugly began playing tapes of his wife's telephone conversations in court, but then suddenly settled his case. It turned out that she had thoughtfully canceled her husband's subscription and had taken out the service in her own name. The professional wiretapper had been unaware of the change because the same wires were used and so his tap became illegal. Meanwhile, in counterassault, Mrs. Wilson had enlisted the aid of a girl known to be friendly with her husband. With a radio transmitter tucked inside her girdle, the girl engaged him in conversation in a bar. The upshot of the battle is obscure, but electronically Mrs. W. clearly came out the superior battler. Today New York has state laws against most kinds of electronic eavesdropping by *private* parties; but a great deal of it still goes on.

A more recent marital battle in the New York courts (1962) exposed a serious deficiency in the Fourth Amendment of the Constitution, which protects citizens against "unreasonable searches and seizures."

The legally separated wife of a Brooklyn doctor was quietly leading her own life in her own little castle on Linden Boulevard when the doctor led a pre-dawn raiding party that produced photographs of her "stark naked" and of a male friend clad only in a

T-shirt. These photographs were introduced in court, over her protests, by the doctor seeking a divorce. The first judge threw out the pictures on the grounds that they were obtained by illegal search and seizure of a private premise. But on appeal a majority of the judges ruled the pictures were admissible since the Constitution's ban against unreasonable search and seizure seemed to them to apply *only* to raids by law officers and not to raids by private individuals!

A dissenting judge grumbled that at least the more minor offense of trespass was involved.

But it is the invasion of the privacy of the home by outsiders that should concern us most There are the non-official intruders, including neighbors, and the official, governmental types. We have permitted the former to become prevalent, and will consider them first.

Among non-official intruding strangers are insurance investigators by the hundreds making their "neighborhood checks." In one such investigator's report that came to my attention, the insured woman in question (unmarried) had been living with a retired colonel for two months. I asked the investigator how on earth he had learned this fact. He replied: "You'd be shocked how simple it was to get this. The information was volunteered by an employee at her apartment house." Some will say that insurance companies need this information to stay in business but it seems a sad comment on our society that such surveillance is deemed necessary.

Prying investigators come, too, from the broadcast rating services. The raters want to know, in making their reports, *who* you are in terms of age, income, occupation, education, number of cars, etc. The head of one well-known rating firm told me that getting an accurate approximation of income is one of the more important points to try to establish. The number of refusals to divulge goes up in March and April when people have their income taxes on their minds and wonder if the caller is a secret agent from the government. But even then only 25 per cent of all the people asked will refuse to answer such a question as, "Is your income between $7500 and $10,000?" During the rest of the year the rate of refusal drops to about 15 per cent.

The rating services are applying their greatest ingenuity, however, to devising ways in which they can learn electronically the station to which you are tuned. This would eliminate the bother of calling or gaining physical entry into your house. Some of the possibilities that are opening up show that Big Brotherism—in which a government could check on the listening habits of its citizens—is already becoming technically possible.

Progress has been phenomenal in the past few years. Before TV producer Dick Powell died, I heard him comment that it was now possible for a technician to drive a special truck up a street and then report what channel each TV user on the street was dialing. I have since learned by checking with five highly knowledgeable sources, including an FCC official, that such a truck is indeed feasible. In fact such trucks have been operating. One that I learned about has been operating in the Spokane-Yakima area and has a sort of radarscope on its roof. A television engineer told me of seeing such a truck in Los Angeles. The operator of this truck stirred up trouble for himself because houses in Los Angeles are so close together that he had devised a 20-foot- long sort of fishpole with a sensing device at the end which he could swing from the top of his truck toward the antenna of each house. The aerial trespassing riled the homeowners. They called the cops; and the man suspended operations, at least in that area of Los Angeles.

The use of trucks is not, however, considered very satisfactory because it would take a lot of roving trucks to give a comprehensive report on viewing choices at any given moment, and a search is on for more efficient ways of making remote checks.

In every TV receiver, for example, there is a low-power communication device, a miniature transmitter—used to beam the

TV signal through the set—that sends out a weak signal and indicates what channel is being received. An official of one of the rating services spoke hopefully of the possibility of arranging for TV set builders to put more powerful transmitters instead of the present very weak ones inside their sets so that the sets in the homes can be monitored from remote electronic stations.

Meanwhile others in the broadcast field think they have a better way of getting an instantaneous report on the station to which every family out of a group of 100,000 or 1,000,000 TV set owners is tuned. Their dreams have been made credible by the launching of charge-TV (or pay-TV) stations and the swift spread of community antenna TV (CATV), in which cables from hilltop towers or master antennas atop apartments carry TV service to hundreds of thousands of homes. The cable is often accompanied by a thin, inexpensive wire that can report what is going on inside each home in terms of listening habits.

Mr. Ira Kamen, technical director of Teleglobe, which has launched a charge-TV experiment in Denver, showed me a perforated tape for a computer-type machine that had been developed. The tape would give an instantaneous report on the viewing of subscribers at any given moment. The first "scan" of the tape through the computers would show "who is on." The second scan would show the channel at which each set owner is looking. The third scan could show what the viewer thinks of the show, since viewers can be requested to express an opinion by twisting a dial on a little box.

It is the first two scans—on who is viewing and what he is viewing—that are of particular interest in connection with the potentialities for privacy invasion. This information can be got automatically. The subscriber doesn't have to turn any dial. Mr. Kamen said: "We can identify everybody's perforation and whether he is on or off. . . . Jones is always the fortieth perforation, Smith is the forty-fifth perforation." Mr. Kamen is interested solely in the information that can be gleaned from his tape for purposes of billing or for ascertaining viewer reaction. He is not interested in any large-scale surveillance. He said: "I personally hate the Big Brother bit. People are entitled to their privacy."

But an operator in the field of cabled TV speaks exuberantly of the ultimate possibility of getting "an instantaneous read-out" home by home of what millions of people are listening to in the entire country in about fifty seconds.

With the development of such electronic wonders, clearly an ominous possibility thus becomes technically conceivable. If a totalitarian-minded group ever attains power in Washington or in the governor's mansion of a state or in Canada or Europe, its leaders might readily be able to spot instantly any household listening to a station deemed too independent or critical for the welfare of the regime.

But let us continue with other electronic developments that are causing millions of dwellers to permit a further nibbling away of their privacy. Some readers—especially city dwellers—will argue that what I am about to describe is a desirable development. They have become so preoccupied with the security of their homes and persons because of theft and assault that they are willing to relinquish a fairly large hunk of privacy for increased security. At any rate I think the swift growth in the use of closed-circuit TV "protective" systems in the apartment houses of many of our cities should be a source of uneasiness and deserves scrutiny.

There are, first of all, the so-called "security" systems in which the doorman or superintendent can keep an eye on everything that goes on at entrances, in elevators, in inner lobbies, and sometimes in corridors. The cameras may or may not be concealed. Residents usually know the system is in operation, but visitors may not.

I looked at a number of these installations on the Upper East Side of Manhattan in the role of a prospective tenant answering the ads. The most impressive layout was on East Sixty-first Street, a posh new apartment building with outdoor rock garden, etc. The handsome uniformed doorman stood beside a panel of six TV monitoring screens that show everything going on in the two elevators, at the rear entrance, at two service entrances, and in the inner lobby.

The magazine *Buildings* featured in its July 1963 issue an article on "advanced concepts" for "Private TV-I's" in apartment house elevators; and on the diagram there was a picture of a monitor that was captioned: "Video Monitor in Super's Apt. Always On." There is no reference to a monitor visible at the entrance. One of its playful subheadings was: "Smile—you're on somebody's camera."

In some New York installations the cameras in elevators are concealed in the ceiling. In most of the ones I saw they were cased vertically in a small compartment about four inches thick near the top of one side of the elevator. Seemingly such a camera could not possibly photograph what was occurring inside the elevator because the lens—which could barely be seen through an aperture—was pointed toward the ceiling. I commented to a superintendent of a new building on Eighty-fourth Street in New York that the camera must not be operating because the lens was pointed upward. He said: "Oh, they're tricky. It's done with mirrors." We were on camera, and I did not know it. I asked if any of the tenants objected to the cameras in the elevators. He laughed. "Only when they're kissing. Some put their hands over the opening." He added that not only are people photographed but what is being said can be heard by the doorman, too, if he becomes suspicious (or curious).

A doorman in the Forties reportedly amuses his friends by inviting them in to watch and listen to the boys and girls necking in the elevators of his building.

One of the most vehement expressions of resentment concerning the TV eyes in the elevators came from a lovely lady who confided to me that she has for years used her moments alone in elevators to do her facial exercises. She demonstrated how she systematically rolls her eyes into five positions and twists her mouth into six positions. She sighed and said with all these hidden cameras she guessed she would have to give up the custom. Some will argue that elevators and corridors of apartment buildings are at least semipublic places so that no one can object to being visually checked by an unseen electronic eye. But must we now go through life assuming we are on camera, except perhaps when we are inside our own dwelling places? Certainly I feel we should at least be given warning.

A quite different type of TV "protection" in apartments brings pictures of visitors right into the tenants' apartments. And these systems are being installed in tens of thousands of apartments in many parts of the nation. This kind of installation, too, has its "security" appeal. But it also permits all one's neighbors to join in the game of people-watching. Here there definitely is no warning to the visitor.

There are two quite different TV systems by which tenants may inspect the callers downstairs. In neither does the caller know he is on camera. The person coming to call on Mrs. Brown goes to the panel where the buzzer buttons are located over each tenant's name. What's new is that these buzzer buttons now are likely to be arranged around a small mirror. It is a two-way mirror, and the caller is looking directly into a TV camera concealed behind it. Or the camera may be in the corner of the ceiling, from where it can photograph the entire lobby. (In some systems the caller can also be observed by tenants while in the elevator.)

The camera hidden in the lobby enables Mrs. Brown to inspect her caller visually before deciding whether or not to acknowledge that she is home by speaking into the intercom or pushing the door-release buzzer. It also enables any curious neighbors in the building to inspect the caller. This system for lobby-watching enables tenants to see what boys are calling on the girls in the building, what creditors are hounding what tenants, what married women are going out with men not their husbands, and what clients are calling on the resident psychiatrist, palmist, or wigmaker. People have long watched their neighbors' callers from their own front porches or by peeking out the windows. But in these situations the caller was at least aware that he was exposed to observation.

The cheaper and simpler system is simply to hook the camera up to the building's master antenna and broadcast the picture over an unused channel. The tenant, hearing his apartment buzzer, turns the dial of his regular TV set to the unused channel.

The University Apartments in Chicago have been using this system for more than two years. A vice-president of the company that owns the apartments advises me that some "fun" has been poked at the management but that tenants generally like it. He said that now a number of residents, "instead of using their television sets to watch one of the local channels, use the closed-circuit TV to see who is visiting their neighbors. One lady told me quite candidly that she just enjoyed watching people rather than shows and this was a wonderful opportunity to do it in the evening."

A shortcoming of this system, if you are interested only in an efficient way to inspect your own callers, and not in people-watching for sport, is that the regular TV set takes forty to sixty seconds to warm up (unless the set is already on).

Bell Television, Inc., has moved aggressively to eliminate this shortcoming. It installs a miniature "Watchdog-TV" set with a five-inch screen placed diagonally into the wall which incorporates the intercom to the lobby. The tenant can get an image of the caller in four seconds by pressing a button because the Watchdog is always on "standby" waiting to be looked at. Bell reports it now has more than 10,000 units installed in the New York metropolitan area and has set up franchises in Boston, Providence, Washington, D.C., Baltimore, northern New Jersey, upstate New York, Long Island, Connecticut, Florida, and will soon have them in Chicago and California.

From the standpoint of privacy invasion there is one fairly

important difference in the two systems of inspecting callers. With a Bell miniature Watchdog TV, if you want to snoop on your neighbor's callers, you have to stand up to do it!

Some of the higher-powered promoters of electronic devices, it might be added, have been seeking to interest suburbanites as well as city folk in the idea that there are other ways that they can have fun snooping by ear. In recent months a number of advertisements aimed at adults have appeared in national magazines, hailing the exciting news that there is now available a remarkable listening device (parabolic mike) called the SNOOPER, which "amplifies sound 1,000,000 times!" It is called "An outgrowth of the fabulous missile-tracking antennas" and can pick up conversations at a distance of "500 feet." Aim it at a group of friends, we are urged. The ad ends with the exhortation "Have Fun!" The cost: $18.95.

As I stared at two of these ads while writing the above paragraph I noticed two interesting coincidences. The ad in *House and Garden* was placed by Madison Electronics, whereas the ad in the *Diner's Club Magazine* for the identical product was placed by Lincoln Electronics. But the headquarters of both companies are listed as being in the same large building in New York. A further coincidence I noted was that the drawing of this wondrous device for grownups apparently was identical in every detail with the BIG EAR, which, as we noted, Gabriel Industries of 184 Fifth Avenue, New York, has been selling to children! Some months later a firm called Telco was advertising in the *Diner's Club Magazine* a device called TELEPHONE SNOOPER ($18.95). It shows a man happily listening to a two-way conversation—perhaps involving his wife or boss—without lifting the receiver from its cradle. He has simply placed the snooper gadget against the phone. The advertisement promises, "Pretty sly little gadget, fits in your pocket without a bulge."

And then there are the private wiretappers, who have been called "a plague on the nation" by Justice Douglas. There have been so many wiretapping cases that I will simply cite the most mammoth case on record to indicate the potentialities for intrusion. That was the now notorious wiretapping factory that operated for two years on East Fifty-fifth Street in New York. At least four men were involved: a detective, an electrical technician, and two telephone-company employees who were making money on the side. They had ready access to the conversations of any one of 100,000 telephone subscribers! This was so because one of the two telephone-company employees was a "main-frame man." He was in a strategic position where he could tie in a spare line to any of the 100,000 lines on which a tap was desired.

Now let us turn to the intrusions into the privacy of family life in modern castles by public officials. Some of the intrusion is remote, not physical. It comes from the passage of unreasonably intrusive laws and regulations.

In my home state of Connecticut the legislature seeks to decree in part the conditions under which every man and wife in the privacy of their bedroom will make love or conceive children. It does this by forbidding the use of contraceptives and prohibiting physicians from giving advice with respect to the use of contraceptives. Many ministers of the state have declared this to be "an invasion of the most intimate aspects of marriage."

The legislature has repeatedly refused to repeal this law, so that it cannot be dismissed as a forgotten hangover from an earlier century. If it were fully enforced, it would require the issuing of hundreds of thousands of search warrants and officers of the law would have to march into as many bedrooms to find out what was going on. And in defending themselves in court the man and wife would have to describe what did go on—which would raise a sticky issue, since a husband and wife can't be required to testify about any of their confidential relationships.

A majority of the U.S. Supreme Court as recently as 1961 refused in test cases to strike down this law as unconstitutional. It based its decision largely on the evidence that such marching into bedrooms has not occurred. The law has been enforced only to the extent that public or private birth-control clinics have not been permitted to operate in the state. Mr. Justice Harlan, in dissenting, stated: "I believe that a statute making it a criminal offense for married couples to use contraceptives is an intolerable and unjustifiable invasion of privacy in the conduct of the most intimate concerns of an individual's personal life." He felt the statute was unconstitutional. Two married couples and a doctor had made the appeal. Harriet Pilpel, to whom this book is dedicated, participated in making this challenge in the Supreme Court and asked that the statute be struck down. After the decision a clinic was opened as a test. A doctor and a social worker were tried and convicted—and a new challenge is under way.

In Cleveland, a mother was arrested and sentenced to a fine and imprisonment for telling her unmarried daughter to use birth-control devices after the daughter had had three illegitimate children. The mother had first told her not to have sex relations at all. And later she had admonished that if she did she should ask her partner "to use something on her" so that she would not become pregnant. By so doing, it was charged, the mother had impaired the morals of her daughter. The case is now on appeal.

Actual physical invasions of the home by law officers and administrative officials without proper search warrants have been happening with uncomfortable frequency, and the laws and court decisions offer the citizen who objects little protection. In fact he may land in jail for blocking such entries.

The wording of the Fourth Amendment of the Constitution would seem to us quite clear and emphatic, at least as far as intrusion by government officials is concerned. It states that people shall be secure in their homes against unreasonable searches and seizures and that a search cannot be made without a proper warrant.

It this is the law, then why is it that in several parts of the U.S. today housing inspectors are insisting they have a right to enter and inspect any home they wish without going through all of this rigmarole of applying for a search warrant?

Furthermore, the inspectors can cite a decision of the U.S. Supreme Court made as recently as 1960. By a vote of 4-4, with one Justice disqualifying himself, the Court affirmed without comment a decision by the Ohio Supreme Court that upheld an ordinance in Dayton, Ohio, requiring homeowners to admit housing inspectors without search warrants. The objecting home-owner, a man in his sixties, had been jailed because he could not put up a $1000 bond. The reasoning, apparently, was that, when no crime is involved, the rules against searching without a war-rant should take greater account of the public interest.

With the United States becoming increasingly urbanized, some cities now have many thousands of housing, health, and fire inspectors on their payrolls. This assumed right of local gov-ernments to inspect premises is likely to become an increasingly acute challenge to the Fourth Amendment. Justice Douglas has observed with some sarcasm, "The requirement that a warrant be issued by a magistrate only on a showing of probable cause has been taken to mean that the police need no warrant to invade the privacy of a home, provided they come in uniforms of health inspectors."[3]

As for the police, one must conclude that they have been viewing too many TV shows in which police and detectives kick in doors of homes to give the TV show some "action." In August 1963 a Manhattan district attorney argued on a network television program in favor of an astonishing bill being submitted to the New York State legislature. It would give a policeman who is armed with a search warrant the right to enter a premise, including a home, without announcing who he is or what he is doing there. He explained that this was the best way to catch some criminals with the goods.

A better way would be to go back to the general writs of assistance issued in colonial days to the King's men, which permitted them to break into and search places any time they chose.

Probably the most outrageous invasions of private homes by police in the history of the United States occurred during the last decade in California. In a number of cases the entries were made by police who climbed through windows or picked locks for the purposes of planting microphones in the hope of obtaining incriminating evidence. For decades legal decisions have held that entry onto premises, even with search warrants, cannot be justified if the search is simply for "evidence." But in California the police often didn't even bother to obtain search warrants. They chose to believe that a California act of 1941 allowing police to use concealed microphones entitled them to gain admittance to plant their microphones in any way that they could.

The planting of microphones, it should be noted, is more pernicious as an invasion of privacy than wiretapping. In wiretapping the conversation is at least with someone outside the physical walls of the home, but a microphone can involve the recording of a conversation of husband and wife in bed. Yet, because of the coincidence that communication by telephone has traditionally been subject to government regulation, there is more legal protection against wiretaps than against microphones in most of the U.S.A.

A case that reached the Supreme Court involved one of the more flagrant invasions of a home by the police of Los Angeles. It concerned a suspected bookmaker named Irvine. While Mr. and Mrs. Irvine were away from home, the police gained entry by use of a specially made key and proceeded to bore a hole through the Irvines' roof in order to run a wire out to a remote listening post. At first the police concealed their microphone in a hallway. This proved to be unsatisfactory, and some days later they again entered the house while the Irvines were away and moved the mike into the Irvines' bedroom. Still later in the month they entered again to move the mike into the bedroom closet. After about a month of listening they got what they felt was incriminating evidence.

Some of the Justices of the Supreme Court suggested that the tactics used by the police violated the principle of the Fourth Amendment; but the majority held that the evidence obained was admissible because California's rules on admissibility should be controlling.[4]

But meanwhile in another court case in California it was revealed that the police felt free to continue climbing in windows. In seeking to gain evidence on a suspected bookmaker named Cahan, Los Angeles policemen climbed through his brother's side window at night to plant a microphone. Then to gain entry to the rented residence of a man suspected of being Cahan's bookkeeper, according to one sworn report, a police official confidentially arranged with the absentee landlord of the premises to notify his tenants that termite inspectors would shortly arrive. The termite inspectors were cordially received by the tenants, and in the course of the inspection one of the "assistants" secretly planted a microphone in the dwelling.

Policemen in the city continued to gather evidence by gaining entry to residences and other private premises through forced or surreptitious means. When the Cahan case finally got into court, the state's own Supreme Court decided matters were getting so flagrantly out of hand that it ruled it would no longer permit illegally seized evidence to be used in the state's courts.[5]

To cite one final form of official invasion of modern-day castles, there is the growing fascination of federal, state, and local governments with mass spraying programs. The results obtained in eliminating pests are in dispute. But what should be more vigorously disputed is the right of any government unit to spray poisons, from airplanes or trucks, that drift upon the yards and homes of private citizens. Can we be permitted to do no more than shake our fists at the airplanes or trucks? Certainly this spreading of poisons should never be undertaken without giving the homeowners who will be affected adequate notice so that they can protest if they desire. In 1963 units of the federal and New York governments sprayed poisons over 100.000 acres in areas surrounding New York City to combat the gypsy moth. Senator Jacob K. Javits of New York asserts that this vast spraying program was half completed before residents knew it had begun.

If these and other invasions continue to spread, then the concept of man's castle will become meaningless indeed!

10. The Unlisted Price of Financial Protection

"This man who plans to marry Subject doesn't know she has been playing around with the two other men that I've seen her with in recent weeks."—Excerpt from report by an insurance investigator assigned to check a young woman who had applied for insurance on a piece of jewelry

Not every investigator, of course, gets to know a Subject better than a prospective marital partner does. But credit and insurance investigators by the tens of thousands do know considerably more about the private lives of millions of U.S. citizens than the citizens realize. They often know considerably more than the Subject has set forth in his application for credit or insurance. These investigators have access to central files; they frequently make telephonic checks; and they often conduct on-the-spot checks in the Subject's neighborhood or bank.

Credit bureaus like to boast, when soliciting local business, that their records stick to a man like a shadow. There is more than a little truth to this, even if the Subject moves to another state. The nation's 2000-odd credit bureaus send one another more than 4,000,000 reports on individuals every year. Each bureau routinely assembles a file on each person who applies to a client company for credit. The file is likely to contain information on jobs, residences, family, income, bank account, legal tangles, debts, speed of paying bills, etc. It adds up to an assessment of background ... credit ... character—the kind of information that helps the businessman selling on credit to determine quickly how much of a chance he is taking. When a client requests a special report (which may cost $15 to $100 or more) the bureau's investigators will probe more thoroughly; and, if the information is deemed pertinent, they can provide such additional items as the Subject's college grades or the stability of his marriage.

Author Hillel Black dug so thoroughly into one giant operation, the Credit Bureau of Greater New York, that it has tried—unsuccessfully—to pull a security curtain around its operations.[1] Black learned that this bureau adds 1,000,000 "derogatory" reports to its files each year. You can be stigmatized with a "derogatory" report for a host of reasons including slowness in paying rent or bills. Much of the unfavorable information is provided by the bureau's member firms. More than two dozen "rush-phone girls" in the bureau's file rooms can give a nervous clerk or credit manager at a client store a report in less than two minutes. The bureau also has about forty investigators who run some type of check on about 250,000 individuals each year. Mostly they work by phone to save time. The average investigator handles about twenty cases a day. He may call a Subject's landlord, neighbors, superiors, or bank and track him through various directories. Retailers Commercial, a subsidiary of the giant Retail Credit Company, is also active in providing credit checks on individuals in many cities.

Both credit investigators and insurance investigators rely greatly upon a special telephone book that is often called "the crisscross book," or "the cross-street book." It is organized by streets, lists the name of each telephone subscriber in the order of his street address, and then lists the phone number. This enables investigators not only to locate the Subject precisely as to his neighborhood but also to learn the identity, within a moment, of his next-door neighbors.

Locating the bank where the Subject has his checking account, I was surprised to learn, is usually a simple matter, even though banks don't give out lists of customers. A Subject who applies for credit at major stores or buys on installment is usually asked to list his bank or banks when opening a charge account or applying for installment credit, and this information routinely passes to the credit bureau. Once the bank is located, a call to an official of the bank by a trusted credit or insurance investigator can often produce quite a bit of information about the Subject's affairs that the Subject may have assumed was confidential, though banks vary in their cooperativeness.

A bank official will ordinarily reveal to an investigator from an accredited agency the following information about a Subject's checking account: the average balances maintained . . . whether the account is borrowing or non-borrowing and if borrowing whether or not it is handled on a secured basis . . . and whether the account has been properly handled by the Subject. If there is a mortgage involved, the official will usually indicate whether there has been any difficulty in maintaining payments. How thoroughly the above is spelled out depends upon the ingenuity of the investigator, how well and favorably his firm is known to the banker, or the cooperativeness of the banker. For example, the bank official may say that the Subject maintains a checking balance in the "low threes" or "high fours." Translated, that means the balance has usually been in the $200-$400 range or in the $7000-$9000 range. A former insurance investigator in the South told me he was usually able to get banking information in "round thousands." Banks, it might be added, are now doing a vast amount of investigating themselves, both for their own information and for the information of customers.

One report on a businessman that was shown to me by an official of a large financial investigative firm in New York carried this sentence concerning the man's standing at his bank: "His account is described as routine, non-borrowing, and properly handled at all times with present balance in a moderate four-figure proportion."

One of the more painful—if useful—services that many credit bureaus perform is the issuance to their client-members of credit bulletins, which list people who have given bouncing checks to any members. I call the listing painful because a good many hundreds of thousands of checks are written on insufficient funds for innocent reasons. Some people are careless bookkeepers. Technically a check based on insufficient funds is not actionable until the writer has had a few days (five in New York) to make good the check. But there are charges that some credit bureaus do not take sufficient pains to distinguish the scatterbrained housewife from the bum-check artist in their credit bulletins. The housewife's best protection is to have a friendly, patient banker who covers for her because he knows she can be trusted to correct the deficit.

And the bureaus issue daily litigation bulletins listing people who have been sued. These clearly, too, are legitimate services to member-clients. But because of the frequent carelessness in failing to discriminate between frauds and nuisance suits that are quickly dropped, these bulletins can unjustly hurt a man's chances of getting a job years later. As we've noted, employers frequently run credit checks as a routine part of pre-employment investigations. The bad check may have been issued carelessly on insufficient funds and may have been made good immediately. And the suit may have been of the picayune variety that was dismissed or not pursued. Stores affiliated with a credit bureau are supposed to notify the bureau if checks are made good, but often neglect to do so. And litigation bureaus are supposed to report the outcome of suits they have listed, but again often fail to do so.

The problem is that while the initial cost of acquiring information about suits is low, the cost of following up on the disposition of suits is vastly greater because of the time and effort involved. In view of this fact, any businessman confronted with a prospective client or borrower should at least call and get the prospect's explanation of the listed lawsuit.

The Credit Bureau of Greater New York requires all clients requesting a litigation report to subscribe to a printed disclaimer. It reads: "The CREDIT BUREAU assumes no liability for any damage which may be sustained by the undersigned . . . resulting from any errors, omissions, inaccuracies or other defects in the Litigation Report. . ."

I met a man who was intimately familiar with credit bureau practices and who discovered that his own credit report at a very large Eastern bureau listed three lawsuits against him. His sense of outrage seems to have been justified. One of the suits went back to the late thirties and was for a magazine subscription he had never ordered. It was a five-dollar scare suit and nothing had come of it. The second one, in the late forties, involved a disagreement he had with a lawyer over a $200 fee. He and the lawyer finally compromised at $50 and the suit was withdrawn. The third involved a disagreement he had had with a client over the value of a service he had performed. This suit came before a jury and the man not only won the case but was awarded attorney's fees.

His credit report did not show the disposition of any of the three suits. It took him two days to dig up the dispositions and present them to the credit bureau. The suits were then erased from his record. He feels strongly that credit bureaus and other reporting organizations should be required automatically to report the disposition of any suit or judgment up to the last ninety days prior to the date the report is made on the Subject.

Financial investigators of all kinds usually experience great frustration when asked to report on a person who doesn't believe in borrowing, living on credit, or establishing charge accounts. In such cases there is no handy credit report with which to start. Wealthy people, especially those coming from Europe or South America, who believe indebtedness is dishonorable, often pose this kind of problem. An investigator who was instructed to check on the financial status of a former member of European nobility now residing in the U.S. stated his frustration in these words: "We have not found any bank account of Subject in New York metropolitan area. There is no record of Subject having utilized or sought credit facilities here. It has not been possible to establish any data which would permit of any evaluation of Subject's financial responsibility."

In the last two or three years efforts have been made to institute a nationwide credit rating service in England similar to the U.S. credit bureaus. The effort has come under fierce criticism from old-fashioned types there who think their privacy is being invaded. They contend that a man's finances should be his own business. Hillel Black cites a British editorial, which complained that since Victorian times the average Briton has regarded his financial standing as a personal affair between himself and his banker and no one else. The editorial added: "The idea that, as in America, [a person] should have some sort of public 'credit rating' is one that [the Briton] properly resents."

Perhaps some Americans are beginning to resent the intrusion, too. At least some merchandisers who sell for cash only seem to feel they can exploit the privacy invasion involved in credit assessments. The Robert Hall clothing chain, in its commercials, stresses that its stores "don't invade your privacy with credit questionnaires." (And they might have added that the questionnaires are often only the beginning of the invasion.)

Not so well known as credit probers but perhaps more omnipresent in the new U.S. society are the firms specializing in insurance investigations. Americans are sufficiently affluent to have hundreds of millions of insurance policies of various sorts. Millions of the applicants for policies are investigated, usually without their knowledge. Ordinarily policies up to $10,000 receive only a routine check unless there are "special circumstances." If there are special reasons for uneasiness even a routine $1500 automobile case will be investigated. An example of a special circumstance would be a married man who applied for life insurance naming as beneficiary a non-related girl. The insurance company might wonder if she could conceivably be a mistress. And that would raise in the minds of the insurers the possibility of an unpredictable factor that they would consider to be a hazard. A few companies now offering lower rates on life policies to non-smokers will often order a neighborhood check to make sure the Subject is indeed a non-smoker.

Company policies apparently vary on the point when applicants are investigated. One former investigator told me that in Louisiana he had been called upon to investigate even $500 policies sought to cover burial expenses.

Some large insurance companies use computers to pull out cases for spot checking. If such a company has 10,000 PPFs (personal property floaters) at $10,000 each, 9500 may get a perfunctory check, but the computer will pull out 500 for a special investigation and 100 (or one per cent) for a full investigation. In general it may be assumed that any applicant for an insurance policy of any kind involving more than $20,000 is going to be very carefully investigated.

An outsider might imagine that the agent arranging the policy with the Subject would be in the best spot to provide all necessary information. The insurance companies, however, assume that the agent's enthusiasm for earning a commission has probably disqualified him for making a tough-minded assessment of risk. Consequently the insurance companies usually prefer to have these investigations conducted by outside "inspection companies."

Since these scrutinies help to protect the innocent we can all applaud them in theory. It is the practices that have developed that concern us, since many of the techniques used by some of the investigating firms are sloppy or invade privacy unreasonably. Further, the investigating firms frequently feel free to sell information from their files to "outside" non-insurance clients, or to use their special position to undertake "outside" assignments. Apparently there are economic reasons for turning to an outside investigative agency that handles a great volume of investigations:

the insurance companies can, by playing one agency against the other, shave pennies off the cost of each investigation.

Among the better-known of the host of insurance investigating or inspection firms in the East are Hooper-Holmes, Service Review, O'Hanlon Reports, Silas R. Franz Company. Most of these operate on a national basis. And then there is the nationwide network of offices of the Retail Credit Company, which is a national organization. Although the Retail Credit Company began as a credit investigating firm, about 86 per cent of its total volume of investigations now involve applications or claims for various forms of insurance. It makes 12,000,000 inspections, including insurance, a year, primarily concerning individuals or small businesses.

The investigations tend to become more exhaustive as the policies become larger, but some companies have some sort of check made on every risk, an official of the Retail Credit Company explained. As a fairly typical kind of case, I inquired what kind of inspection would likely be made of a routine application for a $5000 life insurance policy. He said the insurance company probably would expect that from two to three interviews might be conducted, depending upon the circumstances. There might be a talk with a neighbor or with an associate or with the applicant's banker or with his employer or with the applicant himself.

Some of the investigating companies such as Retail Credit pay their inspectors salaries, others pay investigators on a piece-work basis. And some cut the piecework price as low as they can in order to attract business from the insurance companies. Many of these big insurance companies try to keep the flat rate prices as low as possible.

Thus an investigating firm may accept a large number of orders at a flat rate of $3.60 for each report based on a check of files and neighborhood. This is the so-called "one- stopper" type of investigation. The human investigator may receive half of this fee, or $1.80. As he has to type each report for this meager fee, it behooves him to be fleet-footed and may tempt him to rely on guesswork on some of the less risky details of the report.

Many investigators are "area specialists." They may handle all cases within, say, a thirty-block area of a city, which greatly cuts down travel time. They may write a report based mainly on ten minutes of chatting with the Subject's janitor, lobby attendant, and elevator man, or with a neighbor sitting on her stoop. Many, fortunately, refuse to talk to investigators in any detail, but many others, who may be bored or lonely or catty, enjoy a chance to exhibit their wisdom. The role that certain elevator men play as informants was mentioned in the middle of an article in the *New York Times* about the impact of automated elevators on elevator men. The reporter commented: "The reliance on automatics also threatens to eliminate those elevator men who have long served as a combination tout, retriever of stray children. . .and professional eavesdropper."

The investigator making a special check on the hazard of theft may wish to get a look at the Subject's apartment or at least an identical one. He wants to inspect the locks, buzzer arrangement, window latches, etc. This is often not too difficult to arrange. If persuasion fails, a superintendent can usually be induced to produce a pass key for a $10 "tip." The superintendent, however, is usually bright enough to know that his management wishes to keep in the good graces of its own insurance company. The investigator's inspection company may well do some investigating for that company, too.

The manager of a little grocery store around the corner is not considered a good prospect for information about a Subject because he is apt to feel a stubborn loyalty to said Subject. Managers of supermarkets are assumed to be less concerned about loyalty. Further, about a third of them grant check-cashing privileges and so may have useful information on how many checks the Subject cashes in a month, and perhaps recall the sources of the money.

Investigators reported that they had at times been able to acquire useful information about the Subject from the gas station nearest to his home. The attendant may freely describe the family, commenting on the wildness of the children or the untidiness of the family car. Or he may say: "Yeah, they let me take care of the car once a month for greasing and checking the brakes." One investigator remarked: "This tells me a lot. My Subject is a solid type who regularly has his car checked. He obviously doesn't get into debt recklessly."

In most insurance investigations the paramount factors to be ascertained are the financial stability of the applicant and whether a moral risk is involved. For example, the philanderer may be shot in the head when caught in *flagrante delicto* by an irate husband in his wife's bedroom. That possibility makes the man a risk to insurers. Heavy drinking makes him a risk, too. Worse, the man may be a conniver and might connive to collect insurance.

When a special investigation is required, the investigator may have a check list of several dozen pieces of information he must obtain. The "special," as it is called in some shops, is regarded as one step more thorough than a "one-stopper" but not as thorough as a "full-dress" investigation, which may require a report of 1000 words. In many instances the investigator will in the course of his probing be authorized to talk with the applicant directly.

The "special" is usually ordered whenever a large policy is involved, or there is a more than average risk, or the prospective policyholder is a prominent person. The mere fact of prominence is presumed to "expose" the person to extra risks. The "special" must be a moderately thorough investigation of the Subject's business career, finances, and personal life; and if the policy is to cover hazards of theft there must be a careful assessment of the person's "exposure." (This must cover kind of locks, vacation habits, a description of all hired help who have access to the premises, the sex and race of any servants and whether they sleep in or out.)

Regarding the Subject's finances, the investigator making a

"special" will be expected to try, at a minimum, to cover these facts: net worth . . . annual income for the past five years . . . exact data on location of each bank and savings account, date opened, average monthly balances, all loans, their purpose and facts on repayment . . . all charge accounts . . . highest amount ever charged in any one month, average time for paving bills, any collection difficulties, credit limits . . . any suits or judgments in past twenty years.

The "personal" section of a "special" report may provide the following information on Subject: a fairly complete life history (except for business and finances covered elsewhere in the report), including racial and nationality extraction. I am advised that until about five years ago the insurance companies were absolutely fierce in their insistence that members of the Jewish race be reported accurately, even if only the grandparents were Jewish or if a name had been changed. This particular insistence, I gather, stemmed from rather virulent prejudices then prevalent among the leaders of the insurance industry. (The insurance industry still ranks near the top among industries that include virtually no Jews in their managerial ranks, though recently there has been a decrease in discrimination and an increase in opportunities.)

Among the "personal" data expected are: complete details on the Subject's education . . . his children . . . age . . . the background and any prior marriages of his wife . . . whether the Subject's marriage has been harmonious or stormy . . . whether Subject or spouse is known, reported, or rumored to have or have had extramarital interest . . . the tenor of relationship between parents and children.

A "special" is likely to include in the personal data a detailed coverage of the Subject's "habits." The report must state whether Subject and spouse are known to live quietly (that's good) or whether they attract attention by their behavior or associations (that's bad). If Subject or spouse is known to be ostentatious or carefree in display of furs, jewelry, or expensive cars, that's bad.

The report should detail the frequency of entertainment in the home, the type of parties staged, and guests invited. And it may state whether the man and wife tend to associate with individuals of their own "class." If the subjects have "night-club exposure" this must be explored with care. There is likely to be a note on the extent to which Subject and spouse use intoxicants. Finally, the investigator must report any inclination by the Subject to gambling or any deviative or eccentric behavior. (In about one case in twelve, according to one estimate, the Subject ot a "special" becomes classified as a "morals risk" because of drinking, credit-risk factors, domestic problems, or deviative behavior.)

The insurance investigating firms are particularly wary of certain Subjects and they use their wariness to excuse the extra steps they take in privacy invasion. For example, the unmarried female of reproductive age who has money or owns a business may be considered risky. Apparently the thinking is that a female might be more likely than a male to become unstable if a love affair went badly. And there is the presumed hazard of pregnancy.

The insurance investigators frequently check with extra thoroughness people who lead unconventional personal lives and people who were born outside the United States. This wariness of the foreign-born may be partly simple xenophobia; or it may spring from the extra difficulty in developing the full life history that may be demanded by the insurer. A widely used manual for appraisal (*Risk Appraisal* by Harry W. Dingman) cites in addition the fact that loreign-born applicants "may not yet have become subscribers to the American scheme of life. Sometimes their ideas of ethics may be non-American."

Certain executives of insurance investigating agencies are also said to have a personal aversion to famous intellectuals and on occasion to go to considerable lengths to try to develop evidence that such Subjects are homosexual or at least "homophile." One instance involved a famous figure in the entertainment world who had applied for $25,000 insurance on personal property and was rumored to be a possible deviate. The investigator assigned to the case checked eleven sources on this single point, and even had a friend pull the Subject's file in the Pentagon for a look. Nothing was developed beyond surmise.

Reports such as this are prepared on a confidential basis for guidance of an insurance company. Employees of the investigating firms are sternly forbidden by law to sell information they assemble in their investigations; but, significantly, the *proprietors* of these firms are under no such restrictions in many states. They can sell information to clients not in the insurance field; and they can use their special facilities and contacts to undertake highly profitable investigations lor non-insurance clients.

In New York State, as an example, there is nothing in the General Business Law, which covers private investigators, to prevent a licensed investigating firm from selling the same information, presumably prepared in confidence for one client, to others.

And throughout the United States there is little assurance that the information we give about ourselves to one organization will not be handed over or sold to others who have quite different motives for wanting the information. This seems an appropriate time to examine the disquieting phenomenon of the massive traffic that has developed in exchanging personal information.

11. The Lively Traffic in Facts About Us

"23,000 women who bought
bust developer .... $14 per thousand"
"48,000 men and women of
large means .... $15 per thousand"
"500,000 newlyweds .... $17 per thousand"
"84,000 older men who bought
gadget to enhance sex life .... $15 per thousand"
—Four lists cited as available for rental in *Dunhill
Mailing List Catalog*

The selling, swapping, and exchange of information about individual U.S. citizens have reached grotesque proportions. Several hundreds of millions of dollars change hands each year in the selling of this material alone.

The business takes two forms. First there is the sale of information about carefully selected groups of people who have some characteristic in common that makes them likely targets for campaigns of persuasion. This type of selling is handled by such rapidly growing enterprises as the Dunhill International List Company, cited above. Second, there is the sale of recorded and presumably confidential information about specific individuals.

Beyond the cash-and-carry trade there are three other kinds of traffic in information about us that deserve note: the exchange of information by governmental bodies that possess confidential records, the swapping of information between private and governmental file builders, and the great amount of swapping between private parties with access to confidential information about us. Let us look at each of these five ways in which information about us passes from hand to hand.

The selling of our names on a bulk basis. A name on a mailing list is a commodity usually worth from one to three cents per use. A few select lists containing only a small number of names command a higher value of perhaps a dollar per head, but these are exceptional.

The relative value of our names—one cent or three—on a large list depends primarily upon how attractive we are to the mass solicitors and how hard it is to assemble the lists. At these modest rates our names and addresses become attractive only because they can be sold over and over again—and on a bulk basis. Our names are usually sold along with those of at least 10,000 other citizens who appear to be inviting targets for a client who has a product, a charity, or a political candidate to sell. Perhaps we are all psychiatrists . . . or known purchasers of blackhead removers . . . or "leading business executives" . . . or perhaps each of us recently moved to a new home.

There is no question about it. In bulk, we are very attractive. Business firms, charities, and political parties now spend about $400,000,000 a year to buy and use our names. In early 1963 the *Wall Street Journal* carried the headline: NAME-SELLING BOOMS AS MAIL ADVERTISERS SEEK LIKELY PROSPECTS. Name-selling, it should be emphasized, is a completely legitimate business—as long as the names are acquired legitimately, which they usually are.

More than 250 firms are in the business of buying and selling names. In addition a great many regular business firms have found that selling or renting the names of their customers can be an enormously profitable side line. The Diner's Club may let you peddle your wares by circularizing (once only) its 680,000 members for a fee of about $17,000. Several sizable magazines will rent their subscription lists; others will rent only lists of their ex-subscribers!

Public officials have leaped into the game of selling names in bulk. Some have official governmental blessing; for others it is a quiet side line. In a large East Coast city a clerk of the Marriage

Bureau was making $60,000 a year. He was selling lists of people who applied for marriage licenses. The law was later changed to curb this practice.

The job of county clerk in hundreds of U.S. counties can be a luscious plum indeed. The county clerk is often legally able not only to keep the two-dollar marriage license fee and some other fees but also to sell lists: of new births, new marriages, newly arrived families, newly arrived companies, and so on. In many counties the clerks are paid no salary, and make their income by collecting fees—perhaps supplementing from the sale of information to the mailing-list people. The county clerk makes a living selling the information. He may not be obligated to give the average citizen the information; he sells it.

Cities openly sell their ta1x rolls to companies such as Dunhill. And every state offers for sale, often to the highest bidder, its lists of individuals holding auto registrations. The giant Reuben H. Donnelley Corporation is usually a strong bidder for these lists of car owners. The information sold includes the make and model of each registrant's car. A recent top bid by a mailing-list firm for New York State's list was $75,000. Donnelley offers advertisers 40,000,000 names of car owners.

I gathered that some of the more attractive lists of names can be obtained only by wirepulling. The mailing-list company seeking to get the list of swimming-pool owners in a metropolitan area may have to offer a "fee" to the building inspection officials. It is not uncommon for list companies to have their own "man" in the local Health Department or the county clerk's office or the boat registry office of a state.

If you are trying to sell forty-foot boats, one mailing-list official has stated, you don't just offer the boat seller a general list of boat enthusiasts. That would be the scatter-gun approach. Instead, he said, "We will get you a list of people who now have thirty- to thirty-five-foot boats. It never goes the other way, and we can get the information from the Coast Guard."

Even more precise are some of the new-mother lists. Many of the mailing-list firms compete to establish a "contact" within major hospitals (often a nurse) who doesn't mind earning extra money or receiving gifts by being first to leak the names of all expectant mothers who check in at the hospital. There are two companies in New York City that sell only new-birth lists. It is important to know, within a few days, the dates when babies are born. "You may have people who want a list of babies no more than ten days old," one official states. "This would include the people selling sanitary disposable diapers. We had one of those cases today. On the other hand there are people who want a list of mothers whose babies are known to be two months old. They may be selling baby food."

One official speaks frankly of the people whose names are his company's raw materials. He states: "Your life is an open book. A mailing-list house can get births. . . . As a child grows up there will be a graduation or an engagement, wedding, death."

There is no way to escape getting your name on an assortment of mailing lists. And there is no escaping the bombardment of mail from merchandisers and other interested parties who have bought your name. Once you are on a list, the mail comes on forever. You cannot even escape the mail on which your name has been garbled by some typist years earlier.

I find in my mailbox—and carry up a long hill—at least 2000 direct-mail solicitations a year. Several dozen of them are addressed to "Vance Richard" at my home address in Connecticut. The address is correct and the first name is correct so I assume a typist was woolgathering on the last name. I am still attempting to discover what the various Vance Richards have in common. I note, for example, that though the *Harvard Business Review* addresses me correctly as a subscriber it addresses me as Vance Richard in its promotional literature.

The promotion department of a publishing firm with whose editors I have long had a cordial personal relationship addresses me as Vance Richard when stamping my name on its book-promotion literature. And still another publisher has been trying to interest me, as Vance Richard, in buying a book called *The Marriage Art, A revelation of sex technique for husband and wife.* From all this one might assume that the slip-up in spelling occured in typing a mailing list for some bookish crowd of people. But if this is so, why do I receive mail addressed to Vance Richard from the American Forestry Association?

The direct-mail merchants, when they buy up a variety of lists, try to search for people who might reasonably be interested in their product. Thus if you have ever sent away to a mail-order house for vitamin pills, this may suggest to the list buyers that you are a hypochondriac and so a good prospect for elixirs or even for a book about virility. If you have got on a list of people who are known to have purchased tranquilizers you obviously are a likely candidate for the mail merchant selling a book on insomnia.

Some college alumni associations sell lists of all their old grads in order to help meet their expenses. A number of mail-order companies carefully hoard all names of people ordering from catalogues. The names become pure gold. Thus one firm is able to offer for rent "500,000 housewives who ordered grapefruit knives." The charge is a cent and a half per housewife.

A great deal of the work of mailing-list firms is devoted to assembling the names and addresses of people certified to have contributed to charity drives or to be well-heeled. Boyd's City Dispatch has sold 13,000 millionaires at slightly more than two cents each.

Recently, too, the mailing-list people have been showing a new interest in youngsters. Dunhill, for example, offers 200,000 girls aged eight to fifteen for two cents each, a fairly stiff price. Youngsters attract the mail marketers for several compelling reasons. There are now tens of millions of youngsters who spend more than $500 a year; they are at a highly impressionable age and are starting to form lifetime buying habits. But the most important reason for the fascination may be a recent discovery. It has been found and solemnly reported in the marketing literature that youngsters still love to open mail addressed to them, even if their names are stamped on by machine!

The sale of eagerly sought records involving specific individuals. This traffic is considerably smaller in terms of dollar value but is likely to represent a much deeper invasion of individual privacy. The procurement of the records is often handled by specialists among private detectives.

It should be understood in what is to follow that private investigators range from hungry, hustling private eyes operating in a twilight world of legality to sober, conscientious businessmen providing what they feel has become an indispensable service in our shifting complex society. Investigators differ in character, manner, and function as drastically as ambulance-chasing lawyers differ from heads of conservative corporate law firms.

A good many of the harder-pressed detectives have been forced into trying to establish monopolistic pipelines to hard-to-get personal information by the intense competition for decent-paying investigative assignments. The television serials, such as *Hawaiian Eye, 77 Sunset Strip, Surfside Six,* and *Peter Gunn,* undoubtedly are partly to blame for the recent glut in private eyes. These shows depict handsome, dashing detectives lolling about private suites staffed by gorgeous secretaries or hopping into their Jaguars to rush to the aid of an heiress in distress. All this glamorizing has helped to produce a glut in private eyes.

The dearth in many states of laws regulating private investigators and their employees and the laxity in enforcing what few laws there are also help to account for the influx of would-be sleuths and for the violent competition for assignments. In a few states, such as New York, where many licensees operate vast enterprises, a fairly sharp scrutiny is maintained on license holders—if not their employees. But in Louisiana anyone, including a man fresh from the penitentiary, has been able to set himself up as a private investigator merely by paying a two-dollar Occupational License Tax. The Private Detective Association of New Jersey has complained that at least 1000 unregistered private eyes were operating in four northern counties of the state.

I did see investigators in richly furnished suites but they were invariably top executives of far-flung organizations. The offices of the top dozen executives of the William J. Burns International Detective Agency, occupying a floor of a New York skyscraper, have wall-to-wall carpeting and tasteful black, white, and maroon decor. But they supervise about 15,000 employees. If a man simply wishes to make money, he can usually make more as a hod carrier than as an employed private eye, who will find that $1.50 to $1.75 an hour is about as much pay as he can expect for routine assignments. (In some of the most respected investigating firms, however, men are paid by the week and an experienced investigator can earn $9000 a year.)

Investigative entrepreneurs with poise and with backgrounds as lawyers can command high fees by undertaking delicate missions for the top managements of major corporations. One man who has only a secretary and a couple of part-time assistants confided that he had taken in $4900 during the past month. Many of the rest who are ambitious try to develop less profitable and more hazardous specialties. They may become specialists in electronic espionage; or they may try to gain access to non-public or hard-to-get documents that are in great demand by lawyers, insurance companies, and so on. Supposedly secret information on accident reports, birth certificates, or a patient's hospital report can, for example, often help a lawyer defeat a troublesome lawsuit, especially when the information is used to trip up witnesses during cross-examination.

In developing these specialties, many investigators find themselves walking a tightrope of legality. Some fall—or get pushed—off the rope.

The "specialists" who sell information obtained from classified, "quasi-classified," or hard-to-get documents that I happened to hear about appear to be of three kinds. These might be called:

—The true specialists. These are the old hands who have managed to obtain access to certain kinds of records and information by developing "contacts" and doing favors for the record-keepers. Generally they are regarded matter-of-factly by colleagues, at least until they get into trouble. They often work on a "standby" basis for the large investigative firms.

—The weasels. These are the unlicensed private eyes— generally scorned as fixers—who specialize in getting hold of public documents by bribing the record-keepers. They try to corner a particular market. One investigator told me: "Once in a big libel suit I needed a certain probation report. I bought it from a weasel who got it from the school."

—The moonlighters. These are public officials, including policemen, who supplement their income by selling information from official non-public or hard-to-get documents to such private clients as investigative firms. Some—for instance, certain of the men working in the document rooms of police departments—receive regular retainers from some of the larger investigative organizations.

In New York City, if you want to get information from any individual's passport application you go to a specialist who has an office in a building next to Grand Central Station. And if you want hospital records on an individual you contact a weasel in the Wall Street area (or you could until very recently). If he said yes to your requests, he would guarantee to deliver the records within four days. The larger investigative firms are likely to have on "standby" one specialist who has quick access to a person's immigration or naturalization files (mostly public records, but you have to know where to get them), another who can deliver a copy of a birth certificate. And they have others who can deliver copies of telegraph messages or unlisted telephone numbers, Treasury Department tax records, or applications for city jobs.

When I asked the head of a New York investigating firm how he obtained records, he said, "You buy them. If I want a man's criminal record, I call a friend on the force. Later I'll send him maybe ten dollars in an envelope. And if I want a credit report, later I'll send the girl five dollars or a bottle."

I have tried to put together a list of some of the prices I heard mentioned as what one would probably have to pay for hard-to-get information in the New York City area. Investigative experts who have read this chapter, I might add, argued vigorously that some figures were too high or too low, or doubted that certain items could be obtained at all; so the list is obviously highly impressionistic and assumes that the party desiring the items could find a seller.

An individual's arrest record...$10

An individual's credit report
(to a non-subscriber)...$5.00 to $10

Contents from police memo pad concerning an accident...$10

Unlisted phone number...$20

Birth certificate.. $15 to $50
($15 each if ordered wholesale by an investigating firm; $25 for a single certificate to an investigator; $50 to lawyers and other "outsiders")

Telephone toll slips, old phone bills, or pair numbers for
tapping..$50 minimum

Complete hospital record on a patient suffering physical
ailment...$300

Mental hospital record on patient..........................$500 min.

Medical examiner's report.....................................$500 min.

A look at an individual's federal income tax
return...$1000 min.

Regarding the last item, it should be noted that the federal files are quite rigorously protected. One former special agent of the Internal Revenue Service told me he couldn't get to these files. However, investigators can at times gain much of the information on a return by indirect routes that involve less cost and risk. A number of states require the filing of income tax returns. In some of these—including New York—the files are somewhat more easily invaded than federal files. And most taxpayers in these states simply copy much of the federal return when making out the state return. I heard reports of people in the New York State income tax office actively seeking income on the side by working for private investigative agencies.

*The exchange of file information on individuals among various governmental grou*ps. Some file material is borrowed or exchanged by government units under official sanction, at least at the beginning of its journey from its home file.

One obvious example of such exchange is the central information pool on many known or suspected criminals being developed by an intelligence unit of the Justice Department. It facilitates the exchange of information accumulated by the FBI, the Immigration and Naturalization Service, the Internal Revenue Service, the Federal Bureau of Narcotics, the Secret Service, the Bureau of Customs, the Bureau of Labor Management Reports, and the Postal Inspectors. Most law-abiding citizens—including those who have reservations about the growth of central indexes in our national life— would probably applaud this effort to combat organized crime.

Another kind of exchange involves the passing about of individual federal income tax returns. This is quite a different, and more disquieting, matter. Most people assume that only the Internal Revenue Service has a right to examine their returns. The fact is that in 1963 nine congressional committees were entitled to call for any tax return filed by any U.S. taxpayer for the past several years—and some for any year since 1947.

Three committees that are responsible for legislation involving taxation—House Ways and Means, Senate Finance, and Joint Congressional Committee on Internal Revenue Taxation—have the right, by law, to inspect returns. Most citizens, I imagine, would accept this as reasonable. But the President had by mid-1963 issued, upon request, Executive Orders authorizing five additional congressional committees to have such access to returns for the duration of the 88th Congress. These were the House and Senate Committees on Government Operations (which are concerned with the efficiency and economy of the government) . . . the Senate Committee on Foreign Relations (which has recently been concerned about some of the lobbying being done on behalf of foreign governments) . . . the House Committee on Public Works (which has been investigating the Federal Aid Highway Program) . . . the Senate Committee on Rules and Administration (which has been investigating business activities of employees and former employees of the Senate) . . . and then there is Executive Order 11109 making "open to inspection" any tax return from 1947 to 1963 to the House Un-American Activities Committee, "or any duly authorized subcommittee thereof, for the purpose of carrying on . . . investigations of subversive and un-American activities and propaganda. . ." Presumably the HUAC would be curious about the source of income or the size of contributions of individuals it considered to be possibly un-American. The legislative purpose such information would serve is less clear.

Any inspection of a return by any of the five committees receiving Executive Orders is supposed to be "confidential," but the regulations add: "*Provided, however,* That any portion thereof relevant or pertinent to the purpose of the investigation may be submitted by the investigating committee to the appropriate house of the Congress" (and thus perhaps be published in the *Congressional Record*).

Congressional committees vary greatly in the degree to which they guard confidential material in their files. The House Un-American Activities Committee has, at least until the last year or so, been notoriously prone to leak much of its file material to ultraconservative columnists, newspapers, and other friends of the committee. Perhaps it is reforming, but in any case one might reasonably agree with a comment the *Washington Post* made in connection with an identical authorization the HUAC received in the preceding Congress (in 1961). It said: "We wonder what the Un-American Activities Committee wants with such information. . . . It is easy enough to think of mischievous purposes which the HUAC could pursue by riffling through tax returns, but not so easy to think of useful purposes. . ."

It has been alleged that individual tax returns—or excerpts from them—have traveled from the Treasury Department to the Department of Defense. Senator Barry Goldwater of Arizona charged on the floor of the Senate that the Deputy Assistant Secretary of Defense for Civil Rights had been using "the full force" of income tax returns to coerce local businessmen into desegregating business establishments near military bases. The Department of Defense denied the charge and the senator's office advises me that while he did receive such reports he is not in a position to identify his informants. In any case, all Americans should be concerned that the individual tax files be guarded against abuse, especially since in coming years information from them will be readily available in cumulative, computerized form.

An example of the way one national agency checks the files of other national agencies for information on individuals is seen in the National Agency Check made by investigators for the Department of Defense. This National Agency Check is a minimum rundown that the Defense people make on anyone considered for a job with access to classified Defense information. In 1962 approximately 675,000 individuals were given a National Agency Check.

Here are the points checked in a National Agency Check:

—The FBI's criminal and subversive files.

—The intelligence or special investigation files of the Army, Navy, and Air Force if the individual in question has ever been in one of these services.

—The Civil Service Commission files, if individual has ever worked for the federal government.

—Immigration and Naturalization Service, if individual may be alien or naturalized citizen.

—The House Un-American Activities Committee, "when pertinent."

—The military Central Index Personnel and Facility Security File, if individual has ever worked for a firm with a classified defense contract.

—Other agencies, "when pertinent."

Most of us would agree that the Department of Defense is being only prudent in checking every possible source of adverse information on an individual available to the federal government. Still, one feels a bit uncomfortable about the prospect—as the federal government continues to expand—of a gigantic bureaucracy achieving an all-seeing eye as a result of its far-flung network of intelligence-gathering agencies.

Some of the federal traffic in documents, dossiers, and information, it should be added, is unauthorized. In late 1963 the State Department removed its chief security evaluations officer, Otto Otepka, because too many purportedly classified documents given to him, it was charged, were turning up in the hands of the chief counsel for the Senate Internal Security Subcommittee. Senator Thomas Dodd, vice-chairman of the Senate subcommittee, angrily denounced Mr. Otepka's removal as an affront to the Senate. Both Mr. Otepka and subcommittee officials defended their traffic in information on grounds of "higher loyalty."

The swapping of information about individuals between government agencies and private investigators or organizations. This seems to be most widespread at the local, county, and state levels. Personnel of federal executive agencies appear to be only rarely involved in such swapping. At the county and city levels of New

York City the swapping and selling of information is apparently not uncommon.

When a detective attached to the district attorney's office of a county in New York City died, his obituary mentioned at the bottom that he was part owner of a private investigation agency. I found that his name also appeared on a list I had compiled of about twenty non-employees who had ready access to the files of one of the leading financial investigating firms in New York City. Officially a district attorney would have to obtain a court order to look at any of this firm's reports on individuals.

As to the supposedly secret Bureau of Criminal Identification file maintained by New York City police, I was told that a number of the major investigating firms have contacts within, or have access to, BCI. And when the security officers of some of the larger department stores want to see if a job applicant is known to the police they simply get on the phone and call a contact at the police department. The contact checks the BCI classified file. In return for these favors the store's security officer may invite his friend on the police force to send his wife into the store for some on-the-house shopping.

Some of the most reputable investigating firms seem to see nothing wrong in having a secret payroll to pay retainers to one or more moonlighting police officers. However, one such firm was indignant when it found that a police detective on its payroll was also working for another big investigating firm in the insurance field. There was a feeling that he had somehow violated a code of honor.

Some may argue that interested private organizations should reasonably have access to police files. It seems to me, however, that any file labeled confidential that is assembled on individuals for a specific official use should remain that way. Otherwise a mass undercover traffic in personal information quickly develops. If society wants the police files on criminals and accidents to be made public, it should act to make them so. Until it does act, those who are curious should be required to proceed on the basis of information that is legitimately obtained.

John Cye Cheasty, the famed investigator, has a small staff but a large "stable" and many "contacts." In his stable he has on call specialists in surveillance, specialists in surreptitious photographs, lie-detector specialists, electronic specialists, accounting specialists, and so on. In addition to specialists, he added, "you have to have contacts in credit information services; you have to have contacts in the various police departments; you have to have contacts in the federal services where you might need information. The FBI gives out absolutely nothing. They are a dead loss to us." (Another investigator put the Treasury in this same class with the FBI.)

A large investigating firm in Manhattan, I was told by a person who should know, has in addition to its sizable staff of investigators a list of "standbys" who are called when their services are needed. They include a man with access to birth certificates, a man who has access to State Department passport applications, etc. And the head of a firm who scorned the use of "paid informers" mentioned a moment later that he did have a man he called upon in Washington who is "very effective in checking out security risks."

The coziness of the relationship between public and private file-keepers is perhaps best illustrated in the case of a file that is not even supposed to exist. This is the so-called KSD file maintained by a police bureau often called the "morals squad"; among other duties, it keeps tabs on sexual deviates who for one reason or other have appeared on a police docket. KSD means "known sexual deviate." (In Washington, D.C., I'm told the police in cooperation with a number of federal offices maintain a comparable secret file known as the KSP or "known sexual pervert" file. The word "pervert" is used out of deference to congressmen who prefer to use the stronger word in referring to sexual deviates.)

In New York it has become a frequent practice for investigating firms, credit departments of major stores, and political organizations to use their "connections" to check people out on KSD. In the course of my research, officials of investigative firms or private investigators showed me or read to me samples of reports they make, to illustrate their working methods. One in particular captured my attention, since it involved gaining access to the KSD file. It ran for ten pages. Here are the four most pertinent developments, in chronological order:

1. A business organization suddenly became concerned—for reasons that are unstated—about the character of three men associated with a firm that was about to make a deal with the organization.

2. An official of the organization asked a private investigating company in the early afternoon to try to run a quick, urgent check on the men.

3. Since the assignment was urgent, the main question for the investigating firm was the fastest way to get information from the Police Department's KSD files. It decided to use an investigator I'll call Pete who had a very good rapport with a non-police law-enforcement official of high rank known to have frequent access to the city's KSD file through a top-ranking police official.

4. This approach was used. Within two hours the nonpolice official was reading to Pete from a file on his lap all that was known about the firm in question and the morals of its officials. (Two of the men were listed as KSDs.)

I asked my informant how Pete had obtained such startling cooperation. He said, "They gave Pete the whole record because he has brought them a lot of useful stuff and they like him."

A more ludicrous situation I encountered was a reverse type of swapping. In 1962 a captain of detectives in New York frequently called upon a private investigator to obtain for him information he needed from a state law-enforcement file. This officer had full authority to request the information directly but that would involve making his request in quintuplicate form and sending it through channels. The desired information would come back in about six days. When he was in a rush to press an investigation he would call John, private investigator. John could get the same information for him within an hour! John could also get him credit reports in an hour instead of the weeks that going through channels would take. The officer would prove his gratitude to John by getting John anything John needed from police files—within reason, of course.

(In Chapter 13, "The Right to Have Unfashionable Opinions," we shall see that investigators involved in the entertainment world's "clearance" business have had ready access to a number of federal file-keepers.)

The swapping of information about us by interested private parties. Major investigating firms in the financial field usually have extensive files and fact-gathering facilities. Often they have information that cannot easily be got elsewhere. This makes them attractive partners for swapping arrangements. The only loser in the swap is the citizen being stripped of his privacy.

This mutual attraction explains why officials of banks will often become more cooperative than is officially authorized in responding to an inquiry about a depositor from a trusted investigating firm. These firms can often reciprocate by giving the bank hard-to-get information about someone who may have an uncomfortably large loan from the bank.

Some newspapers open their morgues and legal files to certain of these investigating firms in exchange for access to the firms' thick dossiers filled with intimate and often startling details about notables in the news.

Even doctors in a few instances will bend their ethics a little to reveal facts about a patient's condition in return for information they may desire about other patients. The investigating firms can readily provide credit information about patients who have not bothered to pay substantial bills. Or a doctor may wish to obtain reliable information about a patient's ability to pay before submitting a bill for major medical treatment. Dentists have the same interest but have less useful information to swap.

Again it should be stressed that some of the more conservative investigating organizations scorn investigators who engage in the kinds of selling and swapping of information I've described. They have developed their own Society of Professional Investigators with high standards for procuring and handling information desired by clients. A good model for guarding its confidential files is set by one leading investigating firm, which in its contract with clients asserts at the outset: "any and all information submitted to you under the terms of this contract is confidential and privileged and not for publication verbally or otherwise to others, strangers to this agreement."

An interesting example of the traffic in filed information about people en masse is seen in the use of opinions gathered by public-opinion survey makers. Efforts have been made to assemble this information into computers to predict political reactions. There is, for example, "The People Machine" that may have helped the Democrats win in 1962. Thomas B. Morgan related in *Harper's* (January 1961) that consultants for the Simulmatics Corporation fed into computers information filed in another kind of memory bank, the Roper Public Opinion Research Center at Williams College. They took information from the Center that had been gained from 100,000 interviews, over several years, came up with 480 "voter- types," and filed into the memory bank millions of pieces of information about the attitudes that had been expressed on a variety of issues by these 480 voter-types. Thus the machine was able to make presumed predictions on the way each of the 480 groups would respond to various campaign appeals. Mr. Morgan concluded by asking: "As we seek more and more data for the machine, can we maintain our tradition for privacy? How much pressure toward conformity will be created by the machine . . . ?" He might also have asked whether by 1984 power might be held by the party with the best computers, or the one most adept at exploiting information stored in computers.

If a private file-keeper is not interested in swapping information, investigators have a variety of strategies and dissimulations with which to try to pry loose the information they desire. I'll simply mention two as typical.

I heard the head of a small but well-known detective firm say over the telephone to one of his operatives: "Tell them you are from the credit department . . . Name of store? Make one up."

Another investigator told me of a ploy he uses when he encounters a corporate personnel official who seems unwilling to give more than minimum information—mere verification of employment—about an employee or ex-employee. He said: "You start out by saying you just want to verify some employment dates, but of course you want more. So in a moment you say, 'Something is wrong here. Could I talk to the personnel manager?' This usually gets you an immediate interview with the personnel manager, whose curiosity and concern are aroused, even if the man is no longer employed there. He will get out the records to check again any garbled information I have made up."

All this maneuvering and swapping and buying of information from the keepers of files is serving to undermine the confidential nature of the information about citizens in many of the files. If these practices continue and grow, citizens will not be able to believe that the information they must entrust to others about their private and intimate affairs will be safeguarded.

When that happens they will have lost not only a large hunk of privacy but also much of their sense of freedom.

PART III

Assaults on Traditional Rights
of Free Citizens

12. The Right to a Private, Unfettered Life

> "This is a newfangled thing, this fool idea that you have
> got the right to travel anywhere and at all times. . . ."
> —U.S. Representative E. L. "Tic" Forrester of Georgia
> (1959)

Most thoughtful Americans accept the fact that it is not feasible
to try to be a recluse in a continent now filled with 190,000,000
people. An authentic recluse, in fact, is likely to be the subject
of considerable curiosity. Still, it should be remembered that the
Founding Fathers of the U.S.A. were contemplating a society in
which a man or woman could have a great deal of latitude about
choosing his style of living.

It was assumed that you were free to lead your own life—if
you were not an unpunished criminal, a certified maniac, or a
conscripted soldier. You could go into solitude when you felt in
the mood for contemplation. You could be footloose, even though
it might endanger your own life in hostile Indian territory. You
could, with general approbation, horsewhip anyone who pried
unduly into your affairs simply to satisfy curiosity or to profit by
feeding idle gossip. And you could live in dignity in any way that
you conceived the term.

Today, with society continually pushing in and the shrinkage
of inviolate places, the idea that one can—or should try to—lead
a private, unfettered life is losing much of its force.

Consider first, as the most obvious invasion of our right to a
private life, the role of intruding noise. If some of the passages in
this part of the book seem more than normally irascible, the tone
may be due in part to the fact that two roaring, lunging power
shovels, a bulldozer, and three men with shrieking power saws are

busy nearby. They are slashing a broad new highway through what was until recently a lovely woodland. This or comparable noise has been afflicting my eardrums for weeks. One must not protest, of course, since the noisemakers are not on my land. And besides, their endeavors will mean profits for a developer and more taxes for the nearby town of Wilton, Connecticut. Altogether, they come under our modern definition of Progress.

However, certain assaults upon the ear are reducible and should be combated. For example there are the office seekers who abuse their freedom of speech by multiplying their voices a hundredfold with the use of sound trucks. There are the tens of thousands of youngsters with transistorized bullhorns. The same company that has been mass-merchandising the Big Ear for youngsters also mass-markets the Big Blast. ("Just squeeze the trigger and send your voice booming over long distances.") And there is the canned music in public places that comes at you without request: at the zoo, at the newer library reading rooms, in hospital rooms, in airplanes.

Finally, and worst, there are the more than 10,000,000 portable transistorized radios in the U.S. alone, and many millions more in at least fifty other countries. Some months ago I had the first opportunity in my life to make an awe-filled trip up the Acropolis of Athens to that most perfect of structures, the Parthenon. There on the steps of the temple sat a young man of unknown nationality with a transistor radio blasting out a Greek version of rock-and-roll music. He seemed surprised when I politely suggested by hand motion that he turn down the volume, but he complied. Writers of letters to the *London Observer* have been lamenting the new pests in England with "these horror boxes."

In an editorial of lament on the nation's rising noise level Norman Cousins told of a remarkable sight he saw at a corner of Madison Avenue.[1] Men were at work putting in some underground cables. "One of them was wearing a headband inside of which was a small radio set," he reported. "On a small ledge was another radio, turned up full force. It had to be: it was competing with two pneumatic drills in full operation only a few yards away."

Quite possibly a good many million people on this planet are developing an addiction to noise. Certainly we see considerable evidence that a great many citizens of the modern world are becoming jaded sensation seekers, Mr. Cousins suggests that if people "accept a high noise level they become noisemakers themselves."

The psychical and physiological damage being done by the fairly continual barrage of sound that reaches millions of citizens probably cannot be accurately assessed for at least a decade. But the surmises are beginning. Psychiatrists are suggesting that a heavy intake of noise can create the kind of tensions leading to emotional disturbance. Audiologist Joseph Krimsky has stated that the capacity of noise to annihilate privacy is not only aggravating life's stresses but can produce pathological changes in the auditory system and reduce "sensitiveness to the nuances of sound and music."

People who like to be alone with their thoughts when traveling are finding this increasingly difficult.

The sales experts who strain to attract the attention of our eyes, ears, or noses have learned that they can improve their odds if they have a captive audience. It is hard for a busload of passengers to shut their ears to the commercials being broadcast between musical interludes. A group of passengers in Washington, D.C., objected to this assault on their ears while riding to work by bus and took the matter to court. The question was whether their privacy was being invaded, since they were essentially a captive audience. In a sense they were appealing for an application of the First Amendment in reverse: the right to be free of the freedom of expression of others. The Supreme Court ruled that they did not have a case.

I found myself the victim of an aural assault while flying on Continental Airlines over Texas. All who travel by air have become accustomed to the rather long-winded "Thank you for flying airline _____ and next time remember to fly airline _____" talks from stewardesses at the end of trips. But this was something additional. While the plane was at perhaps 10,000 feet in mid-flight, the pilot spent several minutes describing all the special features that made his plane and airline the best for the discriminating traveler.

In 1962 a historic occasion of sorts occurred on the New Haven Railroad when male models began walking up and down the aisles demonstrating—for Phillips-Van Heusen Corp.—Bermuda shorts, sports shirts, business shirts, etc. A former baseball star carried on a running vocal commentary, while hundreds of passengers tried in vain to concentrate on their newspapers.

And people who feel that their own homes can be places for retreat, work, or contemplation are also finding the going harder. The promoters of intimate person-to-person selling are turning increasingly to attempts to gain entry into each man's castle by way of door-to-door salesmen and telephone solicitors, whose ranks are growing.

As youngsters most Americans are admonished by their parents to be nice to people who call them on the telephone. This ingrained habit has proved a boon to today's hordes of telephone solicitors. People put up with being called from the shower or dinner table or from a nap by a man offering to check on whether the roof is ailing. The calls are especially bothersome to those people who work by night and sleep by day. Their friends know this and don't bother them, but the solicitors don't know and do bother. New brides are solicited by furniture and silverware sales ladies . . . new mothers are besieged by diaper services and perambulator makers . . . new homeowners are beset by people offering insurance, air conditioners, or rugs. During the months after I had had a fire in my home I was called, I would guess, by the representatives of virtually every fire-alarm manufacturer within a hundred miles.

Soliciting by phone has become so profitable, in terms of effort required, that a dragnet approach is often used for such items as women's hosiery. The callers simply buzz every telephone subscriber listed in a residential area including, unavoidably, the occasional bachelor. Spokesmen in the hosiery field claim they have had a phenomenal success.

My publisher relates that he has twice been excitedly advised by telephone solicitors: "You are the lucky recipient of six free dancing lessons." A corporate vice-president complained to me that he had been called to the phone that morning by someone who started by saying, "We are doing a survey in this building of consumer habits." It turned out the person was really a milk company representative who in addition to his little "survey" was making a pitch for new customers.

Most homes in metropolitan areas receive several telephone solicitations a week. A woman's-page reporter of the *New York Times* told of a young Linden, New Jersey, woman who took the calls politely in stride until one morning shortly after she had her first baby. On that morning between eight-thirty and eleven-thirty she was summoned to the telephone eight times by as many different salesmen. She decided that enough was enough and called the telephone company to request an unlisted telephone number.

Many phone companies have no policy against telephone solicitations. They prefer to assume that as long as the phone is used legally it is none of their business. Furthermore telephone soliciting helps push up their volume of calls. Now, however, they are becoming distressed by the rush to unlisted phone numbers. Some people want an unlisted number for status, but a great many are just weary of being bothered by soliciting strangers. In some of the larger cities more than 15 per cent of all phones are now unlisted.

Some merchandisers have been exploring the marvels of modern electronics to increase their sales volume. There have been reports from several parts of the nation of motorcar merchants obligingly leaving the man and wife alone to discuss their finances and reach a private consensus on how enthusiastic they are about the car in question before trying to clinch a sale. The considerate salesman then discreetly returns to see if they can arrive at a meeting of minds. In the final maneuvering of terms he has one considerable advantage. He knows what this particular market will bear in terms of prices because he listened in on the couple's private huddle via a hidden microphone.

In a minor but annoying way the privacy of many people is being stripped away, too, by the prurient and by practical jokers armed with tape recorders, microphone-transmitters, and flash cameras. Stores in California advertise that you can be the life of the party if you buy one of their pocket recorders and play back at parties what people have been saying without knowing they were being recorded. At a leading bar in Oakland the bartender amuses his patrons by tuning in conversations and other sounds occurring in the washroom.

A nightclub owner in New York revealed inadvertently during union negotiations that he had a microphone installed in the ladies' lounge to collect gossip that he could pass on to columnists, presumably in exchange for plugs for his establishment. There have been reports that concealed microphones are used extensively in Las Vegas to record embarrassing conversations purely to provide fun for others.

In Wisconsin a bartender snapped a picture of a woman while she was in the rest room of the establishment and, thanks to the marvels of instant photography, was soon showing the photograph to patrons of the bar. The lady in question was not amused and took the matter to court. She was denied any recovery because, the state Supreme Court ruled, there was no common-law right of privacy in Wisconsin that could be based on judicial precedent; and the state legislature had never bothered to enact a law protecting one's right to privacy.[2]

In another more recently reported case in the West, a woman went to the police to file charges that she had been assaulted. A male police officer told her that pictures would have to be taken to show injury. She protested that pictures would show nothing, but he insisted that she strip and pose in several indecent positions while he photographed her. Later the pictures were circulated among the personnel of the police department. She charged in court that her privacy had been invaded, and the Court was sympathetic to her charge.

The use of tape recorders by professional consultants, though with far worthier motives, is tending to undermine the confidentiality of conversations in many settings. A number of psychoanalysts record their patients' disclosures while on the couch, not only so that they can play back passages to search for insights but so that the tape of a puzzling case can be played for their control analysts or group meetings. In such meetings the patient is identified only by sex, age, and symptoms; but many remarks may be dropped in the discussion that could conceivably lead to educated guesses as to the identity of the subject.

Samuel Dash reported that during his investigation of eavesdropping in Philadelphia he encountered a pocket-recorder representative who revealed that one woman had rented a small recorder from him at the suggestion of her psychiatrist. She explained that her psychiatrist had asked her to record secretly her husband's sexual advances, to help him determine where her problems lay.

According to a report of a New York State joint legislative committee, the deliberations of a jury in a federal court in a Western state were secretly recorded. This was done in the interest of research: the taping was part of a project of the University of Chicago Law School. The judge and opposing counsel had all agreed to the secret recording. The only people who were not consulted were the twelve guinea pigs on the jury who assumed they were conducting a secret deliberation.

The role played by some sections of the mass media (newspapers. magazines, broadcasters) must also be examined in any assessment of the extent to which individual privacy is being undermined today. We should face at the outset that here there can be a conflict of interests, both legally and philosophically. The body of laws specifically protecting one's right to privacy is still puny, mostly state statutes and common laws. It was only in 1890 that a general right to privacy—a right to be let alone—was first seriously discussed in U.S. legal circles. The now classic article, "The Right to Privacy," by Samuel D. Warren and Louis D. Brandeis appeared in the December issue of the *Harvard Law Review*. The Constitution did not establish any protection for privacy as such but covered aspects of privacy by various provisions, such as the protection against unreasonable search and seizure; the guarantees that a person could "not be deprived of life, liberty, or property" without "due process of law"; the guaranteed right to freedom of speech.

On the other hand the First Amendment specifically guarantees that Congress will make no law abridging freedom of the press. This presumes the right of the public to have access to facts even if those facts are extremely embarrassing to citizens who are subjects of the disclosure. As Mr. Dooley commented: "What's one man's news is another man's throubles."

One person who argues that the ordinary citizen isn't fighting a hopeless battle in his right to be let alone by the press is Creed C. Black, chairman of the Freedom of Information Committee of the American Society of Newspaper Editors. The public and press, he contends, are not interested in "the mundane affairs of ordinary, private citizens." To make his point he likes to cite a quip that comedian Herb Shriner made about his home town in Indiana. Herb said his town was so small that everybody knew what everybody else was doing and bought the paper only to see who got caught at it.

Still, a great deal of embarrassing or anguish-producing information about the private affairs of individuals is publicized for profit—especially in gossip columns and the sensational magazines. Our forefathers could not have had juicy pap in mind when speaking of "the press." But judges have been extremely lenient about permitting dissemination of information as long as a charge of libel cannot be sustained. Harriet F. Pilpel, an authority on what can and cannot be published, has summed up the approximate situation now existing after the courts have spent years groping toward a body of law, in these words:[3]

"By and large, today the right of privacy has been interpreted to prevent only or at least primarily commercial exploitation of a person's name or picture to sell something other than the facts about him presented as such. Generally speaking, a fictionalized or dramatized version of the facts is held to be a species of commercial exploitation." (Libel, of course, is another matter.)

Protection against commercial exploitation, at least, is not quite as weak today as it was in 1902 when a girl named Abigail Roberson found her lovely innocent face adorning sacks of flour. Advertising was just starting to feel its power. When she sued to stop this misuse of her face by a flour company, the judges searched the law books, scratched their heads, and said she had no case. This was just one of several outrages that were committed by advertisers at the turn of the century. The *New York Times* vigorously protested the Court's opinion that the public had no right of privacy. Within a few months the New York State legislature created a right-of-privacy act. The law, which stands today, simply protects a person from having his name, portrait, or picture used for advertising or "purposes of trade."

Even this is not always enforced. A few years ago a tennis star found that a news account of one of his matches—in which his name appeared several times—was reproduced on a playful, patchwork-type fabric used in making pajamas and underwear for girls. He objected to the use of his name "in juxtaposition to intimate parts of bodies. . . ." His case was thrown out by a New York court on the grounds that the use of his name was "a mere incidental commercial use." Mrs. Pilpel commented that this was "the first case we know of involving the wearing of the free press."

An interesting symptom of our times has been the success of the TV show *Candid Camera* in which people are caught, unaware they are on camera, in revealing and often foolish behavior. The widow of one subject so caught has sued. He was shown in a subway episode in which a stranger (a TV performer) tried to squeeze in between him and a woman on the seat. The complaint, still pending at this writing, is that members of the family suffered public ridicule, mental anguish, humiliation. Perhaps one reason there have not been more suits is that an aide assigned to the show seeks to obtain on-the-spot releases from the people photographed. Their usual first reaction, I'm told, is one of being flattered to think they may appear before a national TV audience. They may not realize until they see the show that they have perhaps exhibited a moronic expression or performed, unwittingly, in some laughable manner. The complaint of the above case alleges that the woman involved was incorrectly identified as the man's wife.

Television's reporters and cameramen have recently been criticized for pressing too hard for raw drama in covering some news events. Television is the most intimate of the media. When the reporter-cameramen teams shove microphones into the faces of people suffering anguish or embarrassment and refuse to let the persons escape without being rude, they are going too far.

Those most likely to suffer from privacy invasion through disclosures by the mass media—and who are legally most naked of defenses—are people who for one reason or another are or have been "public figures." Alan Schwartz, an authority on the law of privacy, comments: "Do movie stars, governors, presidents, people who are in the public eye by choice most of their adult lives . . . ever get their privacy back? Thus far, the tentative answer seems to be 'no.' Short of using their pictures to advertise soap-suds or the like, the so-called public figure is fair game for the mass media."

Broadway actors are usually shocked to find that they have less chance for privacy when they go to Hollywood. Helicopters fly over their patios to shoot pictures of the stars. Certain of the "screen" magazines have sent photographers disguised as decorators into the homes of stars in order to obtain photographs of their bedrooms—and any signs in the homes of unmarried actresses of visitations by males. Stars have complained in vain about photographers with telescopic lenses taking their pictures from nearby hilltops.

In one instance related to me by a lawyer in Hollywood, a male and female star were in a bedroom engaged in the ultimate in intimate conduct. She was married to another man. Most of the pictures were too raw to be published, but perhaps they still had their uses. At least one Hollywood periodical has got advertisements in exchange for not printing material that invaded the privacy of the stars.

If a picture taken from beyond the borders of a famous person's property is not libelous, there is apparently little that can be done to prevent its publication. Some years ago a majority opinion of the Supreme Court, in an aside on the On Lee case, stated: "The use of bifocals, field glasses or telescope to magnify object of witness's vision is not a forbidden 'search and seizure' even if they focus without [the subject's] knowledge or consent upon what one supposes to be private indiscretions."

Maximilian Schell is one actor who has had the courage to assail photographers and reporters who invade the privacy of public figures. He protested that the laws of Europe and the United States were not adequate to preserve even a minimum of privacy. Mr. Schell said he has had to contend with treetop photographers outside his residences, especially in Europe.

Shortly before Marilyn Monroe committed suicide, she

made some comments about privacy that indicated a depth of wisdom and perception that gave many people a new respect for her. Speaking of the difficulties of being an actor, she commented: "Goethe said, 'Talent is developed in privacy,' you know? And it is really true. There is a need for aloneness which I don't think most people realize for an actor. It's almost having certain kinds of secrets for yourself that you'll let the whole world in on only for a moment, when you're acting. But everybody is always tugging at you. They'd all like sort of a chunk of you. . . ."[4]

Another actress whose life has been wrenched by people peeking and tugging at her—until perhaps she has become numb to it-—is Elizabeth Taylor. While she and Richard Burton were both married to other people, they were photographed, by telescopic lens, in an exceedingly warm embrace. They thought they were alone offshore in a small craft. This photograph was widely reproduced around the world. I asked a lawyer familiar with Miss Taylor's problems if she had considered suing anyone for invasion of her privacy. He shrugged. "A boat probably is not a private place. If this had been the first instance of intimacy with Burton there might have been grounds for suit on invasion of privacy. But whom do you sue? Most of the photographers in Europe are freelance." When Elizabeth was in Paris, everywhere she went she was followed by at least twenty-five photographers trying to get pictures to peddle to magazines or syndicates. When magazines buy pictures they often require a warranty of indemnification from the photographers, so that there is really little protection, and she is constantly annoyed.

She was encouraged to file a suit in quite a different connection: she sued a chain of stores for $1,000,000 for selling "Elizabeth Taylor blouses" and other items that promised to give the wearer the "Liz Look." Her lawyers had already spent more than $4000 in gathering evidence. Although it was really a privacy-invasion case, the stores were being charged with "unfair competition." In essence she is defending a private property, her right to the publicity value of her name and likeness, which is about all a notable person has left of his privacy to defend.

Other celebrities, too, have brought suits. The motion picture actor Kirk Douglas and his two sons were invited to producer Walt Disney's home for what Mr. Douglas assumed was a purely private Sunday afternoon social visit. That may well have been the intent. But in any case during the afternoon Mr. Disney took home movies of Mr. Douglas and his sons on Mr. Disney's toy train. Apparently the Douglases had a whale of a time on the train and the film delighted Mr. Disney. Two years later a film of their train ride was televised nationally on the *Disneyland* show. Mr. Douglas objected and reportedly was assured the film would not be repeated, but somehow it was. Mr. Douglas became angry enough to sue. He claimed not only that his right to privacy had been invaded but also that his right to publicity of his image was invaded and demanded compensation for his services as an actor. On the basis of the skirmishes in preliminary pleadings the judge favored Mr. Douglas' argument but apparently more on the basis of his claim to a right to publicity value than to a right to privacy.

Another privacy problem that has confronted actresses in particular in the last two years is the growing expectation of producers that the girls—after contracting to play roles—will pose nude or partly nude for a brief film sequence. The sequence is usually conceived as audience bait to promote the picture. Although completely nude shots are prohibited in any U.S.-made motion pictures that hope to gain the industry's seal of approval for the domestic market, a number of independent producers have been shooting some scenes involving the actress in two versions. For the U.S. market the actress will wear a bra; for the foreign market, which tends to be more tolerant of nudity, she may be asked to pose with her breasts bare, or to take a skinny dip in a pool. (Other offenders have been the producers of so-called "nudie" shows who advertise for beautiful young girls without disclosing that they will be required to work in the nude.)

A number of established actresses who discovered, after accepting roles, that they were expected to expose all or large parts of their bodies to the camera protested to the Screen Actors Guild. Others, more exhibitionistic or eager for work, have not objected. The Guild became disturbed by the trend. I am advised by Buck Harris of the Guild that it will seek to protect any actress working for any producer with a Guild contract if she is required "to work in the nude against her wishes." Dana Andrews, the new president of the Guild, has warned that unless there is a public reaction enormous pressure will be exerted on actresses to work in the nude.

A troublesome question involving the boundaries of privacy for people who have achieved—or been thrust into—the public limelight arises from the practice of the mass media of retelling dramatic past events. Frequently these events have involved deep anguish for individuals involved. It is noteworthy, however, that on this particular facet of the right to privacy the courts do seem to be moving toward a more protective attitude.

In two of the early, classic cases of suits being brought, the once public figures were told they had lost their right of privacy. In the 1930s a former child prodigy, William James Sidis, contended that The *New Yorker* magazine had invaded his privacy with a "Where Are They Now?" article. In adult life—twenty years after his early fame—Mr. Sidis had become a fanatical recluse. The Court held for the magazine. In a reported case in the early fifties NBC in *The Big Story* recreated the heroic manner in which an intrepid lady reporter had sprung a man from a death cell more than a decade earlier by proving that his conviction was erroneous. He sued NBC for invading his privacy even though his name was not specifically mentioned and the dramatization was not an exact recapitulation. Again the Court held for the defendant, largely because there was a question as to how many viewers had identified him with the program. But it indicated that if he was identifiable the question then would be whether the instance involved "unwarranted" disclosure or "unreasonable" public identification.

During the sixties, however, protesting plaintiffs seem to be getting a more sympathetic hearing. In 1962 a New York court awarded a family $175,000 in damages because of a photo story *Life* magazine ran in the mid-fifties which purportedly recreated a dramatic news event that had occurred three years earlier. The family had been held captive in their home outside Philadelphia by some escaped convicts. When a play called *The Desperate Hours* opened, apparently based in part on the experiences of the family, *Life* used the occasion to present its story under the title "True Crime Inspires Tense Play." The magazine took actors from the play to the actual house, which the family had vacated, and shot pictures from the play. The family contended that some of the depicted episodes from the play were at least partly fictional. But the heart of their contention was that the article was a commercial exploitation of their name rather than a legitimate news use. At this writing, a new trial that will be confined solely to the amount of the damages has been ordered; and the attorneys for the plaintiff are going on the assumption that the publisher will seek to appeal the whole issue of liability to a higher court.

The recent case that most frightened proprietors of the mass media and those believing in freedom of the press occurred in Chicago. It involved the retelling by two detective-story magazines of a crime only five or six months after its occurrence. Many magazines require three or four months to assign and get out an article on a subject. In this case a teen-age girl had been slain and disposed of in a gruesome manner. One of the magazines, *Startling Detective*, titled its story "Frozen Corpse in Lovers' Lane." The girl's mother subsequently sued for libel. This suit was turned down because the statute of limitations had run out by the time the mother initiated her suit. But the U.S. Court of Appeals reversed that decision and ordered the case to go to trial on the grounds of invasion of privacy. The judge, speaking for the Court, wrote: "When the news media have served their proper function in reporting the current events, private individuals involved therein sink back into the solitude which is the right of every person."

However, a few weeks later the same Court reversed itself upon being reminded that at the approximate time the articles appeared the murderer was coming up for trial. Thus the murder was still newsworthy. It was a narrow escape for the two magazines, since they survive largely on the basis of re-creating vivid crimes. But, more important, it was a narrow escape for the mass media generally, since the judge in his defense of the right to solitude had not confined himself to the re-creation of lurid crimes or even crimes in general. He had applied the test of whether or not the news was current and so reportable without danger of liability.

My own view is that the courts should indeed move to protect the right to solitude of people from the revival years later of gruesome episodes that had once thrust them into the limelight, if the rehashing is done primarily to shock or titillate. But I also think that if time limits are to be set the media should work to win legal sanction for greater latitude in alluding to past episodes of legitimate public interest. Otherwise historians, biographers, and even lawyers offering citations of criminal cases settled many years ago might find themselves in trouble.

Great Britain has recently been plagued even more than the United States by problems involving invasion of privacy by the mass media. Although the United States took its system of justice from Britain, that country has not yet evolved any protection of the right of privacy even to the rudimentary extent that exists in some states of the U.S.A. Perhaps the traditional strong sense of decency and decorum in England made such a doctrine seem unnecessary.

But in recent years the British appear to have been going through an upheaval in moral attitudes. Some call it a "sexual revolution." The mass media have helped the revolution along by tearing aside traditional restraints. Some of the results have been as blatant in their excesses as were New York's tabloids in the late twenties. One paper revealed excitedly "What the Queen Looks at When She Takes a Bath." (It proved to be her bamboo-type wallpaper.)[5]

The climax in baring all came during the now notorious Profumo case that nearly toppled Prime Minister Macmillan. Whether the case deserved all the hullabaloo it received is debatable. But it is unquestionably true that some of the more sensational London newspapers—by fighting to get and perhaps hold for maximum impact the confessions of call girls—played a crucial role in shaping the form the crisis took.

To return to the United States, the right of Americans to travel where they please as long as they can pay the fare is another traditional right that is being undermined by bureaucrats in the State Department, with the encouragement of xenophobic congressmen. The U.S. Supreme Court has observed that freedom to travel where one pleases is a "natural and constitutional right." It has held that "the freedom to travel is a part of the liberty to which the citizen cannot be deprived without due process of law."[8]

Nonetheless since 1940 there have been many efforts to qualify the right to travel. A number have succeeded, and the once clear legal right to travel as implied in the First and Fifth Amendments has become cloudy indeed.

All three of the most recent Presidents of the United States have called for an increase in travel and communication between countries with a greater interchange of ideas as the competition of ideas replaces the competition of weapons. Yet steadfastly through most of it all the State Department has sought to declare certain countries out of bounds to travelers. Russia, once out of bounds, is now open; but oddly, Americans are forbidden to travel to China, Albania, or Cuba unless it "is in the best interests of the United States" for them to do so. All are poverty-stricken, dictator-ridden countries that would appear to be in a weak position to convert travelers from free and affluent America.

One explanation the State Department gives for declaring entire countries out of bounds is that it cannot protect American citizens who might fall into trouble in such countries. The United States Government did not feel impelled to offer protection to pioneers who went through the Blackfoot country en route to the unsettled and disputed Northwest or through Apache country to Spanish-controlled California. Further, today's State Department has resolutely refused to permit citizens to waive any right to protection and take their chances.

In a few instances the State Department has felt impelled to make exceptions. A Greek scholar from New York City, a Mr. George Martin, was planning a tour of Greek ruins with a group of British and Continental scholars. One of the greatest of all Greek ruins happens to be in the present-day Albanian city of Durres. The State Department decreed that Mr. Martin would have to remain aboard the ship while his European colleagues went down the gangplank to visit Durres. It was only after Mr. Martin's congressman, Representative John V. Lindsay, waged a long fight to persuade the State Department of the preposterousness of its stand that the department relented and permitted Mr. Martin to join his fellow scholars on the one-day tour.

The State Department was sternly unforgiving, however, when fifty-seven Americans, mostly college students, visited Cuba recently without obtaining specially validated passports. Four of the leaders of the group were indicted.

In addition to general bans on travel to specific areas, the State Department has persistently sought to forbid certain Americans to travel anywhere beyond the nation's borders. It has tried to deny a passport to anyone suspected of having, or having had, Communist affiliations. It is the opinion of many people, Congressman Emanuel Celler, for one, that a real Soviet spy would not bother to seek a U.S. passport.

Congressmen have sought to give the State Department specific legislative authority to curtail the right of some Americans to travel by offering dozens of bills. It was during a debate on one such bill that Representative Forrester scoffed at the idea that any American, including alleged Communists, had a right to travel "anywhere" as a "fool idea."

The American Civil Liberties Union, in opposing the bill in question, reminded the congressmen that any citizen has a right to travel unless he is involved in a court action requiring that he remain within the country or unless his country is engaged in a hot war. Congress never could agree on a law. But then the Supreme Court compromised its earlier strong stand in *Kent v. Dulles*, perhaps inadvertently, by a decision that was not concerned directly with the issue of passports and travel and did not allude to the issue of passports. It upheld the provision of the 1950 Subversive Activities Control Act that requires members of Communist organizations to register under the act. Section 6a of this Control Act *automatically* bars anyone required to register under the act from either applying for a passport or seeking renewal of one—and makes it a crime for any government officer to issue a passport to him! This section clearly seems unconstitutional, but the State Department has fallen back on it to withhold passports.

At first the State Department simply appended to each application for a passport a warning about the section's provision. The department now, at this writing, has taken the more drastic stand of requiring all applicants for passports to state under oath that they have not belonged, within the past twelve months, to any group that has a "final order" to register under the act. The constitutionality of this question is being challenged in the courts, with the ACLU supporting the challenge with a friend-of-the-court brief, and was scheduled to be squarely before the Supreme Court in the spring of 1964. The recent arrangement is considered especially objectionable because it eliminates a person's right to confront the government's confidential informants who claim that an organization to which he belongs has been a Communist front. If the applicant answers "yes" to the question of whether he has belonged to the group labeled as a front, his answer automatically makes it a crime for him to apply for a passport.

If our government falls into the habit of assuming it can prevent all Americans from traveling to certain places abroad—and can prevent certain Americans from traveling to all places—we shall all be in danger of losing a part of our freedom to lead our own lives. There would be much to gain, and little to lose, by practicing what we preach and letting all certified citizens of the United States travel freely. The Communist countries have little to offer in the way of attractiveness when compared with the world's free countries that are geographically near them.

13. The Right to Have Unfashionable Opinions

"If a man does not keep pace with his companions, perhaps it is because he hears a different drummer. Let him step to the music which he hears, however measured or far away."—Henry David Thoreau

Just as talent is developed in privacy, so is bold, independent thinking developed in the privacy of one's circle of colleagues and friends. If anyone can be torn from this environment at any moment and forced to explain any of his thoughts before a panel of grim-faced strangers—fearful, narrow-minded private groups or certain congressmen who are either chronically suspicious or lovers of publicity—then bold or unorthodox thoughts will dry up in this land. This is particularly true if one must not only confess his own unorthodox thoughts but identify every acquaintance who shares similar thoughts.

In recent years we've had an uncomfortably large number of such spectacles. Senator Dodd, a former FBI man, of the Senate Internal Security subcommittee, demanded that Dr. Linus Pauling, now two-time winner of Nobel prizes, turn over to him the names of any American scientists who helped Dr. Pauling circulate petitions in opposition to nuclear testing. The same senator also played a role in hauling before the committee the officials of a small, frequently experimental radio network consisting of three stations dedicated to exploring the spectrum of provocative ideas (WBAI, New York; KPFK, Los Angeles; KPEA, San Francisco). These stations were offering a forum to all people with unorthodox ideas, ranging from a leading representative of the John Birch Society and of the American Nazi Party to a spokesman for the Communists in Southern California. And, perhaps worst of all from Senator Dodd's viewpoint, they had given air time to a disgruntled ex-FBI man. They also offer the kind of drama, music, and poetry difficult to find on mass-appeal stations. Their appeal has been to a relatively small band of intellectuals. The network, sponsored by the Pacifica Foundation, is non-profit and depends for existence on contributions from its listeners. Pacifica's early guiding spirit, Louis Schweitzer, once described himself to editor James A. Wechsler as "a nut about the Bill of Rights."[1] Officials of the network, instead of being cowed, reminded the inquisitorial senators that "Such radio stations exist nowhere else in the world. They could not exist under a Communist or Fascist government— nor under any government which cannot abide freedom or anything but the official position in matters where it counts." As an upshot to the commotion created by the Senate subcommittee the Federal Communications Commission threatened to force the three stations off the air. It took the extraordinary position of demanding that the foundation's officials fill out questionnaires about past as well as present political affiliations, and this they refused to do. The *New York Times* editorially noted that the stations were devoted to "symphonies and symposiums" and commented: "After all the noble statements about wastelands [on the air] and the need for more educational and controversial programs, is the FCC going to nullify its preachments by a witch-hunting approach to stations that offer a place on the airwaves for unpopular views?" A threat to diversity on the airwaves was posed by the federal intervention triggered by the Senate subcommittee's action in this case, but fortunately the FCC backed down and granted the Pacifica license.

Another congressional group that has been hauling before it unorthodox thinkers by the thousands is the House Un-American Activities Committee. When a wealthy if unorthodox Cleveland industrial baron, Cyrus Eaton, proclaimed views critical of the

FBI, the committee's then chairman, the late Representative Francis Walter, immediately signed a subpoena requiring Eaton to explain himself before the committee. This was so preposterous that something or someone—possibly an envoy from the FBI— persuaded the chairman not to have the subpoena served.[2]

Attorney Frank J. Donner, a critic of the HUAC, has made this important—and creditable—charge: "The Committee's major achievement has been the transformation of the hearing into a public identification device which destroys the privacy essential to freedom. Because it strikes at the preconditions of freedom, the ever-present threat of being dropped into the Committee's goldfish bowl has been more stifling than all the repressive legislation on the books."[3]

Recently the House Un-American Activities Committee, under its new chairman, Representative Edwin Willis of Louisiana, has been following a somewhat more moderate approach, and if it must exist at all let us hope that it moves toward more responsible procedures and develops a more responsible concept of its legislative justification.

The poisonous legacy of all the terror generated by private and official rampages in search of offbeat thinkers, which reached a peak in the so-called McCarthy era of 1948-54, is still with us, however. It is less evident in the field of newspapers, books, and magazines—which perhaps are less vulnerable to hammerlocks applied by pressure groups; but it is still very evident in the production of motion pictures and television and, in some areas, painfully evident in the operation of public schools.

Dore Schary, who has spent most of his adult life in the making of motion pictures and plays, told me: "The fear is still enormous. The producers of motion pictures and TV shows will tackle daring sex themes but not daring social themes. We are being inhibited not only as a result of the McCarthy hearings, but because of the massive drive to produce items that will be all things to all men. We must not irritate or alienate the South, nor the veterans, nor the Catholics, Jews, Protestants—what we have been giving up is a basic right, the right of moral indignation and its consequent prerogative to offend." And recently Supreme Court Justice Douglas observed: "Radio and TV stations often fear their advertisers, who in turn fear non-conformists."

The focus of most of the campaigns to expose unorthodox thinking has been on the so-called "subversive." Originally the word connoted the Communist, the former Communist, the Communist sympathizer, the Communist dupe. And the "suspected subversive" was a person who had associated with or been related by blood to an alleged Communist. Today the meaning of "subversive" has splattered out to cover pacifists, opponents of nuclear testing, and many others. In the eyes of John Birchers a "com-symp" can apparently be anyone who approves of the United Nations or of integration of schools.

But let us concentrate on the original meaning of the word "subversive." All thoughtful citizens recognize that the combination of Soviet and Red Chinese ambitions and the ghastly potency of atomic weapons have produced a hazardous situation that will be with us for some time. They recognize the need for continuing vigilance. They are properly appalled when an occasional American turns out to be feeding U.S. military secrets to Soviet agents (whether for ideological reasons or for money). And they are gratified that Americans—with the help of the FBI and military intelligence agents—have apparently reduced their losses of really critical secrets to a relatively small trickle in the past few years.

At the same time, these thoughtful Americans hope that the continuing vigilance can be achieved within the framework of personal freedom and privacy enunciated in the Bill of Rights. Hysteria does not contribute to vigilance; nor does chronic suspiciousness of people's opinions.

Virtually all of the few real American spies who have been caught supplying secrets to the Soviets were elaborately careful to be tight-lipped and to pose as loyal Americans possessing only the most orthodox of opinions. It is doubtful that the we're-more-loyal-than-thou private vigilante groups or the congressional committees investigating possible subversives have ever, in the past decade of shouting or grilling, been initially responsible for uncovering a single spy who was subsequently convicted. This is a job that has been done vastly more effectively, and quietly, by executive law-enforcement agencies.

It should be noted that the first congressional committee in modern times to be concerned with un-American activities—the Dickstein Committee of the early thirties—was scrupulously careful to protect the rights of individual witnesses. It had three entrances to protect people when it held secret hearings. And the reports of the secret hearings were really secret, with a large 'SECRET' stamped at the top and bottom of the cover. In those instances where secret hearings were followed by public hearings, the witness was given a certified transcript of the secret hearing and permitted to enter his corrections or explanations on the public record. Furthermore, he could not be questioned on any subject not covered in the secret hearings. This committee served an important legislative function: it produced the Foreign Agents' Registration Act.

One member of that committee was a Texan named Martin Dies. When in due course he rose to become head of an officially designated House Un-American Activities Committee, he turned it into a trial-by-publicity circus. This tack proved to be so gratifying, politically, that it was followed assiduously by the HUAC for a quarter of a century. A sub-sequent chairman, J. Parnell Thomas, stated: "The chief function of the Committee .. . has always been the exposure of un-American individuals and their un-American activities." The HUAC sought to bring public shame upon individuals for their views. Mr. Thomas, a flamboyant man who later served a jail sentence for corruption, was probably unaware of a unanimous Supreme Court verdict in 1881 which held that Congress possessed no "general power of making inquiry into the private affairs of the citizen."[4] Recent Congresses have refused to be confined by this opinion, and the Supreme Court in recent years has not forced them to be so.

Legislative committees concerned with alleged "un-American" activities have moved in to create a fourth branch of the government. They began to persecute the individuals who could not be prosecuted. An individual in this land still can usually not be prosecuted simply for having unorthodox views, even if those views seem bizarre, foolish, or misguided. The HUAC rushed in to fill what it felt was a gap overlooked by the Founding Fathers. In its fashion it has indicted, it has prosecuted, it has judged wrong thinkers. It has set its own rules, which have left the witness vastly more naked of procedural rights than if he were a criminal. The witness hasn't been able to cross-examine his accusers. Often he hasn't even been advised in advance of the charges. And in our society the charge against him of being a possible "Commie" or onetime Commie or Commie sympathizer has become a more terrible charge than being accused of being a thief, a con man, a draft dodger, or other common criminal.

A witness before the HUAC soon learned that his best chance of escaping public disgrace—and probable loss of his job—was to be a "friendly" witness. He confessed all, he publicly repented his sins of wrong thinking, he demonstrated that he had taken *affirmative* action to prove his conversion to orthodoxy. One way he did this was by naming everyone he knew who shared his old, wrong views. (A man in Hollywood named 162 acquaintances, apparently a record.)

The HUAC usually didn't bother to call the people named —unless they sounded particularly interesting—because it just didn't have the time. But it needed the names for another purpose: to offer as weapons to its conservative allies, the private vigilante groups who supported its works and helped it get ever larger appropriations. Names were the weapons. Once the names were added to lists and printed in an official congressional report, all the people named were fair game for anyone in their community or nation to charge them with being Reds or at least fellow travelers. There was little chance the person named could strike back with a libel suit. Probably the biggest list of all put out under the HUAC label was a 2000-page, seven-volume summary of suspected organizations and individuals issued by a subcommittee in 1944. The index contained 22,000 names, mostly individuals, many of whom admittedly were neither Reds nor fellow travelers. It was such a grab-bag list that the full committee re-portedly ordered it suppressed, but only after many copies had got out to private and governmental agencies that began using it as a check list.[5]

Who were the Communists in those days? My impressions from that turbulent era (1934-46), and from what I've learned about it since, are that a good many Americans became fully, partially, or innocently involved with Communism for reasons other than a desire to overthrow the U.S. form of government. It is my impression that some, though I think they were misguided and often duped, were primarily trying to demonstrate their opposition to the Nazi-Fascist advances in Europe. In the late thirties, until Premier Stalin of Russia made his cynical pact with Hitler at the outset of World War II, the Communists at home and abroad were taking the lead in pressing for a "Popular Front" of all democratic parties against fascism. And for three years starting in 1942, lest we forget, the Soviet Union was officially an ally of the United States in fighting world fascism.

Justice Douglas, in speaking of such factors, states: "From reading many records in cases involving Communists, I gather that many who joined may not have had subversion as a purpose. Some seemed to be sheer sentimentalists; others seemed utterly confused. Yet there has been a readiness to identify all who joined the party at any period of its existence with all of the aims espoused by it. That is guilt by association—a concept which is foreign to our history."[6]

Later not only the HUAC but other congressional committees began compiling and printing lists of alleged Communists and possible sympathizers, and so did several state legislative committees. The list with the strongest ring of authority was issued by U.S. Attorney General Tom Clark in 1947. This was a list not of individuals but rather of organizations that the Justice Department was convinced were subversive. This list has regularly been revised. As first drawn up it was presented as one factor in evaluating an individual's total record. But quickly it became the ultimate in Bibles for security clearance. In 1961 Mr. Clark, by then a Supreme Court Justice, offered a confession to Columbia University law students. He said: "Perhaps we should, as I look at it now, have given the parties an opportunity to be heard before we issued it."

Congressional investigators discovered in the late forties that the happiest hunting ground for dangerous thinkers was in the entertainment world. This world, dedicated largely to fantasy, had more than its share of emotionally oriented people who in the world of crisis of the 1935-45 decade had lent their names to anti-fascist or humanitarian causes that were taken over by, or set up by, Communists. More important, perhaps, was the fact that these people in entertainment were Big Names with glamor and sex appeal who could assure the congressional probers daily front-page headlines. Foray after foray was made into Hollywood, and at this writing some congressmen are talking of the need for still another.

From the first, in 1947, came the famous list of the unfriendly Hollywood Ten. The ten had refused to cooperate with the HUAC, and so were indicted and jailed for contempt of Congress. Actually there had been nineteen unfriendlies but the committee hadn't bothered to prosecute the other nine. By the time the HUAC reopened its Hollywood hearings in 1951 black-listing or gray-listing was rampant. There were not only the HUAC lists, but the American Legion sumitted to producers a list of 300 names. John Cogley reports that a Legion official later "cheerfully admitted that the list was compiled from 'scattered public sources.'"[7]

After considerable anguish and, for many, periods of "unemployability," the great majority of the people on the Legion list managed to satisfy the Legion officials that they were not to be considered risks. Usually they did this by writing a letter to the Legion office or paying a visit.

One analysis of the Legion's activities published in the *Stanford Law Review* concluded that the Legion's test for spotlighting Hollywood personages with unfavorable publicity included all people "who have been at any time in any way associated with an activity in which members of the Communist party were in some way also associated."[8]

Another list of suspects was built on the basis of Hollywood personages who signed a "Committee for the First Amendment" advertisement protesting the abuse of constitutional rights then going on in Hollywood.

By the time of the 1951 hearings, many of the unfriendlies were learning that their only hope of salvaging their careers was to become "friendly" HUAC witnesses. The case of a Hollywood personality who had been known as an unfriendly has become a classic. He went before the HUAC, confessed his sin of having once during the war been a Communist, but explained he had withdrawn from the Party five years earlier. Then came the demand that he name names of all persons he had known as Communists during that earlier wartime period. He protested that virtually all had since withdrawn from the Party and so it would needlessly injure them. One leading HUAC committeeman wondered why there was a need to force him to name names since the committee already apparently had all the names. But the committee counsel insisted that he name the names. The actor made a final anguished plea: "Please don't present me with the choice of either being in contempt of this committee and going to jail or forcing me to really crawl through the mud to be an informer, for what purpose. . . . I don't think this is American justice."

After an executive conference, he gave up and named names. Furthermore, two years later, as a part of the ritual of proving his conversion, he felt impelled to write the committee a letter explaining he hadn't really meant what he blurted out about crawling through the mud.

Meanwhile personalities in radio and television were coming under fire, not so much from congressional committees—though they played a role—as from frightened sponsors. Veterans' groups and other right-wing groups learned to their delight that sponsors panicked very easily. And so here, too, the list-makers went to work digging through the multitudes of published—and thus libel-free—legislative lists. The most celebrated list, called *Red Channels*, contained the names of 151 radio-TV personages who were alleged to have left-wing associations. It was published in 1950 as a "special report" ($1.00 per copy to the public) by three men associated with American Business Consultants, which also published a weekly newsletter called *Counterattack, the Newsletter of Facts on Communism*. ABC was strongly staffed by ex-FBI men. The editors were careful to libel-proof their *Red Channels* by pointing out that some of the activities listed may well have been innocent. Soon it was known as "the Bible of Madison Avenue." A CBS official was reported to have exclaimed: "My God, it's straight out of Kafka, isn't it? These three gents have the whole damn industry stymied. . . ."[9] Other gray and black lists quickly appeared, including *Firing Line*, a listing compiled by Syracuse Post No. 41 of the American Legion. The post happened to have a most powerful and militant ally in Syracuse named Laurence Johnson, who controlled several supermarkets. He frequently bombarded sponsors, advertising agencies, and networks with warnings implying a boycott whenever a program sponsored by any of the thousands of food producers using his shelf space employed personalities that he felt might be Communists or supporters of Communist causes.

A number of the major networks and agencies reacted to all these pressures by setting up "security" officers, dropping controversial personalities, and arranging for the screening of talent being considered for future shows.

I had an opportunity to confer with a man who screened more than 2000 actors or other entertainers, primarily for certain popular TV entertainment shows. I'll call him Mr. Diggs. He was paid by one of the nation's larger advertising agencies. In some instances he would be asked to make a check because of a specific query about a performer's "desirability." In several instances such queries originated with a certain influential religious figure and would reach Mr. Diggs by the following route: the eminent cleric would get in touch with the wife of the chairman of the company sponsoring the program in question . . . who would tell her husband . . . who would pass it on to one of his vice-presidents . . . who would advise the vice-president in charge of radio and TV of the advertising agency . . . who would inform Mr. Diggs's special, confidential contact at the agency. As the system evolved, however, just about every performer not on Mr. Diggs's "known-to-be-clear" list would get a check.

Mr. Diggs riffled through his files and pulled out twelve reports he had made on well-known performers. One was an accordionist, one a dancer, one a singer, one a comic, one a comedienne, and so on.

Many of these reports began with a standard, agreed phrase: "None of the government or private specialist records consulted regularly list the subject's name." It meant he had—-as instructed—checked the following:

1. The HUAC's cumulative indices of all the tens of thousands of individuals who for one reason or another over two decades had gotten themselves on an HUAC index.

2. The cumulative index of the Senate Internal Security subcommittee (Judiciary). (About 36,000 names.)

3. The cumulative index of witnesses who had appeared before any congressional or state legislative committee concerned with subversive activities. (Among the states where hearings have been held: California, Michigan, Pennsylvania, and Ohio.) The California group, incidentally, had come up with some of the wildest "subversive" charges on record (e.g., Thomas Mann and Dr. Albert Einstein).

4. The index of the permanent Subcommittee on Investigations of the Senate Committee on Government Operations. This includes the notorious witch hunts conducted on behalf of Senator Joseph McCarthy by his brash young counsel Roy Cohn. (About 4000 names.)

5. Report on the Army-McCarthy hearings. (3000 names.)

6. The Attorney General's list of subversive organizations.

7. The HUAC's special list of alleged subversive organizations and publications.

8. The 1952 annual report of the State of California Joint Legislative Committee to Investigate Un-American Activities. This contained all that committee's mish-mash from 1945 to 1952 inclusive.

9. *Red Channels.*

After this standardized check of records, Mr. Diggs would probe as the circumstances indicated. In ten of the twelve cases he checked a contact at the American Legion, and in eight cases he checked Aware, Inc., the vigilante group dedicated to fighting "the Communist conspiracy in entertainment-communications." In five cases he checked "Investigator for syndicated columnist with voluminous files."... In four cases he checked "The personnel security official of a major network."... In five cases he checked "The personnel security specialist for major national sponsors ... In two cases he checked a contact at "The Catholic War Veterans."... And in several instances he checked "the writer's confidential contact" at the HUAC and at the Senate Internal Security subcommittee in Washington.

In the beginning the checking was just for "our special interest"—politics. But later the advertising agency also wanted to know about the performer's morals and whether he or she had any criminal record. Mr. Diggs explained: "It all started with the political investigations. The moral and criminal investigations would never have started if it had not been for the political interest."

Thus it was that one of his twelve reports was devoted almost entirely to an extremely intimate description of a celebrated actress'"psychiatric condition" produced by spells of depression over feelings of professional failure. In one of the twelve reports there was mention of an actress who was "red-flagged" at the insurance companies because of fur and jewelry losses; in another he told of an actor's tax problems; and in still another of the fact that the wife of the performer was overusing "stimulants."

The result of all this was that though Mr. Diggs reported to the agency that only one of the twelve personalities (a playwright) was an "absolute risk" for the performance in question (on political grounds), he gave only three performers unqualified okays. All the rest (eight) were okayed with qualifications. They were safe for the specific performance in'question, but further checks should be made—by Mr. Diggs, of course—if further uses of the personality were contemplated.

A report Mr. Diggs made in 1958 on a dancer illustrates the maddening problem you face in getting work if you are on an important list of wrong thinkers. I'll call the dancer Mary Fixx. Five years earlier, Mr. Diggs had reported to the agency that Mary was on a confidential list of the HUAC as a onetime Communist Party member and was due to be called before the committee. Therefore she was an absolute risk for the performance in question. In 1957 (after four years) he was asked to make a second report on her. This report indicated that the HUAC still had her name on the back of its stove, but since it hadn't got around to calling her an official had assured Mr. Diggs that the committee would not publicly protest her employment for the specific performance in question.

The pertinency of Miss Fixx's past political thinking to her present capabilities as a dancing performer was never considered a factor of consequence. She was "controversial," period.

Now in 1958 Mr. Diggs was again asked to make soundings because she was wanted for a show. He reported that the American Legion was "no longer actively interested in Subject." He further reported that he had learned from his "confidential source in Security Section of the U.S. State Department's Passport Division" that Mary had got a passport without difficulty and so obviously was not now red-flagged there. He also gathered that Miss Fixx had had one of those ritualistic "come clean" talks with an FBI representative and had satisfied the FBI official that she was now, at least, a good loyal citizen. Furthermore Mr. Diggs's contact at the Senate Internal Security subcommittee said that that group had no current interest in Mary.

But the HUAC was still unwilling to say that it had lost interest in her. It still had her on that list. And though it was true it hadn't got to her in five years it might still "at some future, unspecified time, want to call her," Mr. Diggs reported. He assured himself, however, that the HUAC could not possibly get to her within the next few months, and so was able to advise the agency that Mary was not an employment risk for the date of performance in question.

In a few instances, Mr. Diggs moved from checking people out to helping them get "clearances," as did many other investigators. One of the people he helped "clear" subsequently won an Oscar, another won a Pulitzer prize, and a third won an Emmy award. The Oscar winner, a beloved, famous star, had been a witness before the Senate Internal Security subcommittee. Mr. Diggs arranged through a female aide he knew on the subcommittee to have a letter containing the standard phrases for clearance placed before the chairman while the chairman was in a pleasant mood.

The letter drafted for the senator's signature was addressed to Mr. Diggs's contact at the advertising agency. It stated: "After a careful examination of the testimony given by Mr. _____ it was and is my conclusion that he testified freely, fully, and frankly, and that any stigma heretofore attached to his reputation was effectively wiped out by his testimony. I further feel that Mr. _____ is a loyal and patriotic American and that it would be unjust to penalize him for any mistakes of judgment he may have made in the past." The chairman signed it.

Teachers, scientists, government employees, journalists, and others with alleged "stigmas" for wrong thinking attached to their reputations have over the years been sharing congressional griddles with entertainers. And the private vigilante groups dedicated to right thinking (as defined by right-wingers) have continued to intimidate TV producers, school officials, corporate employers, and some newspaper proprietors with their power to denounce as dangerous anyone of whom they disapprove.

Some of the more virulent symptoms of antagonism toward political wrong thinking began to subside in much of the United States with the belated overthrow of Senator Joe McCarthy. Several specific developments in recent years have meanwhile helped to moderate the excesses of both the congressional mind-watchers and the private name-callers, in most parts of the country.

The Supreme Court in two decisions has offered some protection to citizens against being unreasonably hounded by congressional committees. In the Watkins case of 1957, the Court held that the resolution under which the HUAC was created was so "vague" that any witness was entitled to insist that the *pertinency* of any question addressed to him be explained and established. Chief Justice Warren stated: "There is no congressional power to expose for the sake of exposure. The public is, of course, entitled to be informed concerning the workings of its government. That cannot be inflated into a general power to expose where the predominant result can only be an invasion of the private rights of individuals."[10]

In a second, more recent decision of importance, a narrow 5-4 one, the Court held in early 1963 that legislative investigators cannot dig freely into the affairs of a group in search of Communist connections unless that group has already been linked clearly with "subversive or other illegal or improper activities." On the other hand, in two other decisions to be discussed (Barenblatt and Wilkinson) the Court encouraged the HUAC in its determination to investigate the private beliefs of citizens in connection with an inquiry into Communist influence.

As for the private groups quick to attach the label "Communist sympathizer," they were given reason for pause by the verdict of a New York jury in June 1962. At issue was a bulletin put out six years earlier by Aware, Inc., which specialized in publishing charges that, whether so intended or not, were frequently used in compiling black lists in the radio and TV industry. The bulletin in this instance charged that a humorous radio and TV performer, John Henry Faulk, had appeared at or sponsored numerous Communist-front functions. Questions about his loyalty were raised. This bulletin was given extra-wide distribution among newspapers, sponsors, networks, etc., and was also brought to the attention of sponsors of programs on which Mr. Faulk appeared through the efforts of Mr. Johnson, the Syracuse supermarket operator. The campaign was viewed by Mr. Faulk as a deliberate smear, since he had been critical of Aware and had run successfully for office in the American Federation of Television and Radio Artists on a middle-of-the-road ticket that was both anti-Communist and anti-black-listing.

Mr. Faulk's career on national radio and television was ruined by the bulletin at a time when he was earning $35,000 a year. He had great difficulty getting TV or radio jobs in various cities where he felt forced to flee, and finally retreated into a small advertising agency in Texas.

He sued Aware, Mr. Johnson, and the author of the bulletin, Vincent Harnett (who had also been a co-author of *Red Channels*), for libel. The defendants were unable to demonstrate the truth of the implications in the bulletin, and the jury awarded Mr. Faulk a total of $3,500,000 in damages, the largest award for libel in history. The judge, in refusing to set aside the award, said it "was evidently intended to express the conscience of the community." Mr. Johnson, a reputed multimillionaire, died a few days before the verdict was rendered. His estate made a settlement with Mr. Faulk for $175,000, all that he has collected so far. As this is written, an appellate court has ordered that unless Mr. Faulk would accept the reduced sum of $550,000 a new trial would have to take place.

During the trial, two noted witnesses who appeared in support of Mr. Faulk offered comments of particular interest. Garry Moore, famed TV master of ceremonies, testified that the black-listing of entertainers was "a little like fighting six men in a closet with the lights out—you can't tell who's hitting you." And producer David Susskind testified that during one period at the height of the black-listing he had been required to submit 5000 names of performers, writers, directors, and even cameramen to the sponsor's advertising agency, Young & Rubicam. He said that about 1500 of the names submitted came back as "politically undesirable."

Today the black-listing has eased. Mr. Faulk is back at work. But *Variety* reports that as of mid-1963 there were still a good many black-listed artists in broadcasting who were finding it extremely difficult to get decent jobs. As for Hollywood, one estimate is that the unofficial black list is now down to about 100 individuals, or less than half its size in the fifties.

A final factor that may have helped to moderate the Red hunting and name calling is publicity about the sad state of the U.S. Communist Party nowadays. A former FBI agent, Jack Levine, has stated that the Party membership has dwindled to 8500, and that nearly 1500 of these dues-payers are undercover FBI agents!

Although much of the virulence and flamboyance has gone out of the Red hunting, we have a heritage of forms. The once high-flying right-wing "clearance boys" of the entertainment world have pretty largely disappeared. But in their place we have the corporate specialists and other official clearance experts. Increasingly broadcasters are demanding that performers sign political affidavits that, among other things, require them to state that they have never been members of the Communist Party. The American Civil Liberties Union, in protesting the affidavits, commented: "It is no secret that the abuse [of black-listing] has been institutionalized and made part of the administrative machinery of program casting." And though, with the elevation of Edwin Willis to the chairmanship, the HUAC has seemingly come uder more responsible leadership and is holding fewer hearings, it managed to get from Congress this past year its largest appropriation on record ($360,000). The vote was 385 to 20.

In early 1963, before Mr. Willis' advancement to the chairman-ship, the HUAC began summoning citizens from many sections of the country for a probe of what it called "Communist infiltration of the peace movement." The ACLU asserted to the HUAC that such an inquiry "will inevitably stifle the voices of those who dissent from government policies in the Cold War. . . . The Civil Liberties Union is not arguing the pros and cons of the program offered by the peace movement, for this is not our organizational concern. However, we do note that the program has been carried out in the open for everyone to see."

All generalizations about the easing of hostility toward un-fashionable opinions must note some conspicuous exceptions. They seemingly prevail in a geographic belt about two hundred miles wide that runs across the southern part of the country. The belt starts on the East Coast between Charleston and Jackson-ville and runs slightly south till it hits mid-Texas and then swings northwesterly until it hits the Pacific between San Diego and Santa Barbara. It includes Montgomery, Jackson, Baton Rouge,

Dallas, and Phoenix on the way. The lack of generosity toward people with differing views can't be entirely a result of warm climate, because most of Florida is below the belt, and when the belt hits the West Coast it seems to swing northward.

Consider the western half of the belt first. We have recently witnessed U.N. Ambassador Adlai Stevenson being spat upon and struck when he went to Dallas to talk about the United Nations. The preceding sentence was written before President Kennedy was assassinated in the same area. Ambassador Stevenson had called the White House to warn that perhaps the President's visit should be canceled because of "the mood of unprecedented madness in Dallas." A Dallas newspaper had commented, after Mr. Stevenson's visit, that it was becoming dangerous for anyone with unpopular views to come to the city and urged the city to reform. It was perhaps an accident of fate that the alleged assassin, a Texan from the fanatic fringe, chose Dallas as his site for shooting, but the *Dallas Times Herald* editorially commented that "first there had to be the seeds of hate. . . ." The state's Governor John Connally deplored the fact that its citizens had permitted extremism to become a fashionable fad. Possibly now residents of the area have been shocked into a more responsible attitude toward dissent. The city's mayor urged the citizens to learn to "enter into controversy without hatred, disagreement without disparagement. . . ."

Some dogmatic Texans might ponder a remark made by civil libertarian Roger Baldwin, who has stated: "My freedom to wave my fist ends where your nose begins."

And we have the president of California's State Board of Education, Thomas Braden, being denounced as a "Communist" by his neighbors in Oceanside, California, because of his efforts to be fair-minded and to resist pressures from the super-patriots to indoctrinate the state's school children. I suspect he was thinking primarily of populous Southern California when he said his state "is rapidly becoming a chamber of political horrors. California has the John Birch Society. It has the Liberty Torch Bearers. It has the Keep America Committee. It has the California Committee to Combat Communism. It has the American Birthright Committee. It has the Citizens for Moral Action and the Network of Patriotic Letter Writers...." He said that scores of "study groups meet in secret to discuss their neighbors and come out in public ... to denounce teachers, editors, ministers, textbooks, Earl Warren, and the twentieth century."[11]

In the political campaign of 1962, the hottest issue in California was the Francis Amendment. It would have deprived any member of a "subversive" group of government employment or tax exemption, and would have left the defining of "subversive" to a great variety of interpreters including county grand juries and U.S. marshals. The amendment would also have subjected to a loyalty test every individual or group seeking to use public property for a public discussion. One powerful promoter of the amendment was the Los Angeles Chamber of Commerce. It failed to pass, thanks to the hard work or good sense of several million Californians who rejected this attack on the Bill of Rights.

As for the eastern half of the belt, there the intolerance of non-conforming views is more notorious, thanks to extensive news coverage of the crises involving civil rights. In Baton Rouge at least fifteen religious leaders are alleged to have been victims of telephone tapping by local segregationists with the help of state officials. The ministers had signed an "affirmation of religious principles" that called racial discrimination "a violation of the divine law of love." One businessman who was charged by a federal grand jury with wiretapping taught Sunday school in the same Baptist church that was headed by a minister who was one of the victims of the tapping.

In Alabama a copy of a presumably private telegram sent out of state via Western Union by a former state president of the National Association for the Advancement of Colored People was presented by an official of the telegraph company, under subpoena, as state's evidence. When a Negro lawyer protested invasion of privacy and demanded that the telegraph official explain how the state had learned about the telegram, the company official would only reply: "I don't know."

The noted editor-columnist from Atlanta, Ralph McGill, commented in 1963: "We are grown used to seeing the hate-twisted faces of young persons and adults in news pictures and on television, crying out the most violent threats and expressing a virulence of venom against their country and its authority. All this is a piece of the mosaic of hate that has poisoned this country...."

The hostility to non-conforming thoughts is probably most intense in Mississippi. A highly respected historian at the University of Mississippi, Dr. James W. Silver, fairly summed up the situation in that state when he described it as a totalitarian society enslaved by "obedience to an official orthodoxy almost identical with the pro-slavery philosophy." He is reported to keep a loaded gun in his home in Oxford, Mississippi. When I visited the campus in late 1962, I chatted with another professor known to be critical of the flagrant way the state had interfered in university affairs by trying to dictate admissions policy. He confided that for the protection of his family he kept a shotgun right by his front door, and had felt forced to teach his wife and children how to use it.

These are the extremes. But it is still shocking that they occur in the land that was the world's foremost fountain-head of liberty. Perhaps it is inevitable that tests of the people's will to freedom occur. Congressman Kastenmeier of Wisconsin has concluded:

"The defense of the freedom to present unconventional ideas is never popular. Yet that freedom is what stands between free men and the totalitarian state."

14. The Right to Be Free of Police Mistreatment

"If the government becomes a lawbreaker, it breeds contempt for the law; it invites every man to become a law unto himself."—Justice Louis D. Brandeis

Justice Brandeis was dissenting in the epochal 1928 Supreme Court decision in the Olmstead case, which upheld police who had resorted to wiretapping. Although the decision represented a great setback for individual liberty and privacy, the argument over it within the court engendered some eloquent warnings in dissent that quite possibly will be cited long after the specific issue involved has been forgotten. Justice Oliver Wendell Holmes warned: "We have to choose, and for my part I think it is less evil that some criminals should escape than that the Government should play an ignoble part." And Justice Brandeis offered this admonition: "Men born to freedom are naturally alert to repel invasion of their liberty by evil-minded rulers. The greatest dangers to liberty lurk in insidious encroachment by men of zeal, well-meaning but without understanding."

More and more often, law enforcers with well-meaning zeal but little understanding have been taking short cuts that violate the constitutional rights or statutory protections of each American citizen. Other practices, though possibly legal, set dismaying examples of unfairness and indecency. Since unpopular figures are usually the victims of these un-constitutional or indecent acts by police, too many Americans have failed to see that their own hard-won rights are threatened.

Such short cuts are taken in the search for evidence, in the grabbing of suspects, in the way suspects are treated once they have been taken into custody. For example, there has been in the past decade heavy reliance upon secret wiretapping and microphoning, particularly the latter, because there are very few laws to curb it. When Samuel Dash, a former district attorney of Philadelphia, made his survey of wiretapping and the beginnings of electronic eavesdropping in the late 1950s he found police in all cities he visited trying to make use of both techniques, and often quite open in acknowledging it. Mr. Dash's findings indicated that the New York police had about 200 plain-clothes men working virtually full time at wiretapping. (And quite a few New York policemen apparently were using their own private tapping equipment to locate bookies and then extort money from them.)

Mr. Dash and his colleagues had this to say of microphoning in Louisiana: "The use of microphones is universal in New Orleans and Baton Rouge. . . . In Baton Rouge all the law-enforcement officers use concealed microphones and transmitters in criminal investigations. Both the state police and the sheriff's offices have indicated that they are presently contemplating purchasing parabolic microphones. All law-enforcement officers are equipped with pocket recorders and make frequent use of them. Practically all the law-enforcement officers use concealed cameras."[1]

Mr. Dash has since conceded that as district attorney he himself engaged in wiretapping in the years before he undertook his study. He said: "A DA, in office, catches an occupational disease. He resents impediments in his way that prevent him from collecting evidence to convict criminals. So the temptation to wiretap is strong." (Wiretapping, incidentally, is reported to be growing in Holland and West Germany.)

Law enforcers in the U.S. at the moment are tending to become more cautious about the use of wiretapping.

Microphoning is another matter. In most states there is little to restrain the police from the use of this kind of electronic surveillance. A few years ago it was disclosed in legislative hearings that the police of the publicly owned New York Transit Authority (in close cooperation with police) had been microphoning the meeting rooms of a union of motormen that the Transit Authority disliked. The bugging had been going on for two years! It continued even after New York State passed a law making microphoning a felony for anyone except "any law enforcement officer while acting lawfully and in his official capacity in the investigation, detection or prosecution of crime." The union was not charged with being a criminal organization; it was a victim of labor spying. What is particularly ironic is that one of the bugged hotel meeting rooms was in a hall known as the Brandeis Room, in honor of the nation's greatest defender of privacy!

In mid-1963, thirty-five years after Justice Brandeis' denunciation of telephone wiretapping by government agents, Justice William J. Brennan felt impelled to make a comparable dissent against use of hidden microphones. In his dissent in a case involving the use of a hidden microphone in Massachusetts by an internal revenue agent trying to record a bribe attempt, Justice Brennan said: "Electronic surveillance . . . makes the police omniscient; and police omniscience is one of the most effective tools of tyranny."

Unknown to most citizens, the U.S. Post Office cooperates with local, state, and federal policing agencies in instituting a form of surveillance called the "mail cover." When a mail cover is placed on you, all first-class mail addressed to you is held aside while a record is made of the sender, his address, and the date of mailing. One such cover quoted to me was issued to a mailman on March 15, 1963, and read: "Effective immediately through April 15 forward all first class mail each day to the supervisor in charge that is addressed to the following: (Name). The mail will be returned to you in time for delivery on the same day."

The legality of the mail cover is clearly dubious but has not yet been specifically tested in the courts, at least in this century. In 1877 the U.S. Supreme Court held that a letter while in the mails is entitled to the same protection as a person's papers in his home. And the United States Code (Sec. 1702, title 18) makes it a crime to take a letter out of a post office or from a letter carrier with design to pry into the business or secrets of another.

We are largely indebted to U.S. Senator Edward V. Long of Missouri for forcing the Post Office Department to disclose its use of this practice. On the Senate floor he charged: "It has come to my attention that the Post Office Department has available to law-enforcement officials an espionage procedure which may be used to interfere with the privacy of the American people.... Information is obtained about the individual which is none of the Government's business. It reminds one of the tactics used in a police state where the Government wants to know who is corresponding with whom." He had earlier demanded full details. While the department was pondering his demand, an unnamed spokesman for the department, questioned by a curious correspondent for the *St. Louis Post-Dispatch* in Senator Long's home state, tried to belittle the mail cover. He said it was used relatively seldom in the last few years and only for apprehension of fugitives.

A month later, however, Senator Long finally got an answer from the department's general counsel, Louis J. Doyle, who disclosed quite a different picture. Mr. Doyle said that currently "the total number of such covers runs between 500 and 750." If each cover is for a month—as was the one I cited—this would suggest that an annual total of 6000 to 9000 orders for covers might be reasonably conceivable. Furthermore it turned out the covers were not confined just to "fugitives." Long reported to the Senate that mail covers were also being used for "investigating mail frauds, use of the mails for pornography, and income-tax violations." In the case of suspected income tax fraud, inspectors could by use of a mail cover trace all persons and companies with whom the suspect was conducting business, and furthermore the inspectors presumably could later question the senders of the letters about the contents of the mail or the suspect's relationship with them.

In defending mail covers, Mr. Doyle contended that no statute deals specifically with mail covers and that an 1893 law permits postmasters to help police track a fugitive from justice. (This may explain the stress that the first, unnamed spokesman placed on fugitives.) Mr. Doyle argued further that an individual's rights are not violated because there is no law requiring a person sending a letter through the mail to put his return address on it!

The military postal officials are apparently even more cooperative with investigators. An officer stationed at New London inadvertently came upon a note in his mailbox which read: "Put a hold on all this man's mail." He was under observation because he is a socialist.

Currently the most flagrant abuses of individual rights by police occur in the way the police apprehend and treat persons suspected of possible involvement in a crime.

Alan Barth, editor and constitutional scholar, points out that arbitrary arrest has long been a measure of despotism. It constituted "one of the bitterest grievances against George III recited in the American Declaration of Independence."[2] These grievances inspired the authors of the Constitution to insist upon the Fourth Amendment provision that a citizen can be arrested only upon "probable cause," meaning only upon reasonable grounds.

Today the hurt inflicted by arbitrary arrest is perhaps greater than it was two centuries ago. As we've noted, both government and industry now tend to ask all job applicants whether they have ever been arrested or "held for investigation." A "yes" answer is apt to become an automatic knockout factor. The district attorney in Los Angeles was quoted a few years ago as conceding: ". . . There is a very real handicap to an applicant for employment by the existence of an arrest record. . . . Many large employers cannot make their determination on an individual employee basis. . . . They adopt a general policy on this matter which requires rejection of any employee having an arrest record regardless of what happened after the prospective employee was arrested; whether he was dismissed . . . etc."

Consider then the prevailing police practices today across the country. All of the reporting of crimes every-hour-on-the-hour has put enormous pressure on the police to prove their "efficiency" by catching the culprit before too many newscasts have passed.

So a dragnet is often thrown out. Everyone who could conceivably be, or know about, the culprit is pulled in; and the police interrogate at leisure. The *Uniform Crime Reports* showing U.S. arrests by categories disclose that in two recent years, 1959 and 1960, the number of arrests on "suspicion" was close to 100,000 each year. As Mr. Barth points out, "suspicion" is not a crime anywhere in the United States. Suspicion is a far cry from the constitutional requirement of "probable cause." In Mr. Barth's view nearly "every one of these arrests was unlawful; nearly every one was in itself a crime." Yet a Senate committee heard testimony in 1962 that there had never been in recent decades a prosecution against a law-enforcement officer for depriving a person of his liberty by arresting him on "suspicion."

The overwhelming majority of people arrested on "suspicion"—and thus given the stigma of an arrest record—are released without being charged with anything. Professor Caleb Foote of the University of Pennsylvania Law School reported that over a four-year period 95 per cent of all persons arrested in Baltimore on suspicion were discharged. He found that of 187 persons arrested for "investigation" during one year in Lincoln, Nebraska, 184 were dismissed.

In Detroit during the late 1950s one third of all arrests were for "investigation" and were made without warrants. ...In Philadelphia the American Civil Liberties Union reported receiving a great many complaints in 1962 of people picked up by the police "on sight" without warrants. Many said the arresting officers told them they were under orders "to pick you up every time we see you," merely on the ground of a past record of gambling. Such arrests helped the police force maintain the appearance of being on its toes in enforcing the anti-gambling laws. ... In Chicago an analysis of 2038 police "arrest slips" made in 1959 by the Illinois Division of the ACLU showed that half of the prisoners produced in felony court had been held without charge for at least seventeen hours. . . . In Washington, D.C., during some recent years virtually none of the thousands of persons arrested "for investigation" was ever charged with any crime. This dragneting practice became so notorious that in 1963 the District of Columbia commissioners promised to put a halt to it.

There has recently been a clear attempt to insinuate the concept that restraints just for interrogation require less justification than "arrests," which require "probable cause." There has been an apparent effort to blur the point at which an "arrest" begins. Logic would suggest that an arrest begins the moment a citizen is forcibly detained. In California the law states that a defendant must be taken before a magistrate "without unnecessary delay" but adds "and in any event, within two days after his arrest, excluding Sundays and holidays . . ."!

In cities where police have been careless in throwing out dragnets and hauling in people with no basis of probable cause, civic groups that are concerned and civil rights committees of bar associations could organize a very effective deterrent. They could provide counsel in the most flagrant cases and initiate a series of suits for false arrest. All they need to do is prove the person was arrested without probable cause. Suits for false arrest can cost city governments tens of thousands of dollars if they are lost and are a great nuisance even if not lost. Several such suits would inspire any city's police department to show a greater respect for individual rights.

And all citizens should be educated to understand that when government officials begin questioning them in their homes, on the street, or in a station house they are under no legal compulsion to respond. This applies whether the questioner is a policeman, a housing inspector, or an investigator checking on a neighbor.

The use of heavy-handed and often illegal tactics in making arrests appears to occur with particular frequency when the suspects are members of racial minority groups. Such manhandling has been especially common when Southern Negroes have been involved in protests against abuse of their civil rights. These abuses of constitutional rights may meet with no serious criticism from the general public if prejudice runs high.

Members of another minority group also are often taken into custody on highly questionable grounds. These are the sexual deviates, who number several million in the population. In the minds of police and other officials in many cities an aura of criminality surrounds the homosexual. Landlords can be subjected to penalties in New York for renting apartments or houses to homosexuals. A police official of Tampa was quoted as saying that he planned to run every homosexual out of town. And within three months there were 130 arrests.

The most dubious of the tactics frequently used against homosexuals by the police is the technique of entrapment. An inspector in Chicago who considers himself an expert on deviates actively tries to lure men into compromising situations by saying, "Come on up, honey." He arrests all who come to the parties he stages. And most subsequently lose their jobs.

In Washington, D.C., detectives of the morals division have been reportedly loitering about parks, posing as homosexuals and inviting pickups, or as derelicts eager to do what is necessary to get a bed for the night.

A national organization concerned with the problems of homophiles, the Mattachine Foundation, has been able in some instances to help deviates in legal battles against charges brought by police when enticement or outright entrapment was involved. Several years ago it helped a man in Los Angeles whom I'll call John Doe be the first homosexual successfully to defend himself against a "lewd vagrancy" charge in the state of California.[3] In this case a member of the vice squad, posing as a homosexual, accosted Doe, who feared the man might be a robber and sought only to get away from him. The man followed Doe for more than a mile and then allegedly elbowed his way into Doe's home. When Doe continued to resist his advances, the stranger started to disrobe and placed Doe's hand on his thigh. Then he arrested Doe for lewd vagrancy.

I imagine that most homosexuals would accept as reasonable the right of the heterosexual majority (by a margin of 20-1) to use the force of law to protect its minors and all unwilling adults from solicitation by homosexuals. Many might concede that the heterosexual majority has a moral basis for discouraging, by police action, conspicuous display of homosexual affection in public places.

But, as I see it, what two consenting adult homosexuals do quietly in the privacy of a home to satisfy their particular deep-seated emotional needs may be of interest to spiritual or medical authorities, but should be of no legitimate interest to the police. And a policeman should have no right to make an arrest after enticing a homosexual into such a private setting.

The legal profession seems to be moving, slowly, toward a more dispassionate and fair-minded view of deviates. In 1962 the American Law Institute, which includes many of the nation's most distinguished legal authorities, unveiled a model penal code that had been ten years in preparation. One provision of the code adopts the view that the criminal law should not punish any kind of sexual relations between consenting adults in private. The drafters of the code recognized that every individual is entitled to protection against state interference in his personal affairs when he is not hurting others. Illinois has, at this writing, moved to adopt the viewpoint expressed in the model code.

Let us return to the general problem of police mistreatment. Manhandling of persons once they have been arrested is certainly not a new phenomenon in criminology. Still, recent episodes—some involving new scientific methods for obtaining evidence—hardly fit our concept of twentieth-century justice and decency. A district court in Los Angeles ruled against a woman who brought a claim of unlawful search and seizure because she was required to disrobe in a police station and submit to a search of body openings. An appeal is being taken.

In New Mexico intoxication was established by withdrawing a sample of blood from a man's body while he was lying unconscious in the emergency room of a hospital after an accident; the evidence was deemed acceptable. On the other hand, the U.S. Supreme Court threw out evidence obtained by a Los Angeles deputy sheriff in the so-called "stomach pump" case involving a man named Rochin.[4] The sheriffs broke into Rochin's bedroom after hearing that he might be in illegal possession of morphine. At the sight of the raiders he put two pills in his mouth. The police tried to force them out of his mouth, but he had swallowed them. So they handcuffed him, under protest, and rushed him to a hospital where a doctor, on police orders, forced an emetic solution into Rochin's stomach against his will. He vomited up evidence of morphine.

The so-called Rochin rule was more recently applied to exclude evidence that had been obtained in trying to prove a man had committed carnal abuse. While police detectives applied a hammerlock to him, a sergeant pulled off his trousers and swabbed his penis with four different chemically treated patches of cotton.

Some policemen have apparently picked up an insight from the Communist brainwashers. It is that you don't have to torture a man, even with a rubber hose, in order to induce him to confess. You simply have interrogators take turns questioning him while depriving him of sleep beyond his normal endurance. In Brooklyn, however, the police in one case went a step too far, in the view of the U.S. Supreme Court.[6] After questioning a murder suspect until he was groggy, the police turned him over to a psychiatrist who told the suspect he was his "doctor." The psychiatrist allegedly lulled the man into at least a mild hypnosis and while the man was in that state he offered to confess to the crime. The police appeared and took the confession.

Perhaps the greatest arrogance of all on the part of the police has been their recent assumption that they can spy upon anyone who comes into a police station, either as a suspect or as a friend or relative of a suspect.

In 1963 I was told by lawyers who should know that the bugging of police interrogation rooms still goes on in Los Angeles. Samuel Dash, in his survey, found that the police building in Los Angeles has "sixty listening posts." All are wired to a sound laboratory. The laboratory manager can switch on, and record on magnetic tape, conversation occurring at virtually every one of the sixty posts. Even police officers often do not know they are being recorded. One interrogation room, Dash reported, has a variety of modern devices (not only a microphone but a one-way mirror and a hidden camera) that can be employed when prisoners assume they are alone in the room. (Dash added that the Philadelphia police also have rooms equipped with one-way mirrors and microphones that are used "at times when two suspects are left alone in a room and allowed to believe that they are unobserved and unheard.")

When the Regan Committee of the California legislature took evidence on police eavesdropping, it heard one supplier testify that his company had installed concealed microphones and recording equipment in police departments throughout California.

In New York City, the headquarters of one district attorney is more up to date. I was authoritatively advised in 1963 that he had installed two hidden closed-circuit TV cameras. Each is in the ceiling—with a mesh cover—behind the head of the interrogation officer and is focused directly on the suspect's chair. In the detectives' room there may be a dozen people—detectives and possible witnesses—listening and watching the show. The DA has a private monitoring setup in his private office for following any interrogations that particularly interest him.

Hidden listening and observation devices also abound in the nation's jails. It might be suggested that we should feel less indignation about this practice since prisoners need to be watched. Granted. But there is still the fact that many prisoners are not convicts, but only suspects who are in prison because they can't afford bail. And there is also the fact that much of the bugging occurs in the visitors' rooms where outsiders come to talk.

At a jail in Brooklyn, New York, there is a TV camera in one of the large prison toilets and also one that can view the chapel. A professor at the University of Minnesota Law School has revealed that at one prison a microphoning device had been installed in a prison room used by priests for hearing confessions of Catholic prisoners.

Many jails and police headquarters that engage in bugging set aside for lawyers one booth or area that is not bugged. The most famous case involving a jail bugging occurred several years ago in the Westchester County, New York, jail when racketeer Joe "Socks" Lanza was being held as a parole violator.

The authorities had bugged the "family" booth where Mr. Lanza held two talks with his wife and one with his brother Harry. One objective of the bugging was to try to develop evidence that improper efforts were being used to spring "Socks" Lanza. When his lawyer came to visit, the lawyer blundered into the bugged "family" booth rather than the bug-free lawyer's facility, and so the lawyer-client talk was recorded.

The tape recordings made of the talk Joe Lanza had with his brother Harry brought *Harry* before a legislative committee investigating shenanigans in the parole system. The committee had a transcript of Harry's talk with Joe. Harry refused to answer the committee's questions and was ultimately sentenced to a year in jail for contempt of the committee! His appeal from this went to the U.S. Supreme Court. The part of his appeal based on the constitutional issue of eavesdropping was rejected 4-3. Justice Potter Stewart said that a "jail shares none of the attributes of privacy of a home, an automobile or hotel room," and Harry's claim was "at best a novel argument."

Meanwhile at the Nassau County, New York, jail a client facing a trial for his life discovered a microphone hidden in a room where he had conferred with his lawyer. (The warden claimed the bug wasn't working at the time of the client-0lawyer conference.) At any rate, the revelation of this and the Lanza episode brought cries of protest from the legal profession.

The outcries inspired a New York State legislative committee that had been trying to mobilize support for privacy of communication to offer this dour comment: "The deplorable jail incidents brought forth a storm of protest from lawyers, some of whom had not previously been audibly concerned about this Legislature's efforts to protect the people's right of privacy. . . ."[6]

In the state of Washington in 1963, on the other hand, the state Supreme Court reversed a conviction against a defendant who had been bugged while forced to remain in jail because he could not post bail. A conference between himself and his attorney had been recorded by the use of a hidden microphone in the jail conference room.

The Court cited the protection given to the right to counsel by the Fifth and Sixth Amendments and noted that "Effective consultation cannot be had without privacy."[7] So in the state of Washington, at least, a prisoner awaiting trial can be assured he is not broadcasting when he has a private talk with a visitor—provided that the visitor is his lawyer of record.

Most of the heavy-handedness, espionage, and dissimulation by police that we have been examining here has been directed toward people in trouble with society or unpopular with society. Many are of low repute. Some are downright scoundrels and would use the same tactics on society if they had a chance. Still, if a free society is to survive, it must defend the fundamental rights of its most disreputable citizens with the same vigor with which it defends its most respectable citizens. The late President John F. Kennedy made a remark in 1963 that is pertinent in this connection. He said that "the rights of every man are diminished when the rights of one man are threatened."

15. The Right to Be Free of Bureaucratic Harassment

"The law requires that the inquiries be answered completely and accurately. . . ."—Warning printed on front of a twelve-page "Household Questionnaire" containing 165 inquiries which was distributed to 16,000,000 U.S. homes during the 1960 Census

The bedeviling of the individual by governmental bureaus has increased substantially in the past fifteen years. During the same fifteen years, there have been a proliferation and an expansion of governmental units at city, state, and national levels. The two trends are almost certainly related.

Some increase in governmental intrusion has been made inevitable by the growth in population and urbanization and by the growth in personal possessions, such as cars and guns, capable of doing injury to others. Also, an ever-greater variety of taxes to support the growing governmental units seems to invite the discovery of new ways to evade taxes. And this of course calls for expanded units to catch the evaders.

Yet much of the governmental intrusion into the lives of citizens is unreasonable by any standard of decency. The bureaucrat assumes that the public loves to fill out forms, keep records, and obey regulations as much as he loves to construct and file forms, check records, and issue regulations. (Sample of the kind of instruction that delights a bureaucrat: "See line 8, subsection D, Section II, of Form 1098B.")

As I see it, legitimate objections by the citizens to the toils of bureaucracy should center primarily on two areas of abuse: (1) the harassment of the citizen by unreasonable forms and regulations and (2) the harassment of the citizen by stigmatizing him with odious labels. We shall consider them—as a good bureaucrat would—in order.

Harassment by unreasonable forms and regulations. The so-called Blue Form or "Household Questionnaire" that the U.S. Bureau of the Census distributed to every fourth house in the land during the 1960 Census springs instantly to mind. An official of the bureau conceded that it would take a citizen a half hour to fill out completely and accurately the form containing the 165 inquiries. Even accepting his extremely conservative estimate of the time required, this meant the bureau was asking American citizens to expend 8,000,000 man-hours wrestling with this form. If you didn't happen to get one, here are a dozen sample questions:

—Do you have a clothes washing machine?

—Do you have an electric or gas clothes dryer?

—Do you have any television sets?

—Do you have any radios?

—Do you have any air conditioning?

—How many bedrooms are in your house or apartment?

—Do you have a home food freezer which is separate from your refrigerator?

—How many bathrooms are in your house or apartment?

—How many passenger automobiles are owned or regularly used by people who live here?

—What is the highest grade of regular school this person has ever attained?

—Has this person been married more than once?

—If married, how many babies has she ever had, not counting stillbirths?

—How much did this person earn in 1959 in wages, salaries, commissions, or tips from all jobs?

A good many citizens balked at filling out the seemingly interminable questionnaire; but one citizen was hauled into court for balking. His offense, apparently, was that he wrote a sizzling article saying why he balked.[1] The man was William F. Ricken-backer, an investment adviser of Briarcliff Manor, New York, and son of Edward V. ("Eddie") Rickenbacker, World War I flying ace and retired executive. He wrote that the questionnaire was "unconscionably long, uncivilly inquisitorial, and absolutely un-constitutional." (The Constitution provides for an "enumeration" of the population every ten years.)

He was fined $100 and given a suspended jail sentence of sixty days. Mr. Rickenbacker not only had to pay the fine, but was admonished by the judge that he would have been sent to prison for the sixty days had it not imposed a special hardship on his family at the time. He evidently spent several thousand dollars appealing his $100 fine.

Mr. Rickenbacker took his appeal up through the United States Court of Appeals and petitioned the U.S. Supreme Court, but his petition was denied. The Justice Department's attorneys simply reminded the Court of Section 221 of Title 13 U.S.C., 68 Stat. 1023, 71 Stat. 484. And that was that! (The section autho-rizes fine or imprisonment for anyone over eighteen years of age who refuses to answer "any of the questions on the schedule sub-mitted to him" in connection with any duly authorized census or survey when requested to do so by the Secretary of Commerce.)

Mr. Rickenbacker advises me that he is sorry he could not get his appeal before the Supreme Court because, he believes, it was "the first case in our history in which an individual raised a constitutional question on the pure grounds of personal privacy under the Fourth Amendment."

Why, one might ask, did the Commerce Department feel it necessary to compel 16,000,000 householders to fill out a twelve-page questionnaire in order to make a "sampling" of U.S. living habits, as it had won authorization from Congress to do? The Nielsen Company has been surveying the television listen-ing habits of Americans to the satisfaction of many of its clients on the basis of sampling about 1200 homes. The Department of

Labor, for its respected monthly report on employment trends throughout the nation, conducts only 35,000 interviews, and without coercion. Mr. George Gallup can predict the outcome of national elections within a couple of percentage points on the basis of a few thousand voluntary interviews.

Behind the compulsory "sample" of 16,000,000 homes lies an interesting tale of commerce. Mr. Rickenbacker in his original accusation charged: "The Bureau probably does not have the honesty to admit that it is collecting statistics for the use of commercial enterprises."

During his trial, he called as a witness Robert W. Burgess, who had been the director of the Bureau of the Census in 1960. Mr. Burgess proved to be a vague witness. He professed to have no clear idea of how many people had refused to answer the questionnaire. Furthermore, the judge had to repeat to him *five* times the question "What was the purpose of getting that particular information?" in the Household Questionnaire before obtaining a comprehensible answer.

It seems that the information was not just for government use. A lot of "users" of Census information "outside" the government had a lot of ideas about questions that should be asked. And these "outside users" met with government committees to plead that all sorts of questions be included. A lot of sifting had to be done to get the questionnaire down to its twelve-page size.

And why was it necessary to require every fourth household— or 16,000,000—to respond? It seems that this was necessary in order for the Commerce Department to develop what it calls "Census tracts." The country is divided into tracts. Each tract contains 4000 to 7000 people. And the Commerce Department can—as a result of the 16,000,000 questionnaires—provide a lot of valuable statistics to interested groups, including business corporations, on the socioeconomic composition of each and every tract.

My own curiosity was piqued when I read Mr. Burgess' references to the "Census tracts." I had heard, while gathering information on the mailing-list industry, that one company, the Reuben H. Donnelley Corporation, had to a large extent built an empire on the basis of buying Census tracts and selling the information. Thus it was that I noted with particular interest the following paragraph in the *Wall Street Journal*, January 7, 1963:

> Reuben H. Donnelley Corp. . . . buys "tracts" from the Census Bureau which list geographic areas containing 4,000 to 7,000 persons with similar education and income. The tracts help Donnelley spot appropriate neighborhoods for the 700,000,000 pieces of direct mail it sends out for its clients annually.

The Donnelley Corporation advises me that each Census tract is homogeneous in character and is likely to contain about 1250 families. The factors about each tract that most interest Donnelley are median income . . . median school years . . . number of children . . . percentage of married couples . . . average age of children . . . percentage of homeowners . . . median value of home and median rent. It adds that most big outfits that have been soliciting by mail have been taking advantage of the "selectivity" made possible by the Census tracts. It calls the tract information relatively inexpensive to buy, as prices go in its industry.

But Donnelley claims it has the big edge in using these Census tracts because it has coded the information into "our mass mailing lists" and "with the advent of the little computers it is now possible to make selectivity quite readily and inexpensively available. . . . The company official added with obvious pride, "To my knowledge no one but the Reuben H. Donnelley Corporation has their mailing lists on tape with the ability for Census tract selectivity."

In view of the foregoing I would suggest that anyone who bothers to sweat over the 1970 "Household Questionnaire" demand that the U.S. Government share with him the revenues obtained from the sale of the information contained therein!

Incidentally a proposal is before the House (H.R. 6386) which would require that in the future such "household" questionnaires be voluntary and be confined to no more than one individual per fifty in the population. It is sponsored by John Ashbrook of Ohio. At this writing, Senator Clifford Case of New Jersey has indicated interest in sponsoring a similar bill in the Senate.

The favorite speech at most business conventions is the slashing attack on the federal government for intervening in the affairs of private business. Yet here we have the situation of business pressing the government to add more and more to compulsory questionnaires that intrude into the lives of private citizens, and to profit from the information gained therefrom. Mr. Rickenbacker, a political conservative, sadly wonders if businessmen know what they are doing. He told me that "it does seem that businessmen are too eager to allow government to get a foot in the door. They mind what they think is their business, says Tocqueville, and ignore what is their chief business, which is to preserve their liberty."

The impertinent or unreasonable questions addressed to U.S. residents come from many governmental sources. Immigration and naturalization authorities set a sad example of the American approach to life in the application form they have devised for United States citizenship. One question asks:

"Have you ever, in the United States or in any other place ... *knowingly* committed any crime, or broken any law, for which you have not been arrested?"

Such a question would give me pause. I recall that a couple of years ago, in an impetuous moment, I drove forty-eight miles an hour in a forty-five-mile-an-hour zone. No one caught me at it, and I don't intend to reveal here what state it occurred in for fear of being prosecuted belatedly. But the question addressed to aspiring citizens is fatuous and unreasonable. In a sense it invites people to prove their desire for citizenship by forgoing the protection of the Fifth Amendment.

The Internal Revenue Service's revised regulations specifying what records must be kept regarding expenditure for travel and entertainment border at times on the preposterous. Let us agree that many taxpayers have in the past got away with outrageous claims. I was told of a small company that several years ago threw a big business party at the beginning of the year. Enough liquor and delicacies were ordered to provide an elegant table for the families who ran this company for a good many months. Nevertheless, the requirements of disclosure are going beyond what any decent society should have to endure.

If you wish to deduct the cost of business entertaining, you must disclose the matters discussed even if highly confidential, the business purpose served, and name of the person who was the recipient of this hospitality while the confidential matter was being discussed. The Blackhawk Restaurant in Chicago moved to meet the new requirements of proof by providing tape recorders that could be placed on the table of each man discussing business with a client.

A friend of mine who went through an income tax audit found himself in the exasperating position of trying to explain to a stern-faced auditor why he had spent $4.50 for supper on a certain night. His itinerary showed that he had arrived at the city that evening in an airplane that served a free dinner. To justify his claim, he found himself disclosing to the auditor that he suffered from an odd ailment that required him, on doctor's orders, not to eat on airplanes.

The tax rules have, in addition to stripping citizens of privacy, produced one clear effect. The requirements for records generated an explosion in business for the credit-card clubs. And the great success of the clubs has had the effect of pushing up the cost to the whole population of dining out at most good restaurants by about seven per cent.

Unquestionably the greatest triumph of the bureaucratic mind, however, has been in its capacity to think of ever-new reasons why people should have permits or licenses in their pursuit of life, liberty, and happiness. The bedevilment of New Yorkers offers a good case in point. There are now more than a thousand activities for which one needs a municipal, state, or federal license or permit. The city's License Department alone takes in more than $1,500,000 in fees for permits and licenses. If you live in New York City, you are officially violating regulations if you try to do any of the following without the proper license, permit, or certificate:

—Keep goats.

—Put a ping-pong table in your home.

—Plant a tree.

—Use a hose to water your lawn or garden.

—Engage in cross-country running around a park.

—Conduct a public dance.

—Engage in fly tying for profit.

—Put up a tent camp.

—Work as a bait dealer.

—Dispose of a dead pet in any Sanitation Department facility.

—Be a doorman or ticket taker at a boxing match.

—Stage a masquerade ball.

—Engage in work at home. This will surprise some of my friends who are writers, but the following is officially required if they work at home in a rented apartment: they must obtain a certificate themselves, their employer must obtain a permit, and until recently their landlord was supposed to obtain a permit! If this were fully enforced, it would certainly fill the sidewalks for many blocks outside the licensing departments.

For many of the thousand-odd licenses and permits required in New York the applicant must submit not only to investigation, but to fingerprinting.

Even social agencies in many parts of the United States are by their regulations tending to manhandle the people they are trying to help. A member of a welfare board in a town in southeastern Connecticut confessed to me her distaste for one aspect of her job. She must visit homes of families on relief at 9 a.m. to make sure the house has been cleaned up and that no men are still sleeping.

In several counties of California, particularly Kern and Alameda, inspectors from welfare agencies have been staging raids late at night or early in the morning at homes receiving state funds for needy children. In one night in mid-1963, raids were conducted on the homes of 500 mothers to see whether a man was in the house—who might be the child's parent or otherwise offering support. If a man is caught sleeping or residing in such a home, the agencies will consider withdrawing aid.

Finally, it might be noted that regulations in my state of Connecticut permit an administrative board of three, upon a majority vote, to sterilize a person. Under the statute no notice need be given. The prospective victim cannot appeal the order or even demand an opportunity to be heard. These medical boards can be established at the state prison, at any of three mental hospitals, or at a school for the mentally retarded. If the officer in charge recommends that an inmate is a person for whom procreation would be inadvisable and the board agrees that the person might produce children with inherited tendencies to crime, mental illness, or mental deficiency, the operation may thereupon be performed by a member of the board.

Harassment by labels that stigmatize the citizen. Social-service agencies are among the most avid form-fillers and record-keepers. Some criminologists working with juvenile delinquency are beginning to feel that the more orthodox social-service agencies often stigmatize youngsters they are trying to help by classifying them in their records as delinquent.

Dr. Charles Slack, who has won fame working with New York's gangs by inventing what he calls Street Corner Research, shares this view. Instead of building up files, he pays unruly youngsters to help him in research that increases the number of "crime-free days." It is his view that delinquents become "stigmatized kids." They may first become stigmatized when hauled into juvenile court and tried, even though not publicly, without due process. They may, after such proceedings, arbitrarily be labeled "disturbed" or "anti-social" and may be referred to social-service agencies in their neighborhood. These agencies, while trying to help the youngsters by treating them as patients, proceed diligently to build up enormous files on them and all people mentioned in the records who happen to be around. Thus in a sense they help further to stigmatize already stigmatized youngsters.

He adds that all these secret records mean to the delinquent kid that decisions are made about him without his knowledge or understanding on the basis of information unavailable to him or his lawyer or friends. Dr. Slack then commented: "It is no wonder that I have never met in all my travels a single adolescent who, having appeared in court, had the faintest idea of what due process of law is or should be. Once they become adjudicated delinquents, these kids have no right of privacy."

The U.S. Congress, in its wisdom, ordered the Post Office Department to create another kind of label that is capable of stigmatizing. It is hung on anyone receiving "Communist political propaganda" from abroad. Congress in early 1963 ordered that the Post Office hold up any non-first-class mail addressed to U.S. residents that comes in from abroad and looks like Communist propaganda. Usually this is unsolicited material. (Congress did this, incidentally, over the opposition of the Post Office, the President, the Justice Department, the Treasury Department, and the U.S. Information Agency.)

The Post Office must now notify the addressee that such mail is being held and that he can have it delivered by filling out a form requesting delivery. If he fills out the form asking to receive it, his name goes on a list of persons who wish to receive Communist propaganda. Thus by the mere act of asking the Post

Office to stop interfering with his mail he gets on a list and is stigmatized by a label.

Three suits challenging the constitutionality of this act of Congress are under way. All are being supported with counsel by the American Civil Liberties Union, which contends that the law violates the First Amendment's assurance of freedom of speech and the due process clause of the Fifth Amendment. One suit was brought by a sixty-five-year-old truck driver in Pasadena, California, who vows that he is anti-Communist but doesn't like to have to sit up and beg —and fill out forms—in order to get his mail. The mail in question, printed in English, was sent to him unsolicited from Tokyo.

A third kind of label that can stigmatize is hung on people by the military services at the time military personnel are discharged from service. Here are six types of discharge that the Army has been giving:

1. HONORABLE DISCHARGE
2. GENERAL DISCHARGE Under Honorable Conditions
3. UNDESIRABLE DISCHARGE
4. DISCHARGE Under Other Than Honorable Conditions
5. BAD CONDUCT DISCHARGE (By Reason of Sentence of a Court-Martial)
6. DISHONORABLE DISCHARGE (By Reason of Sentence of a General Court-Martial)

All but the first of these may serve as labels to stigmatize and handicap the people receiving them for the rest of their lives. This practice is creating unjustified hardships. After all, in today's militarized society every young man is subject to conscription if he meets the military's needs. Many young men obviously are able—by their orderliness, conformity, and instant obedience— to please the military mind better than others, especially those who rebel at regimentation. Yet when the men are released into civilian life, they have an evaluative label on them. This is in addition to the label inherent in the rank they have attained, which should certainly constitute a clear enough label for all who have completed their term of service on a conscripted basis and have not been court-martialed.

Increasingly, as we've seen, employers have fallen into the habit of asking to see a man's military label (discharge status) before hiring him. If it is less than the No. 1 label, they may wonder about his manliness or the possibility of his having radical ideas or being a troublemaker.

The military label, furthermore, may be based on more than the man's record while in active service. The armed services during much of the 1950s sought the right to take into account pre-induction political associations and political activities after separation but while maintaining an inactive status. Such a power of surveillance could have a stifling effect on the political thinking of all American men during their entire early manhood. The courts in specific decisions have ordered that the military services cannot take pre-induction political activity into consideration in deciding on the form of discharge; but questions still arise, particularly in regard to a man's activities while in inactive service.

An ominous situation developed some years ago, incidentally, when a question arose as to whether a veteran holding an honorable discharge could be recalled to active service for the sole purpose of subjecting him to court-martial. The offense for which he was facing prosecution had occurred prior to his discharge. Fortunately the U.S. Supreme Court ruled that he could not be recalled in such circumstances.[2] Chief Justice Earl Warren later commented that the issue of the case had enormous significance in view of the fact that more than 22,000,000 Americans are veterans and that if the decision had been adverse to the veteran it would have meant that millions of former servicemen would be left helpless "before some latter-day revival of old military charges."

We should note a final and terrible power to stigmatize through labeling that has rested with the Department of

Defense. This is the power to label anyone working for private defense contractors—which include universities—as a security risk without offering him clear assurance of a chance to confront his accusers. Several millions of Americans have been subject to this power to stigmatize. And the labeling as a "risk" can be based not only on factors of individual loyalty, but on where one's relatives live, on one's health, or on any associations that suggest to surveillance-minded people that the individual may not be reliable.

Obviously the Department of Defense must have the power to protect its classified information. But in evolving the protections, flagrant abuses of individual rights have occurred. And the worst injustices centered on the inability to question or even see one's accusers. When the first Federal Employees' Loyalty Program was set up in 1947, President Harry Truman left vague the degree to which anyone accused of being a security risk had a right to confront people raising derogatory questions about him. The first chairman thought there should be a right of confrontation; but the FBI made it very clear that it would not cooperate unless the facts that were received in confidence by its investigators were kept entirely confidential. Attorney Joseph Rauh, Jr., recalls:

"So it began. The principle of nonconfrontation spread from the federal loyalty program to all the other loyalty-security programs in the nation: to the screening of millions of employees in defense plants with access to classified information. . . ."[3] Not only were the professional federal investigators who developed derogatory evidence against a person unavailable for cross-examination; so were the casual informants. These included "acquaintances, ex-wives, neighbors, landlords, gossips, village idiots," to use Mr. Rauh's words.

The first case involving this right to confrontation of accusers that brought a decision by the Supreme Court involved a man named Greene, who was general manager of a fairly small private company making electronic products for the Navy. He personally had developed much of his company's "secret" information and the question was, to use Mr. Rauh's sardonic words, "whether he could be trusted with it." Although he had received security clearance four times, the Navy in 1953 decided he could no longer be permitted to have access to his company's classified information. He was soon discharged. The bulk of the charges against him pertained to his marriage with an ex-wife whom he had divorced and the associations he had developed while married to her. She was apparently under suspicion for her political views or associations.

In 1959 the Supreme Court upheld Greene in his charge that he had been unfairly cut off from his source of livelihood without a right to confront his accusers.[4] In its momentous decision the Court commented:

"Certain principles have remained relatively immutable in our jurisprudence. One of these is that where governmental action seriously injures an individual and the reasonableness of the actions depends on fact findings, the evidence used to prove the Government's case must be dis-closed to the individual so that he has an opportunity to show that it is untrue. . . . We have formalized these protections in the requirements of confrontation and cross-examination. These have ancient roots."

Instead of ruling specifically on the constitutional right to confrontation, the Court upheld Greene simply because neither the President nor Congress had authorized an industrial security program that withheld confrontation. However, the vigor of the allusions by the majority opinions to traditional and constitutional rights made it seem evident that at least five of the Justices (Warren, Black, Douglas, Brennan, and Stewart)—all still on the Court—felt that the "ancient roots" should be protected if a clear issue involving confrontation ever came before them.

This decision did not sit well with a good many congressmen, and several efforts have since been made in Congress—with evident support, at times, from friends in the Pentagon—to trim back some of these ancient roots. Congress sought to provide the statutes authorizing nonconfrontation that the Court had observed were lacking.

Repeated efforts were made in 1962 to stampede through the House, with no discussion, a bill that would sharply narrow a defense worker's or scientist's right to confront and cross-examine his accusers or to appeal charges against himself. This bill provided that *ordinarily* the accused might have the rights to confront and cross-examine but that these rights could be suspended if it was decided at the Pentagon that such confrontation and cross-examination were not consistent with national security. In that case the accused might simply be shown a "summary" of the charges with, perhaps, no identification of his accusers. Young Representative John Lindsay of New York twice stood *alone* in the House chamber to prevent its passage by unanimous consent. A few weeks later, when three votes were required to strike the bill from the consent calendar, Mr. Lindsay was able to gain three allies out of the 436 House members. The managers of the bill were forced finally to agree to a suspension-of-rules arrangement permitting each side twenty minutes of debate, with a two-thirds vote necessary for passage. Supporters of the right to confrontation such as the AFL-CIO, the ACLU, and groups within the League of Women Voters meanwhile had been seeking to alert congressmen to the importance of the right to confrontation.

Mr. Lindsay made his case before the House with considerable eloquence. He said: "One of the greatest dangers to the American way of life is government supervision of the private arena and of the relations between employer and employee. A vast and growing section of private institutions are engaged in classified work and are subject to the regulations of the industrial security program." He felt that if defense work was permitted to become a justification for unlimited government regulation of the private area, then America faced a grave threat indeed.

Congressman Lindsay noted that Congressman Gordon H. Scherer of Ohio had argued that the President "should be able to prevent a person from having classified information if he doesn't like the way he parts his hair," because such information is the property of the government.

Mr. Lindsay went on to say: "If this point of view should ever come to pass, then we will be one step nearer to the horrible world vision so powerfully expressed in Franz Kafka's terrifying novel, *The Trial.* In that frightening allegory of modern life, we are exposed to a world where an apparently innocent man is arrested for a crime whose nature he is never able to ascertain, and then put to death by a capricious, anonymous bureaucracy without ever determining the reasons for his punishment or ever being able to confront his accusers."

When the vote came, Mr. Lindsay found himself with enough allies—and six to spare—to beat back the measure for the time being. But we have not heard the last of such measures.

Meanwhile the executive branch took note of the Supreme Court's comment that the President had never authorized an industrial security program that lacked a right to confrontation. With presidential authorization (Executive Order 10865), the Department of Defense in 1960 issued its Directive 5220.6 containing thirty pages of detailed procedures for reviewing security cases that involve "industrial" personnel. It provides for appeal and for the right of the accused to confront witnesses who have supplied derogatory information about him. But it also provides for several broad and vague exceptions to this rule of confrontation. An informant who has supplied damaging information may not be required to appear for cross-examination (1) if the department head supplying the informant feels it is not in the national interest to reveal his identity, (2) if the informant cannot reasonably be produced for reason of illness or similar cause, (3) if the Secretary of Defense feels there are "good and sufficient" reasons why the informant should not be identified or cross-examined. Those are three big "ifs."

In actual practice, the Department of Defense in the last two years has seemed anxious to provide cross-examination wherever possible, and has indeed permitted it in most cases. Furthermore, the department's executive in charge of security policy, Walter T. Skallerup, Jr., has shown a gratifying concern for the private rights of individuals involved in the defense program.

Still, one's right to cross-examine one's accusers is officially only vaguely protected. The millions of people working for defense contractors can only hope that the ancient roots so badly torn during the past decade can be nurtured and given a chance to grow deeper before a new wave of popular hysteria strikes.

16. The Right to Be Free of Mind Manipulation

"Here at our disposal, to be used wisely or unwisely, is an increasing array of agents that manipulate human beings."—John B. deC. M. Saunders, dean of the School of Medicine, University of California

The control of the human mind is quite rapidly emerging as a fascinating new science. New phrases are coming into our language: "psychobiological control," "biocontrol," "chemo-psychiatric control," "psychopharmacological control," and "psychotomimetic effects" (induced experiences "mimicking" psychosis). Dean Saunders stated that though there is great optimism that scientists are on "the threshold leading to a fuller understanding of the mind ... there is, especially among thoughtful physicians, a deep sense of disquiet."[1] Disquieted or not, many social scientists, biologists, and medical scientists have been plunging ahead to explore methods of attaining control. A few years ago, a group of sixteen distinguished scientists were called together by Dr. James G. Miller, psychiatrist and psychologist at the University of Michigan. They concluded: "We must assume the probability of a breakthrough in the control of the attitudes and beliefs of human beings through exceptionally effective educational techniques, drugs, subliminal stimulation, manipulation of motives or some as yet unrecognized medium." They suggested that the potentialities of this science of mind control far outweigh those of the hydrogen bomb. And so what did they do? They called for funds to help develop a science of human behavior. Their thinking followed the usual rationale: if we didn't, the Communists might beat us to it.

A good many social scientists have found that by employing their insights they can point to ways of attaining some degree of control over human behavior. They have shown marketers how to play upon the human subconscious in order to move goods; they have shown management how to spot conformists who will be good team players; they have discovered the kind of people most likely to confess during interrogation under the right kinds of pressures. Social scientists from the University of Texas who studied the anatomy of conformity described "the key factors that are likely to produce maximum suggestibility for any given individual." They reported; "A personality profile of the kind of individual who is least able to resist conformity pressures, and probably interrogation pressures as well, includes such characteristics as submissiveness, lack of self-confidence, lack of originality, lack of achievement motivation, desire for social approval, and being uncritical, conventional and authoritarian."[2] That, to a large extent, describes many of the young drones who have been chosen for management training by bureaucratic organizations, including many modern corporations. Such individuals are adept at accepting the group's views as their own. It is true that the same insights could be used to spot non-conformists (or help reduce suggestibility during interrogation). The sad truth is, however, that as far as conformity is concerned, personnel managers of large bureaucracies——who are in a better position than most of us to help shape society—are much more interested in identifying and selecting conformists than non-conformists.

Joost A. M. Meerloo, psychiatrist and psychologist, has warned: "All knowledge can be used either for good or for evil, and psychology is not immune to this general law. Psychology has delivered up to man new means of torture and intrusion into the mind."[3] But his is a relatively lonely voice.

At the other extreme, Harvard's influential B. F. Skinner heads a school of social scientists who are enthusiastic about getting into behavioral engineering. Dr. Skinner is the father of teaching machines.

Social scientists working alone could have only a limited effect in this engineering of behavior on a mass basis. Quite a different and more ominous picture opens up, however, when the would-be behavioral engineers of whatever science are given the new tools resulting from medical research. I refer to techniques for applying electrical stimulation to the emotional centers of the brain and to the discovery of behavior-changing drugs.

In 1957 I concluded a report on the new fascination with mass persuasion through psychological manipulation by offering the fanciful suggestion that by A.D. 2000 electronics experts might be capable of taking over much of any manipulation desired. This mention of a highly visionary possibility was inspired by some speculations at an electronics conference in Chicago and by some experiments with rats in Toronto. Today, after only seven years, the mechanics are already well developed for obtaining a substantial measure of control through electrical and electrochemical stimulation of the brain.

Some of the most remarkable feats in modification of behavior by remote control have been achieved by a Spanish-born physiologist who has been at Yale since 1950. He is Dr. Jose M. R. Delgado, a Charter Fellow of the American College of Neuropsychopharmacology.

Much of his work has been with a colony of monkeys. By surgery he has implanted thin, hairlike electrodes into various areas of the brain. These are connected to a socket outside the scalp, which in turn is connected to a small transistorized radio receiver strapped to each monkey's back. Thus Dr. Delgado can remain in another room and maintain two-way radio contact with his free-moving monkeys. There is no apparent discomfort to the monkeys. By pushbutton Dr. Delgado can make his monkeys walk, vocalize, cower, fight like fury, become ravenously hungry or violently amorous.

Dr. Delgado, furthermore, has made enough "preliminary tests" of electrode implantation on mentally ill humans, for therapeutic purposes, to know that changes can be produced in humans, too. He has been able to evoke such human responses as affection, laughter, fear, and fuzziness. A writer for the *Yale Daily*

News of April 24, 1963, described his discoveries about humans in these words: "Modern technology has created instruments able to stimulate electrically a cerebral structure in a fully conscious human. Electricity influences the nerves, can direct the brain to produce movements, emotions, hallucinations, drives, hostility, friendliness, and is even able to modify basic thoughts and transform ideas."

Recently Dr. Delgado has refined his control of monkeys by adding drugs. Into the brain of his monkeys he inserts an assembly formed of two fine tubings and two electrodes. He calls the assembly "chemitrodes." A tiny electrochemical pump activated by the radio receiver will pump on signal minute quantities of drugs into various areas of the brain. The drugs are stored in a small capsule attached to each monkey's neck. Last summer he described to a pharmacological meeting in Prague how he could temporarily change the social structure of the monkey colony by equipping just the boss monkey, Ali, with chemitrodes plus radio receiver. The other monkeys soon learned they could convert Ali from a bullying boss into a docile creature by pressing a lever.

A longer-term experimental project in modifying human behavior by electrical stimulation of various brain areas has been going forward at Tulane University's School of Medicine. Dr. Robert G. Heath of the Department of Psychiatry and Neurology has in the past several years equipped a number of mental and other patients, many seemingly hopelessly ill, with portable self-stimulators. Usually the patient wears a device containing three pushbuttons on his belt. These buttons activate electrodes placed in the brain. Ordinarily the patient tends to favor the button that yields the most pleasurable results. In certain instances when patients have been in the midst of violent psychotic seizures, Dr. Heath has activated electrodes without their knowledge. One such patient was changed quite quickly from a state of uncontrollable rage to a mild euphoria.

Some of the responses that have been observed to occur in patients after a button has been pushed, he reported in mid-1963, are frustration, anger, fearfulness, a feeling of being sick, happy feelings, and sexual ecstasy.[4] The button activating an electrode in the septal region of the brain has, in a number of instances, produced such ecstatic feelings. One patient would often introduce a sexual subject as a topic of conversation "with a broad grin" soon after pressing the septal button. Another liked the "good" feeling that came from pressing the septal button. He said it was as if he were building up to a sexual orgasm. The response to the button, however, wasn't completely satisfactory. The man was unable to achieve the orgasmic end point and would explain that the reason he sometimes pushed the button frantically was in an attempt to reach that point. The stimulation of other areas of the brain, however, produces in some patients "happy feelings" with no associated sexual thoughts.

Meanwhile, spectacular results are being achieved in modification of human behavior by straightforward administration of drugs, usually in pill form. When Aldous Huxley created his futuristic *Brave New World* in 1931, he conceived an ingenious dictator some centuries hence, who kept his subjects contented in their technocracy with tablets called "soma." The old destructive bliss-producers, alcohol, opium, cocaine, etc., were outmoded. The dictator did not have to force soma on his subjects: they cried for it. Huxley in the fifties described his marvelous, imaginary soma as "one of the most powerful instruments of rule in the dictator's armory. . . . The daily soma ration was an insurance against personal maladjustment, social unrest, and the spread of subversive ideas."[5]

The bliss-producing soma had four magical powers: it tranquilized . . . it stimulated . . . it produced visions when taken in large amounts . . . and it heightened suggestibility. This last characteristic helped the dictator get across his propaganda.

A single tablet with all of soma's powers still has to be devised; but all four of its magical powers for behavioral modification have been chemically perfected. And most of the drugs that will provide these powers appear to be relatively free of dangerously destructive side effects.

Tranquilizers from mild to powerful are, of course, already taken as commonly as candy in millions of U.S. households and thousands of hospitals. In some Midwestern cities they account for a fifth of all drug prescriptions.

Stimulants are almost as readily available. Amphetamine (benzedrine) and a number of other pep-producers are available. When overused, however, they may lead to wakefulness, jitteriness, or even addiction. In Japan, where evidence of high physical and psychic energy is greatly esteemed, there are said to be many hundreds of thousands of amphetamine addicts. A newer type of stimulant, iproniazid, an anti-depressant, works much more slowly (two weeks) but produces in many a general euphoric and energized state.

Vision-producers are being bootlegged as well as imported onto dozens of U.S. campuses, where students and some professors have been taking them for the thrill as well as for serious experimentation. LSD-25 and psilocybin are the most potent of these hallucinogens that "free the mind" and create psychotomimetic effects. A Technicolor world opens up to persons sampling such drugs. Everything becomes more vivid. The mind soars into fantasies and undergoes mystical experiences. *Religious Education* carried a report in mid-1963 by psychologist Timothy Leary and Walter Houston Clark of Andover Newton Theological School on the reactions of a number of religious people who experienced the effects of psilocybin. Many of these people reported "that their spiritual sensitivities have . . . been expanded. Biblical passages or religious terms formerly meaningless or pale have suddenly acquired vivid meaning."

Dr. Leary speaks of the drugs as "consciousness-expanding." He contends that they "unplug the ego . . . and the mind. What is left is something that Western culture knows little about. The open mind. The uncensored cortex, alert and open to a broad sweep."

He contends that there have been no physical or psychological "casualties" among more than 400 volunteer subjects who have taken the drugs under controlled conditions. A number of medical authorities have taken a dimmer view of what they call indiscriminate overuse of these drugs, especially when used by latent psychotics. Dr. Leary and his associate, Dr. Richard Alpert, were released from Harvard for what was considered to be overenthusiastic experimentation.

Their group began issuing from Cambridge the *Psychedelic Review* and set up an "Educational Center" in Los Angeles. Dr. Leary advised me that his group wants to qualify as a sponsor of a government research project (the only way to gain access to LSD and psilocybin). He added that mescaline and morning-glory seeds, the more common and older-type consciousness-expanders, are in the gray area of government supervision. Meanwhile Leary and Alpert moved their headquarters from Cambridge to an estate at Millbrook, New York, and while waiting for authorization to conduct research concentrated on reporting their findings.

Suggestibility-enhancing drugs also appear to be available. Scopolamine, sodium amytal, and pentothal apparently have some potentialities in this area. They have reportedly been used as so-called "truth serums" in some countries by police and the military in an effort to elicit information or confessions. In many cases they apparently do make people more talkative; but they also make the people more disoriented, so that the information that emerges from them may be partly fanciful. Jean Rolin in his book *Police Drugs* condemns the use of such drugs on the grounds of both reliability and ethics. He calls their use the moral equivalent of torture.

They may be more effective in bringing out confessions. Huxley states that pentothal may have the effect of "suggesting confessions to" a suspect being questioned.

There is speculation also that scopolamine has been used in some of the famous "brainwashing" cases by making the subject extraordinarily suggestible to ideas while in a state of twilight sleep. Whatever the present effectiveness of drugs in enhancing suggestibility, it seems virtually inevitable that drugs for this purpose will be perfected in the coming years.

Nearly all the drugs and the techniques for electrical and electrochemical stimulation of the brain that we have been examining were developed for worthy medical purposes. They relieve anxieties and depressions and have had the happy result of bringing relief or cure to tragically disturbed persons.

Unfortunately, many of them also have the potentiality, if abused, to intrude tragically upon the privacy and liberty of individuals, and to destroy the uniqueness of individuals.

What if our society, twenty years from now—1984—comes under the dominance of political leaders who are enthusiastic about the concepts of behavioral engineering espoused by some social scientists? Quite possibly such leaders might say, "Give us your children for a while," at special nurseries devoted to Preparation for Life. The experiments at Yale in modifying behavior by electrical or chemical stimulation would indicate that, after an individual's brain has been subjected to repeated stimulation, modifications of behavior may become permanent. In short, the altered personality pattern of the children—as desired by the political leaders—might very well jell for life.

Or let's assume that twenty years hence every citizen carries in his pillbox a supply of tranquilizers, energizers, and vision-producers. And let's assume he has on his belt an electronic pushbutton arrangement for activating instant feelings of bliss or sexual ecstasy. Will such people produce a strong and interesting society? Many of the world's most colorful figures, most inspired leaders, and most creative people were anxiety-ridden neurotics. Wouldn't the world be made more drab by their absence?

When the chairman of the U.S. Atomic Energy Commission, Dr. Glenn T. Seaborg, was asked some months ago to list the fifteen most revolutionary discoveries he expected to see in the coming generation, one change that he predicted was: "Pharmaceuticals that change and maintain human personality at any desired level." And he added: "It may . . . become necessary to establish new legal and moral codes to govern those who prescribe use of these materials."

More ominous than the individual pushbuttons and pillboxes are the potentialities for mass application of behavior-modifying techniques. Perhaps we shouldn't really be willing to queue up for our daily ration of soma as Huxley imagined. But it is now readily conceivable that potent behavior-modifying chemicals can be put into the table salt that we all must have or the water we must drink or the air we must breathe. A start down the road to forced medication is seen by some in government decisions to fluoridate water. The earlier chlorination of water was simply to purify the water, but fluoridation involves the concept of positive medication through the drinking water available in the areas affected. As one doctor has commented: "Individuals will have no choice but to swallow what the state presents."

Army spokesmen have hinted that the Army may have aerosol sprays that would be able to control the minds of human beings during war. Properly applied, apparently the mist could douse the courage of opponents. It seems reasonable to wonder whether the military has also shown an interest in chemicals or other means that could induce a ferocious fichting spirit in its own personnel, such as Dr. Delgado has produced in experiments with his monkeys. It might be worth noting that the Office of Naval Research is reported to have been financial sponsor of much of the work done by Dr. Delgado and others at Yale.

And what is our assurance that twenty years from now a government may not, in peacetime, be tempted to use the potent psychochemicals to control at least a little bit the minds or moods of its own people? The first experimental use of such psychochemicals would presumably come at a time of great domestic turmoil, recrimination, and restlessness, to help save democracy. *The Bulletin of Atomic Scientists* carried an article in early 1962 by Dr. James Lieberman of the James Jackson Putnam Children's Center in Boston speculating on this possibility. He took the gloomy view that the government might well be tempted to use psycho-chemicals as instruments of coercion and control. And then he added:

"Under such circumstances, a government could outwardly uphold the noblest statutes of political freedom, while subtly extinguishing the actual expression of individual liberty."

That would be close to the ultimate conceivable horror.

PART IV

If Personal Liberty Is to Be Sustained

17. The Bill of Rights Under Siege

"Today, as rarely before, case after case comes to the Court which finds the individual battling to vindicate a claim under the Bill of Rights against the powers of government, federal and state."—Justice William J. Brennan, Jr.

The Preamble to the United States Constitution states: "We the People of the United States, in Order to form a more perfect Union, establish Justice, ensure domestic Tranquillity, provide for the common defence, promote the general Welfare, *and secure the Blessings of Liberty to ourselves and our Posterity,* do ordain and establish this CONSTITUTION for the United States of America." (Italics supplied.)

As first adopted, the Constitution did provide a number of guarantees designed to "secure the Blessings of Liberty." It included, for example, the right to a speedy hearing before a magistrate, protection against retroactive laws, and a prohibition against religious tests. But many of the nation's Founders, especially James Madison, were apprehensive that the Blessings of Liberty had not been sufficiently secured, so they began the amending process. Specific guarantees that the government would not intrude unreasonably into the private life of the citizen were drafted. The first ten amendments, drawn up by Madison and quickly adopted, have come to be known collectively as the Bill of Rights.

Today, with the onslaughts of new technologies, ever mounting surveillance, ever widening bureaucratic controls and other forces we've examined, the guarantees of the Bill of Rights are being both diluted and often ignored. The most somber statement of the modern challenge to the Bill of Rights is contained in the James Madison Lectures, which four of the Supreme Court's most consistent libertarians—Chief Justice Warren, and Justices Black, Brennan, and Douglas—gave at New York University.[1]

Justice Douglas, for example, commented: "The fences have been broken down. . . . The Bill of Rights—with the judicial gloss it has acquired—plainly is not adequate to protect the individual against the growing bureaucracy." Much of the smashing of fences protecting individual liberties is being done in the name of order or of "balance." Instead of accepting the amendments as mandates, judges have increasingly talked of balancing them against needs of security, needs to combat crime, etc. Chief Justice Earl Warren commented on this trend toward balancing social against individual rights: "Legislative or executive action eroding our citizens' rights in the name of security cannot be placed on a scale that weighs the public's interest against that of the individual in a sort of 'count the heads' fashion." Chief Justice Warren has expressed doubt that the Bill of Rights could be adopted if it came before Congress today. And it is far from certain that the general public would support the ratification of these rights, or even knows what they are. Justice Douglas in his lecture doubted that most school boards or Parent-Teacher Associations could pass a test on the Bill of Rights.

The importance of our "Blessings of Liberty" presumably is taught in our schools, yet it is questionable whether this has been done effectively. The nationwide 1960 poll of the attitudes of high school students toward civil liberties made by the Purdue Opinion Panel found wide favor for the repression of some individual rights.[2] The report on the poll stated, for example: "Today's teenager readily endorses censorship." Here are four of the specific responses:

—Forty-one per cent agreed, or would "probably agree," with the statement: "People who have wild ideas and don't use good sense should not have the right to vote."

—A third of them agreed with the statement: "In some cases, the police should be allowed to search a person or his home even though they do not have a warrant."

—Two thirds of them agreed or were "uncertain" on the statement: "The police or FBI may sometimes be right in giving a man the 'third degree' to get him to talk."

—Two thirds of them agreed or were uncertain on the statement: "Some of the petitions which have been circulated should not be allowed by the government."

And it is questionable whether further education brings any significant increase in understanding of or belief in the mandates of the Bill of Rights. In fact, there may be a decline. Attorney Edward Bennett Williams tells of a poll of students majoring in political science at a large Midwestern university. The major principles embodied in the Bill of Rights were set forth as matter-of-fact statements in modern phraseology. Students were invited to indicate whether they believed in each statement. Williams relates:

"To the amazement and the chagrin of the professors, about half of the students indicated they did not believe in the right of all Americans to peaceable assembly. They did not believe in the right of every accused to meet his accuser face to face and subject him to cross-examination, and they did not believe in the privilege against self-incrimination."[3] Yet, Mr. Williams added, every one of the students said he believed in the Bill of Rights!

Let us examine those great guarantees in the Bill of Rights that were designed to protect the private life of the individual citizen and which have been most flagrantly ignored or eroded in recent years. These are the First, Fifth, Sixth, and—most particularly—Fourth Amendments. Where do we stand in regard to their observance and implementation? And what actions seem particularly needed to maintain these rights as vital protective forces in our modern society?

FIRST AMENDMENT

Congress shall make no law respecting an establishment of religion, or prohibiting the free exercise thereof; or abridging the freedom of speech or of the press; or of the right of the people peaceably to assemble, and to petition the government for a redress of grievances.

Justice Brennan has observed recently that the right of privacy "would mean little if it were limited to a person's solitary thoughts, and so fostered secretiveness. It must embrace a concept of the liberty of one's communications, and historically it has."

To communicate freely one needs freedom of expression, and the First Amendment specifies that the citizen's freedom of speech shall not be abridged. Yet it often is.

We've seen an abridging of freedom of speech in the extreme hazard to livelihood, and even to life and limb, that has arisen in the past decade for many who have sought to express opinions unfashionable in their areas. We've seen this abridging in the hundreds of requirements that citizens submit to test oaths in order to hold jobs. Justice Douglas has stated: "Foremost is the command of the First Amendment that government will make no law penalizing the citizen for his beliefs, his conscience, and his utterances. A loyalty order that casts a citizen into the outer darkness because of his speeches or beliefs does just that."[4]

The spirit of the First Amendment clearly should bar the Congress from probing an individual's beliefs and associations, but we've seen a vast amount of such probing in recent years. And furthermore, a Supreme Court majority has consistently refused to act to halt such probing by congressional committees provided that the questions are "pertinent." In 1959 in the Barenblatt case involving a college instructor, the Court held that the compelling need for national security at times outweighed First Amendment guarantees of individual rights of speech and association, so congressional interrogations in this area have wide power.[5] A number of cases that reached the high court involved people prosecuted for contempt of Congress for refusing to answer political questions. The House Un-American Activities Committee, in pursuing its mandate to investigate that elusive element "un-American propaganda," is often challenging the right of Americans to a free expression of opinion.

Then in 1961 a particularly flagrant use of congressional inquisitorial power to probe individual beliefs and associations reached the Court for review. A man named Wilkinson had been convicted of contempt of Congress for refusing to answer questions about himself put by the House Un-American Activities Committee.[6] What made the case seemingly so flagrant was that Wilkinson had not been subpoenaed until after the HUAC learned he had gone to Atlanta to use his freedom of expression to try to develop sentiment that would induce Congress to call off the committee's hearings in that city. The HUAC would clearly seem to have used its power to hound a critic. Yet in this case the Supreme Court, by a 5-4 vote, affirmed Wilkinson's conviction. The American Civil Liberties Union, which had undertaken to provide Wilkinson with legal defense, commented: "The practical effect of the majority's statement is to silence all critics not prepared to testify about their motivations."

Justice Black in his dissent was even sharper. He said: "I think it is clear that this case involves nothing more or less than an attempt by the Un-American Activities Committee to use the contempt power of the House of Representatives as a weapon against those who dare to criticize it."

Other provisions of the First Amendment have also been abridged in recent years. We have seen an abridgment of the right peaceably to assemble in the many requirements that citizens sign affidavits listing all organizations to which they belong.

And we have seen an abridgment of the right to petition the government for a redress of grievances in such incidents as the shocking treatment by state police of the professors at

State University College of Education at Brockport, New York. Their only offense was that they had sought to petition their government.

FOURTH AMENDMENT

The right of the people to be secure in their persons, houses, papers, and effects, against unreasonable searches and seizures, shall not be violated, and no warrants shall issue but upon probable cause, supported by oath or affirmation, and particularly describing the place to be searched, and the persons or things to be seized.

Of all the guarantees of the Bill of Rights, the guarantees of this amendment deal most directly and intimately with the individual's right to privacy. And of all the guarantees in the Bill of Rights, these are the most often violated.

We have the hundreds of thousands of citizens unreasonably seized merely on "suspicion." . . . We've seen the growing wave of unreasonable searches without warrants by administrative officials. . . . We've seen the thousands of unreasonable seizures of our papers in the "mail covers." . . . And we've seen the host of unreasonable searches without warrants made of one's home or premises by the new electronic surveillance equipment. Justice Douglas has said that wiretapping is "far worse than ransacking one's desk and closets." And microphoning is even more of an invasion than wiretapping.

Let us examine where we stand in terms of crucial decisions and laws bearing on unreasonable search and seizure. Perhaps it will simplify the examination if we consider separately the three kinds of search or seizure that have been subject to the greatest abuses.

1. Physical searches and seizures by government agents and others.

We are speaking here of searches by people who appear in person, rather than via surreptitiously placed electronic devices.

The question of who has a right to enter and search your home without permission has long been a sore one. The issue as much as anything touched off the American Revolution.

In colonial days American settlers lived under the laws of England. The right of the government to search homes and other private properties was a burning issue, both in England and in the colonies, in the years immediately preceding the Revolution. In England the great battles were fought over the right of officers of the Crown to issue "general warrants," often to try to find and silence critics of the regime. With a general warrant, the officers could search and seize anyone in the realm—along with his papers—who they felt was connected with a specified offense. In 1762 the king's officials in England sought to find and seize the anonymous author of an especially critical pamphlet by giving the agents a general warrant. Forty-nine persons were seized, including the real author, John Wilkes, along with a mass of his uninventoried papers, among which was his will. He challenged the warrant and was upheld by Chief Justice Pratt, later Lord Camden, who stated:

"To enter a man's house by virtue of a nameless warrant, in order to procure evidences is worse than the Spanish Inquisition; a law under which no Englishman would wish to live an hour."

In the colonies the main cause of grievance was the writ of assistance, used primarily in the search for goods smuggled past the customs officials. The writs did not authorize arrest, but otherwise they were even broader permits to snoop than the general warrants. They authorized the sovereign's officers to search anywhere, anytime, for uncustomed goods as long as the sovereign lived. After George II died, Boston merchants sought a hearing against the granting of new writs. James Otis, in 1762, made the plea on the merchants' behalf, but lost his case. John Adams later remarked: ". . . Mr. Otis's oration against the Writs of Assistance breathed into this nation the breath of life. . . . Then and there the child Independence was born."

The writs and general warrants were very much on the minds of the new nation's citizens when—after Independence—they adopted the Fourth Amendment. This amendment, we'll recall, required that warrants could be issued only on probable cause and must specify the place to be searched and persons or things to be seized.

In the past two decades the U.S. Supreme Court has permitted several significant dilutions of this amendment. In 1947 it gave its approval (by a narrow 5-4 margin) to searches made without warrants if they were "incidental" to a lawful arrest.[7] Justice Frank Murphy in his dissent charged that as a result of this exception "a warrant for arrest is the equivalent to a general search warrant or writ of assistance."

In recent years a major issue in cases involving police searches has centered on the question of whether evidence seized in violation of the Fourth Amendment might be admitted in court. From a liberal position in 1914 that such evidence would not be permitted in federal courts,[8] the Court swung to a permissive attitude in 1949 by permitting such evidence in the courts of states that did not exclude such evidence.[9] So many flagrant injustices followed that the Court decided in 1961 that its ruling of 1949 had been erroneous and outlawed such illegally seized evidence in both federal and state courts.[10]

The U.S. Supreme Court has been considerably less protective of citizens, however, in the matter of administrative searches. These involve the rights of the ordinary citizen faced with the great variety of bureaucratic inspectors who have emerged as our society has become more urbanized. The trend quite clearly has been against the individual homeowner in favor of the administrative officers of government.

Even more disturbing has been the rationale used to assert that the Fourth Amendment may mean less when invoked to protect an individual's privacy in his home than when used to protect an individual against incriminating evidence. Some members of the Supreme Court have assumed a difference in kind between civil searches and criminal searches.

This distinction was made by Justice Frankfurter, speaking for the majority, in a case involving the power of a Baltimore health officer to enter a home without a warrant over the objection of the homeowner.[11] The inspector was looking for rats, and apparently had some reason to assume rats might be in residence. The theory of the Court's majority was that the state's interest in health overbalanced the homeowner's insistence that the invading official must have a warrant.

Justice Douglas—joined by Chief Justice Warren and Justices Black and Brennan—took sharp issue with this line of reasoning. He argued that the history and spirit of the Fourth Amendment show that the privacy of the individual is protected from invasion by "officious" government officials without distinguishing whether the searches were for evidence of violating "civil" regulations or "criminal" statutes. It is quite possible that health inspectors can serve as advance scouts for the police by reporting dwellings where there is probable cause for police raids. In fact, such inci-dents have been reported from two Midwestern cities, though it is not clear that there was organized collaboration between the health inspectors and the police. We've seen earlier, in the case of the housing inspection in Dayton, Ohio (Chapter 9), that not even probable cause was claimed in demanding entry.

Most citizens will gladly permit a well-mannered inspector who identifies himself to enter their homes upon request without a warrant if his mission seems reasonable. If the courts would uphold the need for a warrant in those few cases where homeowners do object to searches, this decent requirement certainly would not seriously impede the administration of health or housing programs. And it would uphold an important constitutional protection against unwanted intrusion. Justice Douglas pointed out that in Great Britain a warrant is required where a householder objects. It is hoped that in coming years the Court will show a willingness to review its position on administrative searches.

*2. Searches by wiretapping telephone conversations made from the
privacy of one's home or premises.*

The main difference between this kind of search and the conventional physical search is that it is inherently surreptitious. A
victim rarely learns about it. Justice Brandeis commented in his
dissent in the Olmstead case: "As a means of espionage, writs of
assistance and general warrants are but puny instruments of tyranny and oppression when compared with wire-tapping."

Yet the Supreme Court has never recognized that wiretapping is a form of unreasonable search that should put it under
the prohibitions of the Fourth Amendment. At present the legal
situation in regard to wiretapping in the United States can best
be described as a shambles. To understand where we stand today
we should start by taking note of that famous, bitterly divided
Olmstead decision of 1928.[12]

A man named Olmstead and fifty others were charged with
being members of a bootleg ring operating out of Seattle. Most
of the evidence against the ring was based on wiretaps placed
on eight telephones over a period of five months. The government produced 775 typewritten pages of notes of conversations
overheard.

The issue put for the first time squarely before the Supreme
Court was this: does the Fourth Amendment's proscription of
"unreasonable searches and seizures" make wiretapping unconstitutional? The answer, by a margin of one vote, was that it did
not. Chief Justice William Howard Taft, writing for the majority,
gave the Fourth Amendment a narrow, literal reading. He held
that:

"The Amendment does not forbid what was done here. There
was no searching. There was no seizure. The evidence was secured
by the use of the sense of hearing and that only. There was no
entry of the houses or offices of the defendants."

It was perhaps unfortunate that this first test of wiretapping
involved the emotion-laden national Prohibition Act.

The enforcement of this act—and a desire to see it work—was very close to the heart of Chief Justice Taft. Mr. Taft's principal biographer, Henry Pringle, wrote: "It sometimes seemed as though there were no lengths to which the Chief Justice would not go, and along which he would not attempt to lead the court, in his determination to uphold prohibition enforcement."[13]

Olmstead has never been overruled. Perhaps one reason is that Congress intervened, apparently accidentally, in 1934 to provide Section 605 of the Federal Communications Act. This act runs about 20,000 words. Its controversial Section 605, if read in its entirety, is an outright nationwide ban on all types of wiretapping. Law-enforcement agencies, including the Justice Department, have chosen, as we've seen, by straining to give it a different, more permissive reading. And the section has only rarely been enforced. But the interesting point is that Section 605 passed without debate or notice. Since then, in most of the Supreme Court decisions dealing with wiretapping, the Court has developed the law on wiretapping by interpreting Section 605, rather than reaching back to the larger constitutional question arising from the Fourth Amendment.

Law-enforcement officers, congressmen, and other proponents of wiretapping frequently refer to "the thirty-one words" of Section 605 as the heart and meaning of the section as it relates to wiretapping. Those thirty-one words, which have been cited hundreds of times, are:

". . . no person not being authorized by the sender shall *intercept* any communication *and divulge* or publish the existence, contents, substance, purport, effect or meaning of such intercepted communication to any person." (Italics supplied.)

These exponents of regulated wiretapping, as we've seen, choose to read those words to mean that a crime is not committed until there are *both* interception *and* divulgence. They insist that anyone is free to intercept as long as he doesn't divulge. And they choose to read "divulge" as meaning a public presentation of the intercepted message (and not something that a federal tapper might pass along to his superior).

Because of all the emphasis upon "the thirty-one words" cited above, few people are aware that a subsequent seventy-five-word clause includes the following:

. . . and no person having received such intercepted communication . . . shall . . . *use* the same or any information therein contained for his own benefit or for the benefit of another not entitled thereto." (Italics supplied.)

If mere *use* is a federal crime, then there is no conceivable legitimate basis for wiretapping by either police or private parties.

In the years immediately after Section 605 became law, the Supreme Court outlawed not only wiretap evidence from federal courts,[14] but any evidence based on *information* gained from wiretapping.[15] Then came two setbacks for the libertarians. The Court ruled that if a defendant had not been a party to a wiretapped conversation at issue he could not prevent its introduction as evidence.[16] And in 1952 it concluded that Section 605 did not prohibit the divulgence of wiretap evidence in *state* courts.[17] This served as a green light to police tapping in states that did not prohibit it.

However, in 1957 the Court did take a stand that made the local tappers considerably more cautious in their approach to wiretapping, and led them to use it more to obtain leads than to obtain evidence to be presented in court. In the Benanti case it ruled that federal courts could not receive evidence obtained by state officials which had been secured by wiretapping.[18] A cloud of doubt was cast over the legality of state laws permitting wiretapping.

In the same year, however, the Court found nothing wrong in permitting another person to listen in on the first person's telephone conversation via an extension line.[19]

The Court has veered toward permissiveness in two major decisions involving wiretapping in the last three years.[20]

One marvel of all this interpreting of Section 605 is that the Court has never, at this writing, offered an opinion on the central—and I believe preposterous—claim that the nation's prosecutors have been making for more than twenty years: that interception of messages is no crime so long as it is not accompanied by "divulgence." If the zigging and zagging of these decisions leaves you somewhat dizzy, be assured that it has left a number of lawyers puzzled, too. New York's prosecutors know, for example, that since their state has a permissive wiretapping statute they can still introduce wiretapped evidence in state cases. But they also have been warned that divulging such evidence is a federal crime!

This is why New York's prosecutors and congressmen in particular began pressing for action by Congress to give the law enforcers clear-cut authorization to tap wires.

The Department of Justice, too, has been increasingly embarrassed by the contorted reading that it has for twenty years been giving to the Section 605 law. Since it has chosen to insist that the intercept-and-divulge wording permits interception as long as there is no divulgence, it has been in a poor position to prosecute any private wiretappers caught listening or using information gained from tapping, or to prosecute law-enforcement officials caught tapping without court orders or using information gained from such tapping. As attorney Edward Bennett Williams told the Senate Subcommittee on Constitutional Rights (Judiciary) in 1961: "You can't tap wires with one hand and prosecute wiretappers with the other."

In the early sixties a number of congressmen presented bills to permit official wiretapping and prohibit private wiretapping. Some of the testimony by law-enforcement agencies before the Senate subcommittee amounted to requests for almost unlimited wiretapping by anyone wearing a police badge. Witness after witness in favor of some official tapping talked about the burden of prosecuting illicit tappers because of those "thirty-one words" of

Section 605 that forbid anyone to intercept *and* divulge. Congressman Robert W. Kas- tenmeier, a critic of all wiretapping, came up with a bill that was brilliant in its simplicity. He proposed that the "and" be changed to "or." That didn't interest the law enforcers at all.

Finally, in 1962 the Department of Justice came out with its own bill, which it is still pressing, and with renewed vigor, at this writing. (Its 1963 label was S. 1308.) It is described as a bill "To prohibit wiretapping by persons *other than duly authorized law enforcement officers* engaged in the investigation or prevention of specified categories of criminal offenses, and for other purposes." (Italics supplied.) The bill provides that:

A. The Justice Department might, upon obtaining a court order from a federal judge, wiretap in the investigation of offenses involving murder, kidnaping, extortion, bribery, transmission of gambling information, travel or transportation in aid of "racketeering" enterprises, narcotics offenses.

B. The Attorney General at his "sole discretion" might order taps, without bothering to get court orders, in cases involving espionage, sabotage, treason, sedition, subversive activities, and unauthorized disclosure of atomic-energy information, if he decided that resort to the court order would be "prejudicial to the national interest." (The phrase "subversive activities," as we've seen, can cover a multitude of assumed sins.)

C. State attorneys general and city prosecuting attorneys might wiretap, after obtaining a court order from a state court judge of competent jurisdiction, in crimes involving murder, kidnaping, extortion, bribery, or narcotics offenses.

There is a seemingly stern section requiring that an annual "full and complete" report be issued on the number of applications made for state and federal court orders. But notably there is no requirement that the Justice Department reveal how many taps the Attorney General authorized at his "sole discretion." The bill also includes the gutting, by rewriting, of Section 605.

In short, wiretapping by state, city, and federal police would for the first time in our history be recognized as legal, when done in compliance with the proposed new "Federal Wire Interception Act." Interestingly, the state and city law enforcers are not particularly happy with this bill because it wouldn't allow them to tap where they have found tapping most fruitful: against gambling and vice offenders.

Furthermore, it develops that a great many state attorneys general have reservations about the wisdom of tapping. When the Senate Subcommittee on Constitutional Rights sought their views, a mere thirteen out of forty-five who responded called for wiretapping authority.

Only a handful of states, incidentally, now authorize any kind of official wiretapping, whereas nearly three dozen states have some sort of curb, often vague, on wiretapping. The remaining states have no law whatsoever on the subject. Mark Lane, assemblyman of New York State, where wiretapping is permitted under court order, told the Senate subcommittee that his state's effort to draw a line between permissible and proscribed tapping had not resulted in any abatement of (1) illegal tapping by police or (2) tapping by private individuals.

In my view, the American people should not permit Section 605 to be scuttled until they have a better assurance that their privacy will be respected than is evident in the Administration's wiretap bill.

Meanwhile, a number of partial remedies for the plague of wiretapping could and should be made. For example:

—Possession of wiretapping equipment should be made a felony in all states that prohibit tapping. California and New Jersey are among the states already making possession a crime.

—Private citizens who find they have been victims of wiretapping should be enabled by statute to sue for punitive damages.

—The Federal Communications Commission should wake up to its responsibilities for policing the nation's telephone lines to ensure privacy. Congressman Kastenmeier has commented, "Quite simply, we have no police to police the police." He is demanding that the FCC actively assume this role by requiring all telephone companies to investigate and report on all evidences of wiretapping. My own feeling is that the telephone companies should also be required to lock all terminal and feeder boxes (where taps often are made). And the FCC should seek to establish criminal penalties for employees of telephone companies who cooperate with wiretappers by providing information.

As things stand the FCC's record of policing the wiretappeis is one of incredible evasiveness. In 1953 it turned over to the FBI the whole problem of investigating complaints of violation of Section 605! The FBI in this instance is scarcely an objective policing agency. Six years after the FCC took this action Attorney General William P. Rogers, who held ultimate responsibility for the FBI, reported, according to Congressman Kastenmeier: "There is no record of prosecution by the Federal Government . . . of local law enforcement officers who have intercepted and divulged..."

3. *The use of microphones to hear and perhaps record the words spoken by individuals when they are within the presumed sanctuary of their own premises.*

When one talks on the telephone, he knows his voice is going to the outside world, with all the obvious hazard of interception that this involves. But when one talks within his home or office, he reasonably assumes he is in a protected area—unless he has come to know that walls can have ears. Thus microphoning is a much more intimate invasion of privacy, and yet the individual has even less legal protection against it than he does against wiretapping. One reason for this, perhaps, is that there is no obvious constitutional link justifying a broad federal law regulating eavesdropping. The law in this area is far behind the technological progress of the eavesdropper.

From a libertarian's viewpoint the Supreme Court's record here has been discouraging. The Court first confronted the hidden microphone as a major issue in the Goldman case in 1942.[21] Federal agents seeking evidence against a lawyer gained entry to an office next to his and placed a "detectaphone" against the dividing wall. The Court found that this involved no unreasonable search that would constitute a violation of the Fourth Amendment. Some observers thought the Court's action might be explained by the fact that it feared creating a rule, in wartime, that might handicap the government's counterintelligence activities.

A decade later (during the Korean War) the Supreme Court was confronted with another even more invasive use of a hidden microphone in the On Lee case, and it again found no violation of the Fourth Amendment.[22] It seems that On Lee, who was suspected of violating the Narcotics Act, was minding his laundry shop in Hoboken, New Jersey, one day when his old friend and former employee, Chin Poy, came in for a chat. What On Lee did not know was that his old friend had become an "undercover agent" for the Narcotics Bureau and was carrying a small radio transmitter in his pocket. A federal agent outside listened to their conversation with a radio receiver and later gave evidence in court that convicted On Lee. The majority of the Supreme Court, in reviewing the case, rejected the idea that any trespass or unreasonable search had occurred, since Chin Poy had been welcomed. It was, however, a close 5-4 decision. One dissenter, Justice Harold H. Burton, contended that the Fourth Amendment's protections clearly should extend to intangible things—conversations—as well as to improperly seized physical objects.

Another nine years were to pass before electronic eavesdroppers received their first major setback. But the circumstances were hardly cheering for those who hoped for a broad reading of the Fourth Amendment. This was the Silverman case, in 1961, involving a spike mike.[23] Police drove a foot-long spike with mike attached into a party wall shared by two houses in Washington, D.C., until it touched a heating duct that acted as a giant reverberator. They were searching for evidence of illegal gambling. Since there had been a physical intrusion the Court ruled unanimously that a violation of the Fourth Amendment had occurred. But the narrow, physical basis for the decision was emphasized by Justice Potter Stewart's assertion: "We find no occasion to reexamine Goldman here, but we decline to go beyond it, by even a fraction of an inch."

All this emphasis upon physical intrusion evades the primary issue of whether citizens are to be secure in carrying on conversations within their private premises. In terms of a right to security, what difference does it make whether the eavesdropping microphone is dropped on a string to a point outside one's apartment window or is placed by physical invasion inside a wall?

In 1963 the Supreme Court faced a case somewhat comparable to On Lee except that the government agent himself went into the individual's premises, wearing a hidden tape recorder, so that eavesdropping is less clearly involved. This was the Lopez case, involving a bribe offer made to an Internal Revenue agent.[24] The tape became in effect a third-party corroboration of the conversation. The Court decided 6-3 against the defendant. But the decision was notable on two counts:

Evidence emerged that a majority of five of the Court might now be willing to reverse itself on its On Lee stand if an opportunity arose. At this writing, attorneys of the American Civil Liberties Union have filed a friend-of-the- court brief with the U.S. Supreme Court asking for a review of a case in California involving the major elements of the On Lee case. A man named Carbo was visited at his hotel room in Los Angeles by a friend who had become a government informant and was wearing a hidden transmitter that was broadcasting to police officials stationed in another room of the hotel.

Also notable in the Lopez decision was Justice Brennan's

ringing dissent. He found it an "intolerable anomaly" that electronic eavesdropping is "wholly beyond the pale of federal law." And he warned: "If electronic surveillance by government becomes sufficiently widespread . . . the hazard that as a people we may become hag-ridden and furtive is not fantasy."

A sample of what apparently is still considered legally permissible is seen in reports that inspectors for the federal Food and Drug Administration have been carrying concealed recorders on many if not all of their plant inspections. Officials of American Dietaids Co., producing special-purpose foods, accidentally discovered that two FDA inspectors who had been voluntarily admitted to one of its facilities were carrying such recorders. Company officials have sought unsuccessfully in court to obtain the tapes and an injunction against future use. The Court of Appeals, in unanimously affirming the district court's denial of the de-mands, mentioned that the government conceded that "such use of recorders is in accord with department practice."[25]

Meanwhile, a groping for remedies through the creation of laws against microphoning has begun. Some influential members of the Senate Judiciary Committee appear to feel that since the offenses are local any laws should be left to the states. The few states that have recognized microphoning at all as an offense—such as Maryland, New York, and Oregon—have mostly enacted prohibitions that exempt bugging by law-enforcement officers acting under court orders.

In the U.S. House of Representatives, however, the enthusiasts of surreptitious microphoning have come up against a formidable foe. Representative Emanuel Celler of New York, chairman of the powerful House Committee on the Judiciary, has introduced a sweeping bill to exclude from federal courts all evidence obtained by microphoning. There is at least one additional way in which Congress could act against microphoning. It could outlaw the shipment across state lines of items clearly and exclusively designed for eavesdropping use. Obvious examples are the spike mike, the wristwatch mike, the parabolic mike, the device that activates tape recorders when voices come over a connecting wire.

Finally the FCC could, and should, tighten its regulations—and require licensing—for all low-powered transmitter devices, and prohibit the use of radio devices for eavesdropping by *anyone* unless specifically authorized by law.

The states, meanwhile, should all be urged to develop right-of-privacy laws that clearly give the average citizen legal recourse for damages if he finds himself the victim of eavesdropping.

Now let us face up to the central question that has been hanging over all judicial and legislative deliberations involving both microphoning and wiretapping: the very reasonable concern about taking any action that would prevent the United States Government from acting with full effectiveness against any clear and direct threat to national security. This would arise in cases involving espionage, sabotage, treason.

This concern almost certainly has had an inhibiting effect when judicial bodies have had to consider whether any form of electronic surveillance of words spoken within a citizen's premises is unconstitutional.

While they have pondered, wiretapping and microphoning have become national scandals. Every citizen's right to privacy is being threatened. The leaders of our government have permitted a disgraceful spread of electronic snooping as they searched for reasons not to enforce Section 605 against wiretapping. Worse, they've searched for reasons not to invoke the Fourth Amendment against both microphoning and wiretapping in cases where these would clearly seem to intrude upon the people's right "to be secure in their persons, houses, papers, and effects, against unreasonable searches and seizures."

Both the Olmstead decision accepting wiretapping and the On Lee decision accepting a form of microphoning were, we'll recall, close ones. There is a possibility that the balance in the present Supreme Court will, if faced with comparable cases, tip to a broad reading of the Fourth Amendment and overrule both On Lee and Olmstead. And it quite conceivably might also overrule the Goldman decision, where the mike was against an outside wall.

Such an overruling of Olmstead, On Lee, and Goldman would bring under the Fourth Amendment virtually all forms of electronic eavesdropping on words uttered inside private premises. Would this mean that all such electronic eavesdropping would automatically become illegal?

Some legal authorities say no. They point out that the Fourth Amendment permits any reasonable search when a search warrant can be obtained. To obtain a warrant they must convince a magistrate that "probable cause" for the search exists. A good deal of wishful thinking has appeared in print on the possibility of obtaining such warrants for electronic surveillance. In several instances well-known lawyers have spoken of search warrants and court orders as if they were substantially identical. They are not.

It is extremely unlikely that a warrant could be obtained or used for most electronic surveillance because:

A warrant cannot be obtained to search for mere evidence. It must be a search for instruments of crime, fruits of crime, or contraband. Certainly microphoning could never meet these requirements and only occasionally could wiretapping conceivably be construed as a search for an instrument of crime.

A warrant must define specific items to be seized. All wiretapping and most eavesdropping uses are by nature indiscriminate.

A warrant must be served on the person whose premises are to be searched, except under very special circumstances. Such notice would inevitably destroy the value of any form of electronic surveillance. Traditional requirements of a legal search would have to be forsaken if such notice was abandoned.

If, then, electronic surveillance without a warrant is declared to be illegal under the Fourth Amendment it seems likely that virtually all kinds of wiretapping and microphoning would be eliminated. At this prospect we should rejoice. But what about the exception we should all like to make for handling the genuine and urgent national security cases? Such exceptions could not at present be made without engaging in the kind of sham thinking that has nullified the Section 605 ban on wiretapping.

There seems, however, to be a possibility of satisfying the general public's urgent need for protection against electronic surveillance while at the same time permitting an exception for clear-cut national-security cases.

Congress should act to ban all wiretapping and all use in federal courts of evidence gained by the microphoning of private premises, but provide that either technique can be used in cases involving espionage, sabotage, or treason. The exceptions should be permitted only when a court order is obtained from a specific federal judge of the district where the use is to be made. If Congress would act promptly to put such a statute on the books before the Supreme Court has to face another major case involving electronic surveillance, the chances seem excellent that the Court would be satisfied to continue interpreting statutes rather than to reach beyond to constitutional questions.

Otherwise the only possibility would be to amend the Constitution to give the federal government broad powers to act in cases of espionage, sabotage, or treason, but this would be an awkward arrangement at best.

The present Bill of Rights represents a magnificent vision for assuring the Blessings of Liberty. This does not mean, however, that the amendments are immutable. The original Bill of Rights has already been expanded by other amendments, and could be again.

Our main concern must be to strengthen the protections long afforded to the citizen by the Fourth Amendment in the light of modern developments.

We have been seeing a serious dilution of rights of privacy long assumed to be protected by the Fourth Amendment. The Court has too frequently read the amendment narrowly to require physical intrusion by an actual trespass onto a person's property by distinguishing between a microphone outside and one partly inside one's wall. This is not realistic in terms of protecting one's right to be secure in one's home against modern eavesdropping techniques. The Court has refused to see wiretapping as an invasion of this right to be secure in one's home and person since there was no physical searching and seizure. It has engrafted the "incidental" search exception to the requirement of a search warrant, and this exception clearly can be abused. It has condoned administrative searches of homes of innocent persons suspected of no crime without a warrant at a time when we're seeing a growth of administrative officers seeking to search homes.

In short, the right of privacy implied by the bold wording of the Fourth Amendment has not received its due recognition. The Court must respond to the new challenges, especially to the many variations of electronic surveillance, and elevate and protect the right of privacy against such innovations.

If the Court finds it cannot do this within the traditional terms of the Fourth Amendment, then it should take a new look at the "liberty" phrase embodied in the due-process clauses of the Fifth (see below) and Fourteenth Amendments. There has been a hopeful trend in arguments and opinions toward taking a fresh look at the "liberty" provision as offering the possibility of giving broad protection to the right of privacy.

Judge George Thomas Washington of the District of Columbia Court of Appeals offered support to this approach in his dissent in the Silverman case, where a spike mike was driven into a wall. He said: "Thus, eavesdropping of the kind which occurred here may be held not to abridge any Fourth Amendment rights. But it does violate, I think, our fundamental concept of ordered liberty, as embodied in the due-process clauses of the Fifth and Fourteenth Amendments."[26]

One final thought is this. Since the Fourth Amendment was not intended to protect the individual from non-governmental intruders, the fifty states have a responsibility to strengthen their laws and their enforcement procedures so as to protect individuals from eavesdropping and unwarranted intrusions by other private citizens.

THE FIFTH AND SIXTH AMENDMENTS
(excerpts)

Amendment V. "No person . . . shall be compelled in any criminal case to be a witness against himself, nor be deprived of life, liberty, or property, without due process of law. . . ."

Amendment VI. "In all criminal prosecutions, the accused shall enjoy the right to a speedy and public trial . . . and to be informed of the nature and cause of the accusation; to be confronted with the witnesses against him; to have compulsory process for obtaining witnesses in his favor, and to have the assistance of counsel for his defense."

The "assistance of counsel" of course is destroyed when— as commonly happens—an accused person is being detained in a room at a police station or jail that contains hidden microphones.

I have listed the Fifth and Sixth Amendments together because the Sixth to some extent spells out the meaning of the "due process of law" phrase used in the Fifth.

The provisions of the Fifth Amendment that I have excerpted are those that have been most frequently assaulted in recent years in cases involving the rights of individual citizens.

In the careless lingo of many Americans the phrase "taking the Fifth" has in the past decade come to be a sneer. It suggests that the person taking it is guilty of something, and in some situations probably is guilty of being a Communist. It signifies confession of guilt by silence. Distinguished jurists, however, have referred to the privilege against self-incrimination as one of the great landmarks of civilized man's struggle to evolve fair legal procedures. It was aimed at giving both innocent and guilty alike a safeguard against manhandling. A perfectly innocent person, it was realized, could be terrified of the thought of prosecution when finding himself at bay before the forces of government, especially if the government was known to be relentless or harsh. And in a police state he could be made to testify against himself to avoid torture.

Today the assaults against this amendment come not from the use of the rack or screw as short cuts to confession in criminal cases, but in the new kinds of trials that have developed. It should be noted that the subsequently enacted Fourteenth Amendment specifies that no state shall "deprive any person of life, liberty, or property without due process of law . . ." There is no suggestion that this requirement is confined to criminal cases.

In these many new quasi-trials the defendant is not accused of a crime; but the prospective penalties of an unfavorable decision can be as terrifying as being declared guilty of a crime. Here are some of the results of these new kinds of trials and scrutinies:

—In the past decade we have seen many thousands of persons subjected to what in effect have been legislative trials. In these sessions they could be jailed for contempt if they gave a wrong answer, and yet were assured none of the safeguards of fair procedure incorporated in the phrase "due process of law."

—We have seen a frightening increase, in the past decade, in the use of lie detectors employed by government representatives to induce persons under examination to be witnesses against themselves. Quite probably chemicals of the so-called "truth serum" variety also have been used.

—We've seen the great growth of test oaths as a condition of public employment. These have often required applicants and jobholders to be witnesses against themselves concerning affiliations in the distant past.

—And we've seen on many fronts a fifteen-year-long battle

to gain for people under administrative accusation the right to cross-examine their accusers. This is basic to due process, but is not always granted.

The Blessings of Liberty would certainly be more secure in this modern world if the Fifth Amendment were amended to provide that its protections apply to all administrative proceedings against individuals when the individual has a substantial stake involved—and not just to criminal cases.

In the meantime, various government bodies could take three steps that would reduce many of the abuses in violation of the spirit of the Fifth Amendment that we have been seeing in recent years. Those steps are:

1. There is an urgent need for the Congress to develop its own uniform code for conducting its quasi-trials when individuals are brought before it under subpoena. Otherwise the individual is at times left to feel as if he has been hauled before a panel of Torquemadas. In 1962 and again in 1963, the Supreme Court felt impelled to reverse convictions for contempt of Congress because elementary procedural rules had not been followed by committees. The Congress should not be content, as one of three equal branches of the national government, to have its ground rules set, bit by bit, by another branch.

2. The right to confront and cross-examine accusers whose testimony threatens a person with dismissal because of governmental charges should be made universal for civilians. We have noted the progress made in gaining a limited right to confrontation for employees of private contractors who are doing business with the government. The Atomic Energy Commission, in 1962, became the first federal unit to offer its own federal employees assurances of this same limited right. And I am advised that, at this writing, the Department of Defense is seriously studying the possibility of offering the same opportunities to its civilian employees. But the weakness of all these programs is that officials of the various agencies involved can refuse to disclose the

identity of accusers on several grounds, including simply "good and sufficient" ones. In any case, when it is alleged that national security would be endangered by confrontation, the facts should at least be reviewed by an independent panel of distinguished citizens.

3. The various states should be encouraged to prohibit the use of lie-detector tests as a condition of private employment. A few states now have such laws, and California has one under consideration.

In one way or another, the right to privacy, per se, should be given more explicit recognition by statute and by constitutional interpretation through the courts. A great many of the states now have laws that offer some—usually minor—recognition of a right to privacy. In view of the fact that our privacy is being assaulted in a hundred insidious forms, it would seem appropriate for the Supreme Court finally to dignify this asserted right by at least pondering it—perhaps as an aspect of ordered liberty—and offering some guidelines.

Morris Ernst and Alan Schwartz concluded from their study of the "young" right to privacy that "individuals will rely on the right more heavily as time goes on in order to keep their own individual outlines from being merged in-distinguishably into the commonweal."

18. What We Can Do to Protect Ourselves

"... a respect for privacy. It is in this as much as in any other single characteristic that the free society differs from the totalitarian state."—Alan Barth[1]

We began this exploration by citing Judge Learned Hand's comment that the defense of liberty must come from the hearts of men and women. In the last several pages we have examined some of the legal remedies that seem obviously to be needed to defend liberty and privacy. But constitutions, laws, and courts, as Judge Hand emphasized, make only a limited contribution at best. Many of the invasions of privacy we have examined are not susceptible to legal restraint. And even if they were, the degree to which the general citizenry is determined to protect the Blessings of Liberty profoundly influences the performance of lawmakers, judges, and law enforcers.

A few years before his death, Aldous Huxley said that the fact that "we are being propelled in the direction of *Brave New World* is obvious. But no less obvious is the fact that we can, if we so desire, refuse to cooperate with the blind forces that are propelling us."

If we determine to resist the "blind forces," inevitably it will be sensed by those who have a measure of control over the forces. They are decent citizens who, like most of us, are influenced by the mood of their times. During the past decade the forces producing massive invasions of privacy have at times been rampant because they were reflecting the times and advancing technology—and because citizens were preoccupied with other problems.

Perhaps I'm being overly hopeful, but today the mood seems to be changing. The continual pushing in on the individual, which

Senator Edward Long noted, is being widely felt, resented, and resisted.

This new mood, for example, may well be causing public officials concerned with security and law enforcement to reexamine their practices and their consciences.

Consider the new emphasis that top officials of the Department of Defense are placing upon private rights. Walter T. Skallerup, Jr., Deputy Assistant Secretary of Defense for security policy, has disclosed a memorandum he has addressed to the Under Secretaries of the Army, Navy, and Air Force. In this memorandum he cited twenty-six kinds of questions that were "improper and irrelevant" in making loyalty investigations. It is not proper, he advised, to ask such questions as:

Do you consider yourself a liberal or a conservative?

Have you ever signed a political petition? Explain.

What are your views on desegregation?

What are your views regarding decisions of the Supreme Court (i.e., prayers in public schools, desegregation, and Communist Party cases)?

Are you an atheist or agnostic?

It is shocking, as the *New York Times* editorially commented, that any security officer should ever have dreamed of asking such questions in the first place as part of a loyalty examination. But it is heartening that a high Defense official has acted to remind security investigators to respect "lawful civil and private rights." The memorandum warned that investigators must not "discourage lawful political activity, or intimidate free expression or thought."

Mr. Skallerup first revealed the existence of this memorandum during a conference he held with leaders of the American Civil Liberties Union. They were discussing possible ways to improve the security program from the viewpoint of individual rights. It is noteworthy that ACLU leaders have also been conferring with chiefs of police in major cities and report finding a new mood of willingness to re-examine police practices in dealing with persons seized. They report a new sensitivity to private rights among police administrators in several cities, such as Detroit and New York.

Philadelphia was the first major city in the nation to set up an Independent Citizens' Police Review Board, which weighs complaints any citizens lodge against the police. Rochester has been a pioneer among the smaller cities in setting up such a citizens' board. Los Angeles doesn't have such a board, but at least it now forwards any written complaints to the Police Commission instead of the police department, as was the procedure in the past. The commission consists of five business and professional men appointed by the mayor.

Possibly some of this evidence of interest in respecting citizens' rights was reinforced by the nation's chief law enforcer, J. Edgar Hoover, director of the FBI. Mr. Hoover has recently urged the nation's law-enforcement officers to develop a code of ethics to eliminate violations of civil rights. Such violations by law-enforcement officers, he said, "seldom stem from evil intent, but rather from officers improperly trained and untutored in the ethics of the profession."

One item of the code of ethics of both law-enforcement and security directors might well involve the responsibility for safeguarding their central index files. Furthermore, both police and security forces should develop and enforce stiffer penalties against personnel with access to such files who—by selling or swapping—pass such information to persons unauthorized to receive it.

All citizens—acting as individual citizens or as persons with special power to exert influence because of their position—can and should work to secure the personal liberties that have recently been under such vigorous assault.

What business and labor leaders can do. Both have sound reasons, from their special viewpoints, for working to help each person associated with their enterprise achieve a sense of personal dignity, fulfillment, and responsibility. But both have, with relatively few exceptions, shown too little interest in doing this in the past.

A number of demeaning privacy-invading practices at companies need to be reassessed and modified.

For example:

Any company that hopes to be known as a decent place to work should completely eliminate lie detectors; and both management and labor leaders should work to achieve that end.

Such a company should also refrain from tape-recording interviews with job applicants unless notice is given.

Any company that respects its personnel will confine its use of undercover agents—if it must use them at all—to the attempt to solve specific crimes against the company, and not use them as a generalized form of "insurance."

Such a company will adopt a completely open policy in regard to any use it makes of cameras or closed-circuit TV systems. Any photographing equipment used will be readily visible and will scan only work areas and entrance areas.

If the company wants key employees to have periodic health checkups, it may reasonably finance those checkups. But it is unreasonable to expect a report of the results. The company should make it emphatically clear that the results of the checkup are a confidential matter between the doctor and the employee.

Any company that is still fascinated by the idea of subjecting key employees to the so-called personality tests should permit use of the tests only in the same way suggested for health checkups. A trained psychologist who enjoys the trust of an employee can often help him become more effective on the job by counseling him; in some instances he may feel he can gain additional insights or reinforce his hunches by using the tests. Such use is not objectionable. But if the company expects a report on either the testing or the counseling, the relationship of trust between psychologist and employee is shattered, and any personality testing then becomes merely a relatively unreliable form of espionage.

What private and public planners can do. New York architect Philip Ives has referred to privacy as "the first essential in an overcrowded world." And one of the most obnoxious features of overcrowding is noise. Since most Americans already live in urban areas, and the motor vehicle population is expected to grow twice as fast as the human population, it is past time to view noise as a major disrupter of privacy.

England is much further ahead on a national campaign to combat "noise pollution" than the U.S.A. It sees noise as a major new civic disease of our time, as distressing as bad housing and dirt. A "noise map" has been constructed of the thirty-six square miles of central London, the first such large-scale map ever compiled in any country.[2] This survey discovered that main roads had become as distressing to the human ear as main railway lines, in some instances even more distressing. Buildings, too, exude distressing noise. From the massive studies ordered by the Minister for Science, radical changes are expected to come in the design of Great Britain's cities. The Committee on Noise is drawing up maximum acceptable levels of external noise for different types of buildings within cities.

It is considered likely that architects and town planners in Britain may now tend to favor courtyard or "cloister" planning for buildings. British common law, incidentally, holds that freedom from noise is essential to the full enjoyment of one's dwelling.[3]

Mitchell Gordon in his study of sick cities, just cited, reports that great progress in restoring municipal quiet has been made in Paris and Mexico City by such measures as stern enforcement of laws against the blowing of automobile horns. And Paris has replaced the noisy metal wheels of subway trains with rubber-tired ones. Mr. Gordon cites estimates that New York City could reduce its noise level by 80 per cent "by compelling trucks and busses to use effective mufflers, getting garbage collectors to install rubber pads on their rear shelves, and convincing home owners to use non-metallic containers for their refuse."

In the United States the Federal Housing Administration now makes available recommendations on how to control noise in any new apartments being built.

The recommendations were prepared by Bolt, Beranek and Newman, acoustical engineers. But these FHA recommendations are optional. Some builders insist they will produce little effect until they are made mandatory, because building competition is too intense, and corner-cutting is the order of the day.

Perhaps the most heartening development in the United States is that in New York City the new city building code, due to go into effect in 1965, will contain mandatory provisions for noiseproofing in new apartment buildings. The city's building commissioner contends that the people who drew up the existing, outdated building code "had no concept of the cacophony produced without limit by a disharmonic symphony of radios, XV, hi-fi sets, washing machines, air conditioners, fans, laundromats and dishwashers. . . . They could not contemplate the sounds of surging waters in hidden bathrooms . . . nor did they consider the disruption caused by loud, boisterous, or discordant neighbors, or the pitter-patter of little feet at three o'clock in the morning."

He added: "'The right to privacy' through 'quiet enjoyment' need not be an abstract legal phrase. . . . An apartment can be a refuge, a peaceful nook where a man can escape the alien contraptions which incessantly seek to attack and destroy his nervous equilibrium."[4] Some of the new apartments in New York already are advertising "soundproofing between floors and walls." At present the only insulation legally required is to retard fire, not sound.

Cities might also start looking at the worst noise generator of all, the motor vehicle. And it might be hoped that the automobile industry, for its own future well-being, will join in the looking. After they have examined the possibilities of reducing automotive noise through insulation and muffler construction they might agree on maximum phon levels of sound that a car or truck would be permitted to make while going, say, thirty miles an hour past a phon meter, measuring sound from fifty feet away.

What educators and scientists can do. Obviously they can do a great many things to strengthen and safeguard our personal liberties. I will mention just a few.

—College faculties should develop a written standard for the kinds of information about students that can reasonably be given to outside investigators and prospective employers, and a standardized form for explaining why they do not consider it appropriate to answer questions about *any* student concerning beliefs, attitudes, associations, etc.

—The officials of secondary schools should examine any surveillance methods they have instituted to control student behavior, and discard any methods that they would not be pleased to describe to a student assembly or to a parent-teachers meeting.

—These same officials should ask to see all "family-background" inventories and "personality" check lists used on students. They should ban all that probe further into the private world of the captive student audience than any public institution has any right, in decency, to do. Such tools should be used only with clearly disturbed children, with parental permission, and preferably by an outside clinical psychologist. The National Education Association could perform a great service if it would establish a distinguished board of educators and social scientists who would evaluate all personality-type tests being used or seriously considered for use in schools. The NEA should later disseminate the board's findings to the nation's schools.

—School administrators at both college and secondary levels should re-examine the quality of instruction being offered on problems involved in the relation of the individual to modern society, and specifically the instruction on the content and meaning of the Bill of Rights. One kind of model is being set, for adult education, by the University of California, Los Angeles Extension. It has been offering a series of lectures on the Bill of Rights entitled "Controversy in the Classroom." Schools and other institutions exerting social influence might well place greater emphasis upon observing the "Bill of Rights Week." The *New York Post* is one newspaper that annually publishes the Bill of Rights during that week. In 1963 the *Post* commented editorially that the bill "embodies the dreams of men in every land where tyranny wounds and suffocates the human spirit."

The problems of scientists are primarily ones of ethics and responsibility. Conceivably they can ultimately exert some control—in cooperation with government and industry—over the development and uses of electronic memory banks by making certain that the instruments are not put to socially dubious uses.

More immediately, scientists certainly can work through their professional associations to develop codes for the use of mind-manipulating techniques. They should work to develop tighter federal laws and regulations that would prohibit all use of certain of these drugs and electrical stimulations except in the medical treatment of specific severe physical and mental ailments.

Dr. Robert S. Morison, director of Medical and Natural Sciences of the Rockefeller Foundation, explained that he has enough confidence in the scientific method to realize that much greater controls over human behavior will ultimately become possible. He believes it is time to start thinking about "how we will handle the increased responsibility which such power will bring with it." And he added: "Actually a good many people feel that we are rather far behind in such thinking already." He has stated that the central question is whether society can devise checks and balances on its scientific power roughly comparable in their effectiveness to the checks and balances "which democratic societies have learned in the last 500 years to apply to political power." He feels there is need for a "clearer recognition that increased knowledge implies increased responsibility."

What every individual can do. We do not need to be antisocial to cherish privacy. Good citizens know they have responsibilities to their community, and delight in filling them. But they also know they are better citizens if they can feel free to keep a part of their lives as uniquely their own.

What can a citizen do to protect himself, for example, from people who may wish to listen in on conversations he conducts in or from his home, by microphoning or wiretapping? He can urge his state or national representatives to get busy and provide realistic legal protection that has a chance of being enforced. Meanwhile, if he needs to discuss a matter that someone would be willing to pay more than $100 to overhear, he must accept the possibility of electronic eavesdropping being used. In that case he should avoid the telephone for important conversations and take prudent action to foil any possible microphoners.

The techniques used by the federal government and by corporations to safeguard conversations are too expensive to be considered by the average citizen. He cannot afford to have special, shielded, wiretap-proof cable strung to his telephone. And unless he is a Texas millionaire like Clint Murchison, Jr., he probably won't feel he can afford to have a voice scrambler system installed for his telephone conversations. And he can't afford, at $25 a room, to have his quarters scanned by professional anti-intrusion experts—with their electronic mops and probing devices—on any regular basis. Even if he could afford to put a special electronic box in his ceiling that would create a cone of silence around the area of the room where he is conversing with others, he couldn't do so as yet. This device is still under development, and probably will be too expensive for individual use anyway.

So what possibilities are left for the citizen? His best bet is to do his conversing near a turned-up radio. The human ear, fortunately, has one enormous advantage over an electronic ear. This human ear automatically filters out background sounds, whereas a microphone cannot. Another possibility is to do any important conversing in a room where you would ordinarily be most unlikely to conduct such conversations, such as in a child's room or in the kitchen.

The person who is concerned about the privacy of his private affairs should make his concern known to people who are likely to be sought out by the usual run of investigators. Such people would include particularly his banker and, if he lives in an apartment, the attendants of his building.

Every American, it might be added, can protect himself to some extent against the nuisances that he feels intrude unreasonably into his life. If he is fed up with finding his mailbox half filled each day with bulky junk mail of no interest to him, he can fight back. He can do this by returning, empty, any business-reply-postage-guaranteed envelopes that are enclosed, and he can mark "refused" any unwanted mail that is stamped "Return Requested."[5] The senders will soon get the hint. I've started doing this with some of the particularly unwanted, particularly bulky mail that seems to have been coming for more than a year. These returns cost the companies receiving them back a minimum of six cents each. If one householder in a hundred who is on a mailing list would adopt this practice of returning unwanted mail or envelopes, the mailing-list industry would find itself with a multimillion-dollar headache, and then would be more careful to select people who might reasonably be interested in their mail.

Our harassed citizen might also refuse on grounds of principle to chat with every investigator who comes along inquiring about the habits of a neighbor or associate. My Dutch publisher says that Hollanders have such a respect for privacy that most of them wouldn't dream of offering such information, even if it was a good friend who was inquiring.

If a citizen is annoyed when he goes to a public beach or park in search of refreshing solitude and finds that someone within a few feet has a transistor radio blaring, he can (1) politely ask the offender to turn down the noise, (2) work to get a local ordinance banning such nuisances, or (3) fight back with his own radio. An expert on electronics explained to me that you can do this simply by dialing your own set to a point 460 kilocycles numerically below the signal that is creating the nuisance. Your set can be silent. The only requirement is that the switch be turned on. (Your own set has within it a small transmitter.) Thus if the offensive rock-and-roll music is on 1060, you dial your radio to 600, and if you are lucky you will hear a squeal issuing from your inconsiderate neighbor's radio.

But enough of petty retaliations.

One important thing we should all strive to do in order to protect our right to lead our own lives is to show a decent tolerance, if not respect, for the views of people with whom we disagree. A republic cannot possibly be weakened by an airing of unpopular views. The danger posed by certain groups on the fanatical right in the U.S. is that they have copied some of the procedural tactics of secrecy, furtiveness, and disguise frequently practiced by the Communists on the fanatical left. But with regard to people who are willing to speak their views openly, the comment of Woodrow Wilson still deserves respect. He said:

"The wisest thing to do with a fool is to encourage him to hire a hall and discourse to his fellow citizens. Nothing chills nonsense like exposure to the air."

All Americans who are concerned about efforts to undermine individual rights in their country might also wish to support organizations that have been leading fights to safeguard those rights. I refer to such organizations as the League of Women Voters, the Americans for Democratic Action, and the American Civil Liberties Union. The ACLU recently found itself in what some people assumed was an odd position, since it has often been publicized for upholding the legal rights of left-wingers who, it felt, had been deprived of constitutional rights. It was defending the right of Mississippi's segregationist governor Ross Barnett to demand a trial by jury when he was to face charges of criminal contempt. Actually there was nothing odd about it at all. The ACLU was simply asking that he be given a right to which every tree American is entitled under the Sixth Amendment of the Bill of Rights. It has also offered to defend the rights of John Buchers, radical right-wingers, to put up posters that called for impeachment of Earl Warren, the Chief Justice of the U.S. Supreme Court.

More than 800 volunteer lawyers in the U.S.A. work without fee, when requested by the ACLU, on cases in which critical constitutional issues seem to be involved. Whitney North Seymour, a former president of the American Bar Association, has stated:

"As a lawyer I have sometimes differed wtih the ACLU's choice of cases and some of its legal positions, but as a citizen I have been glad there was a group ready to perform the often unpopular task of contesting every inch of ground in defense of basic liberties."[6]

And if we want to uphold our right to privacy, let us stop fearing to stand alone. We must stop worrying about whether our necks are out, or whether someone will consider us out of line. Let us be ourselves and speak our minds and act on both our convictions and our indignations.

A dedicated country doctor on the island of Martha's Vineyard, Massachusetts, who has cared for my family, became indignant a few months ago. This man is a native of the island, a lifelong Republican and conservative who has been so absorbed in his practice that he has shown relatively little interest in civic matters or national problems. But what he read about gross affronts to human dignity in Williamston, North Carolina, impelled him to do something completely untypical for him. He left his island and rode in a car thirty-six hours without sleeping until he reached Williamston, where he joined in passive demonstrations and did what he could to help the morale of citizens involved in a local struggle for human dignity. When at the end he went to the bus station to return home, he was physically assaulted by two men who used ugly words to him.

Some people in New England thought he had gone seven hundred miles out of his way to "look for trouble." 1 gather that he believes the experience made him a better, more enlightened citizen. I feel that our urgent need today is for more people like him who will stand up for human integrity even if it means great personal inconvenience and the possibility of personal trouble. Such people might meet Henry David Thoreau's specification: "Oh for a man who is a man and . . . has a bone in his back which you cannot pass your hand through!"

Finally, the most important thing that every American can do to protect his heritage of a right to privacy is to see that the right is respected in his own home. This means that parents should knock or call before they enter the room of a child who has his door closed. This is simple decency. Goethe, we'll recall, said that talent develops in privacy. His actual words were "*Es bildet ein Talent sich in der Stille,*" which might also be translated freely as "Talent develops in unseen solitude." Whether it is privacy or solitude, it is also true that dreams and plans and self-reliance and a sense of being trusted—as well as talent—flourish in such an atmosphere. A child raised in an environment where his individuality is respected will have more inner resources to draw upon when he becomes an adult.

And in the world in which he is going to become an adult, respect for privacy and individuality will clearly be an increasingly important problem.

Alan Schwartz suggests that concern for privacy is a manifestation of a relatively sophisticated, thoughtful society. He reminds us that privacy is "unknown in most primitive societies and unknown in all dictatorships—save for the privacy of the dictator himself."[7]

He makes a further, and I think profoundly important, point. Concern for one's right to privacy, he states, "represents a basic alienation between the individual and his society, an alienation which, I suggest, is at the core of all our civil liberties. To the extent that a society not only tolerates, but encourages, this human antagonism within its midst, it can truly be said to be a democratic society."

Perhaps most of us will never be able to prove Emerson's contention that the private life of each person should be a more illustrious monarchy than any kingdom.

But we should have the opportunity to try.

REFERENCE NOTES

CHAPTER 1

1. Ralph S. Brown, Jr., *Loyalty and Security: Employment Tests in the United States* (New Haven: Yale University Press, 1958), p. 181.
2. From information supplied by Walter T. Skallerup, Jr., Deputy Assistant Secretary of Defense, Security Policy.
3. Samuel Dash with Richard F. Schwartz and Robert E. Knowlton, *The Eavesdroppers* (New Brunswick: Rutgers University Press, 1959). Study sponsored by the Pennsylvania Bar Association Endowment Fund.

CHAPTER 2

1. Morris L. Ernst and Alan U. Schwartz, *Privacy: The Right to Be Left Alone*, Milestones of Law Series (New York: The Macmillan Company, 1962).

CHAPTER 3

1. Remark made by Dr. Robert McMurry of The McMurry Company. For amplification see Chapter 4 of *The Pyramid Climbers* by Vance Packard (New York: McGraw-Hill Book Co., 1962).
2. Richard A. Sternbach, Lawrence A. Gustafson, and Ronald L. Colier, "Don't Trust the Lie Detector," *Harvard Business Review*, November-December 1962.
3. All of the following, as examples, contain one or more chapters that discuss the uses of personality tests in the business world: *The Brain Watchers*, by Martin L. Gross; *Life in the Crystal Palace*, by Alan Harrington; *The Tyranny of Testing*, by Banesh Hoffman; *The Pyramid Climbers*, by Vance Packard; and *The Organization Man*, by William H. Whyte, Jr.

CHAPTER 4

1. *Wall Street Journal*, June 21, 1963, 279

CHAPTER 5

1. *Management Review*, May 1957. Report on survey made by Lydia Strong.
2. Frederick Herzberg, Bernard Mausner, and Barbara Block Snyderman, *The Motivation to Work* (New York: John Wiley & Sons, 1962). p. 130.
3. Chris Argyris, *Interpersonal Competence and Organizational Effectiveness* (Homewood, 111.: Irwin-Dorsey, 1962).

CHAPTER 7

1. Excerpts of letter published in *AAUP Bulletin*, Summer 1961, reprinting from *Newsweek*, May 22, 1961.
2. C. Vann Woodward, "The Unreported Crisis in Southern Colleges," *Harper's*, October 1962.
3. *Life*, April 26, 1963.
4. Louis Joughin, "Scrutiny of Professors," *Bulletin of the American Association of University Professors*, Spring 1958.

CHAPTER 8

1. From Notice of Meeting of the Representative Assembly, University of California, October 28, 1958.
2. For the full policy statement see *School and Society*, October 7, 1961.
3. Martin Gross, *The Brain Watchers* (New York: Random House, 1962), p. 166.
4. Hillel Black, *They Shall Not Pass* (New York: WilliamMorrow, 1963), p. 133.

CHAPTER 9

1. United States vs. On Lee, C.A., N.Y. 1951, 193 F. 2nd, 306, 315.

2. *New York Times*, August 11, 1963. Grace and Fred Hechinger are co-authors of the book *Teen-Age Tyranny*.

3. Frank v. Maryland, 359 U.S. 360 (1959). Cited by Justice Douglas in his lecture reprinted in *The Great Rights* (New York: The Macmillan Company, 1963).

4. Irvine v. California, 347 U.S. 128 (1954).

5. People v. Cahan, 44 Cal. 2nd 434 (1955).

CHAPTER 10

1. Hillel Black, *Buy Now, Pay Later* (New York: William Morrow, 1961).

CHAPTER 12

1. Norman Cousins, "The Noise Level Is Rising," *Saturday Review*, December 8, 1962.

2. Yoeckel v. Samonig, 272 Wise. 430, 75 N.W. 2nd 925 (1956).

3. Harriet F. Pilpel, "What Will They Think of Next?" *Publishers' Weekly*, July 31, 1961.

4. "Remember Marilyn," *Life*, August 17, 1962.

5. *Time*, May 10, 1963.

6. Kent v. Dulles, 357 U.S. 116 (1958).

CHAPTER 13

1. James A. Wechsler, "News Control," *New York Post*, March 11, 1963.

2. Edward Bennett Williams, *One Man's Freedom* (New York: Atheneum, 1962), p. 77.

3. Frank J. Donner, *The Un-Americans* (New York: Ballantine Books, 1961), p. 59.

4. Kiibourn v. Thompson, 103 U.S. 168, 190.

5. Robert K. Carr, *The House Committee on Un-American Activities*, 1945-1950 (Ithaca: Cornell University Press, 1952), p. 328.

6. Justice William O. Douglas, *The Right of the People* (New York:

Pyramid Publications, p. 61; reprint of Doubleday edition first published January 1958).

7. John Cogley, Report on Blacklisting—1 Movies, The Fund for the Republic, 1956. See also his Report II on blacklisting in radio-TV.

8. Harold Horowitz, "Loyalty Tests for Employment in the Motion Picture Industry," *Stanford Law Review* (1954), 6: 438.

9. Merle Miller, *The Judges and the Judged* (New York: Doubleday & Co., 1952).

10. Watkins v. United States, 354 U.S. 178 (1957).

11. Tom Braden, "I Was the Target of a Hate Campaign," *Look*, October 22, 1963.

CHAPTER 14

1. Samuel Dash, et al., op. cit., p. 135.

2. Alan Barth, *The Price of Liberty* (New York: Viking Press, 1961), p. 11.

3. R. E. L. Masters, The Homosexual Revolution (New York: Julian Press, 1962), pp. 186-88.

4. Rochin v. California, 342 U.S. 165, 170 (1952).

5. Leyra v. Denno, 347 U.S. 556 (1954).

6. 1958 Report of the New York State Joint Legislative Com-mittee on Privacy of Communication and Licensure of Private Investigators, p. 25.

7. *American Bar Association Journal*, October 1963, p. 1015.

CHAPTER 15

1. William F. Rickenbacker, "The Fourth House," National Review, May 21, 1960.

2. United States ex rel. Toth v. Quarles, 350 U.S. 11 (1955).

3. Joseph L. Rauh, Jr., "Nonconfrontation in Security Cases: The Greene Decision," *Virginia Law Review*, Vol. 45, No. 7, 1959.

4. Greene v. McElroy, 360 U.S. 474 (1959).

CHAPTER 16

1. *Control of the Mind*, edited by Seymour M. Farber and Roger H. L. Wilson (New York: McGraw-Hill Book Company, 1961), p. xii.
2. *The Manipulation of Human Behavior*, edited by Albert D. Biderman and Herbert Zimmer (New York: John Wiley & Sons, 1961), p. 267. From report on "The Experimental Investigation of Interpersonal Influence," by Robert R. Blake and Jane S. Mouton.
3. Joost A. M. Meerloo, *The Rape of the Mind* (Cleveland: World Publishing Co., 1956), p. 27.
4. Robert G. Heath, "Electrical Self-Stimulation of the Brain in Man," *American Journal of Psychiatry* (1963), 120:571.
5. Aldous Huxley, *Brave New World Revisited* (New York: Harper & Bro., 1958), pp. 85-86.

CHAPTER 17

1. The four lectures are contained in *The Great Rights*, edited by Edmond Cahn (New York: The Macmillan Company, 1963). Justice Brennan's comment stated at the outset of this chapter came from his lecture.
2. Report on Poll 61 of the Purdue Opinion Panel, November 1960, Division of Educational Reference, Purdue University, Lafayette, Indiana.
3. Edward Bennett Williams, op. cit., p. 8.
4. Justice William O. Douglas, op. cit., p. 79.
5. Barenblatt v. United States, 360 U.S. 109 (1959).
6. Wilkinson v. United States, 365 U.S. 399 (1961).
7. Harris v. United States, 331 U.S. 145 (1947).
8. Weeks v. United States, 232 U.S. 383 (1914).
9. Wolf v. Colorado, 338 U.S. 25 (1949).
10. Mapp v. Ohio, 367 U.S. 643 (1961).
11. Frank v. Maryland, 359 U.S. 360 (1959).
12. Olmstead v. United States, 277 U.S. 438 (1928).
13. Henry Pringle, *The Life and Times of William Howard*

Taft (New York: Farrar, 1939), p. 989.

14. Nardone v. United States, 302 U.S. 379 (1937).

15. Nardone v. United States, 308 U.S. 338 (1939).

16. Goldstein v. United States, 316 U.S. 114 (1942).

17. Schwartz v. Texas, 344 U.S. 199 (1952).

18. Benanti v. United States, 355 U.S. 96 (1957).

19. Rathbun v. United States, 355 U.S. 107 (1957).

20. Pugach v. Dollinger, 365 U.S. 458 (1961), and People v. Dinan, 371 U.S. 877 (1962).

21. Goldman v. United States, 316 U.S. 129 (1942).

22. On Lee v. United States, 343 U.S. 747 (1952).

23. Silverman v. United States, 365 U.S. 505 (1961).

24. Lopez v. United States, 373 U.S. 427 (1963).

25. 317 F. 2nd 658 (2nd Cir. 1963).

26. 275 F. 2nd at 179 D.C. Cir. 7, in comments of Judge George Thomas Washington of the District of Columbia Court of Appeals

.

CHAPTER 18

1. Alan Barth, op. cit., p. 75.

2. "New House Rules Mean Changes in Building Design," *London Observer,* May 19, 1963.

3. Mitchell Gordon, *Sick Cities* (New York: The Macmillan Co., 1963), p. 224.

4. *New York Times*, September 12, 1963.

5. Sam Blum, "The List Makers—How They Find You," Pageant, August 1962.

6. *Wall Street Journal*, October 30, 1963.

7. From a paper prepared by Alan U. Schwartz entitled "Privacy— The Right to Be Let Alone," for a compilation being made of views on "The Right of Privacy and the Mass Media" by the School of Journalism at Penn State University.

ARTICLES IN ADDITION TO,
AND IN AMENDMENT OF,
THE CONSTITUTION OF THE UNITED STATES OF
AMERICA
TEN ORIGINAL AMENDMENTS—
THE BILL OF RIGHTS

ARTICLE I.

Congress shall make no law respecting an establishment of religion, or prohibiting the free exercise thereof; or abridging the freedom of speech, or of the press; or of the right of the people peaceably to assemble, and to petition the Government for a redress of grievances.

ARTICLE II.

A well-regulated militia, being necessary to the security of a free State, the right of the people to keep and bear arms, shall not be infringed.

ARTICLE III.

No soldier shall, in time of peace be quartered in any house, without the consent of the owner, nor in time of war, but in a manner to be prescribed by law.

ARTICLE IV.

The right of the people to be secure in their persons, houses, papers, and effects, against unreasonable searches and seizures, shall not be violated, and no warrants shall issue, but upon probable cause, supported by oath or affirmation, and particularly describing the place to be searched, and the persons or things to be seized.

ARTICLE V.

No person shall be held to answer for a capital, or otherwise infamous crime, unless on a presentment or indictment of a Grand

Jury, except in cases arising in the land or naval forces, or in the militia, when in active service in time of war or public danger; nor shall any person be subject for the same offense to be twice put in jeopardy of life or limb; nor shall be compelled in any criminal case to be a witness against himself, nor be deprived of life, liberty, or property, without due process of law; nor shall private property be taken for public use, without just compensation.

ARTICLE VI.

In all criminal prosecutions, the accused shall enjoy the right to a speedy and public trial, by an impartial jury of the State and district wherein the crime shall have been committed, which district shall have been previously ascertained by law, and to be informed of the nature and cause of the accusation; to be confronted with the witnesses against him; to have compulsory process for obtaining witnesses in his favor, and to have the assistance of counsel for his defense.

ARTICLE VII.

In suits at common law, where the value in controversy shall exceed twenty dollars, the right of trial by jury shall be preserved, and no fact tried by a jury, shall be otherwise reexamined in any court of the United States, than according to the rules of the common law.

ARTICLE VIII.

Excessive bail shall not be required, nor excessive fines imposed, nor cruel and unusual punishments inflicted.

ARTICLE IX.

The enumeration in the Constitution, of certain rights, shall not be construed to deny or disparage others retained by the people.

ARTICLE X.

The powers not delegated to the United States by the Constitution, nor prohibited by it to the States, are reserved to the States respectively, or to the people.

ACKNOWLEDGMENTS

I have become indebted to so many people in the process of assembling material for this book that it is difficult to decide where to start, or stop, in expressing my appreciation. A great many people patiently answered my inquiries, and often provided me with material and insights that had not occurred to me. Some would, I know, not wish to be acknowledged. I shall simply try to list here a few dozen to whom I feel especially indebted.

My thoughts go first of all to the officers of two associations that were of immense help. I particularly want to thank John de J. Pemberton, Jr., Alan Reitman, Melvin L. Wulf, Lawrence Speiser, and Eason Monroe of the American Civil Liberties Union and William P. Fidler and Louis Joughin of the American Association of University Professors. From here perhaps it would simplify matters if I tried to categorize those to whom I feel particular indebtedness.

People from the legal profession: Dean Frank C. Newman of the University of California School of Law; Samuel Dash of Philadelphia; Joseph L. Rauh, Jr., of Washington, D.C.; Edward Mosk of Hollywood; Morris L. Ernst, Harriet F. Pilpel, Alan U. Schwartz, William D. Zabel, Nancy F. Wechsler, Julia Perles, and Leonard Garment of New York City.

People from the federal government: Senator Edward V. Long of Missouri; Representatives John V. Lindsay of New York, Robert W. Kastenmeier of Wisconsin, and John M. Ashbrook of Ohio; congressional staff directors William Creech, Bess E. Dick, and Samuel J. Archibald; Walter T. Skallerup, Jr., and

Charles M. Trammell, Jr., of the Department of Defense; Edwin O. Guthman of the Department of Justice; P. L. Rothchild of the Department of the Treasury; Lee C. White of the White House staff; and John C. Harrington of the Federal Communications Commission.

Medical and social scientists: Dr. Robert S. Morison of the Rockefeller Foundation; Robert G. Heath, M.D., of Tulane University; Dr. Chris Argyris of Yale University; Dr. Jay L. Otis of Western Reserve University; Dr. Abraham Maslow of Brandeis University; Dr. Jerry Weisbrodt of Purdue University; and Dr. Timothy Leary, psychologist.

People from organizations concerned with investigation or security: N. Morgan Woods of the Claims Bureau of the Association of Casualty & Surety Companies; William M. Chiariello of Bishop's Service; T. Hutchison Leath of the Retail Credit Company; Norman Jaspan of Norman Jaspan Associates; Vincent W. Gillen of Fidelifacts; W. Sherman Burns of the William J. Burns International Detective Agency; R. M. Walker of the American Society for Industrial Security; G. Ralph Kiel of the Wackenhut Corporation; George W. Lindberg of John E. Reid and Associates; John Cye Cheasty (of his own organization); and Leonard S. Lowell of the Dale System, Inc.

Officials of organizations making or supplying investigative or surveillance equipment: Coleman London and Ralph V. Ward of Mosler Research Products, Inc.; Lee Bunting of Bell Television, Inc.; Max J. Kanter of ITV, Inc.; Raymond Farrell of Bondwitt Sound Engineering Company; N. M. Marshall of General Precision Laboratory; Harry Cowan of Regiscope Corporation of America.

People from the world of mass media and entertainment: Creed C. Black of the Wilmington News-Journal and chairman of the Freedom of Information Committee of the American Society of Newspaper Editors; Buck Harris of the Screen Actors Guild; Dore Schary; Frank Stisser of C. E. Hooper, Inc.; Richard Doan of the New York Herald Tribune: Irving Kahn of TelePrompTer; and Ira Kamen of Teleglobe.

Others who defy categorizing: Theodore McNulty of the Educational Testing Service; Bernard S. Benson of Benson-Lehner Corp.; Arthur H. Kuriloff of Non-Linear Systems; Ralph E. Peterson of the National Council of the Churches of Christ; Wesley McCune of Group Research Inc.; William F. Rickenbacker; Stanley Warren of Muzak; Edward J. Van Allen of East Meadow, L.I.; Richard Banks of Yale University; James Mills of Home Facts, Inc.; Dr. James K. Feibleman of Tulane University; Andrew J. Biemiller of the AFL-CIO; Mrs. Alexander P. Guyol of the League of Women Voters; Mrs. G. A. Cunningham.

Readers may safely assume that some of the people I've listed above would not agree with all the thoughts I have advanced in this book.

I wish to thank a number of people who helped me with major contributions at certain phases of the research and preparation of the manuscript. I express my appreciation to Guenther Reinhardt, who drew upon thirty years of federal and private investigative experience to help orient me, at the outset of my research in 1962, regarding modern investigative techniques and practices. Later, from time to time, he offered information. Marion Fuller and Ann Bridgman again were of immense help in preparing the final manuscript, as was my son Randall. My daughter Cynthia Ann undertook cheerfully the laborious task of classifying my printed source materials and copies of unpublished papers furnished to me.

Finally I wish to express my gratitude to Kay and Jack Tebbel, Nancy and Charles Saxon, Jane and Edward Eager, Audrey and William Roos, Eleanor and Kennett Rawson, my son Vance, and my wife Virginia for their criticism, encouragement, and suggestions.

VANCE PACKARD
New Canaan, Connecticut
February 3, 1964